Tikal Report 34
Part A

ADDITIONS AND ALTERATIONS
A Commentary on the Architecture of the North Acropolis, Tikal, Guatemala

North Acropolis from Temple I looking NW 1966.

North Acropolis from Great Plaza looking N 1966.

University Museum Monograph 128

Tikal Report 34
Part A

ADDITIONS AND ALTERATIONS
A Commentary on the Architecture of the North Acropolis, Tikal, Guatemala

H. Stanley Loten

Series Editors
William A. Haviland
Christopher Jones

UNIVERSITY OF PENNSYLVANIA MUSEUM
of Archaeology and Anthropology
Philadelphia

Copyright © 2007
By the University of Pennsylvania Museum
of Archaeology and Anthropology
3260 South Street
Philadelphia, PA 19104

Cataloging-in-Publication Data
Loten, H. Stanley.
Additions and alterations : a commentary on the architecture of the north acropolis, Tikal, Guatemala / H. Stanley Loten.
p. cm. – (University Museum monograph) (Tikal report ; no. 34, pt. A)
Includes bibliographical references and index.
ISBN 1-931707-98-7 (hardcover : alk. paper)
1. Tikal Site (Guatemala) 2. Maya architecture–Guatemala. 3. Temples–Guatemala. 4. Excavations (Archaeology)–Guatemala. 5. Guatemala–Antiquities. I. University of Pennsylvania. Museum of Archaeology and Anthropology. II. Title.
F1435.1.T5L67 2007
972.81--dc22
2007010638

H. Stanley Loten is an architect and former faculty member of Carleton University.

Printed in Canada on acid-free paper.

Contents

Preface and Acknowledgments x

Introduction xii

Chapter 1. Platform 5D-4-10th 1

Chapter 2. Platform 5D-4-9th 5

Chapter 3. Platform 5D-4-8th 11

Chapter 4. Platform 5D-4-7th 21

Chapter 5. Platform 5D-4-6th 29

Chapter 6. Platform 5D-4-5th 35

Chapter 7. Platform 5D-4-4th 39

Chapter 8. Platform 5D-4-3rd 51

Chapter 9. Platform 5D-4-2nd 57

Chapter 10. Platform 5D-4-1st 63

Conclusions 69

Bibliography 73

Appendix 1. Content of Architectural Episodes 79

Appendix 2. Glossary of Architectural Terms 81

Index 89

Illustrations

Figures

1	Map of Maya Area	xiii
2	Central Part of Tikal Map	xiv
3	Main Trench Location	xv
4	North Acropolis Perspective	xvi
5	Platform 5D-4-10th-A	2
6	Platform 5D-4-10th-A	2
7	Platform 5-D-4-9th-B	6
8	Platform 5D-4-9th-B	7
9	Platform 5D-4-9th	8
10	Platform 5D-4-9th	9
11	Platform 5D-4-8th-D	12
12	Platform 5D-4-8th-C	13
13	Platform 5D-4-8th-B	14
14	Platform 5D-4-8th-A	15
15	Structure 5D-Sub.1-1st	16
16	Structure 5D-Sub.1-1st rear facade	17
17	Structure 5D-Sub.1-1st building walls	18
18	Platform 5D-4-8th-A	19
19	Platform 5D-4-7th-C	22
20	Platform 5D-4-7th-C: view from SW	22
21	Platform 5D-4-7th-C	23
22	Platform 5D-4-7th-A	23
23	Platform 5D-4-7th-A	24
24	Platform 5D-4-7th-A	25
25	Platform 5D-4-7th-A	26
26	Platform 5D-4-6th	30
27	Platform 5D-4-6th	30
28	Platform 5D-4-6th	31
29	Platform 5D-4-6th	32
30	Platform 5D-4-6th	33
31	Platform 5D-4-5th	36
32	Platform 5D-4-5th	36
33	Platform 5D-4-5th	37
34	Platform 5D-4-4th-B	40
35	Platform 5D-4-4th-B/A	41
36	Platform 5D-4-4th-A	42
37	Platform 5D-4-4th-A	43
38	Platform 5D-4-4th-A	44
39	Platform 5D-4-4th-A	45
40	Structure 5D-22-3rd-E	46
41	Structure 5D-22-3rd-D	47
42	Platform 5D-4-4th-A	48
43	Structure 5D-23-1st-B	49
44	Platform 5D-4-3rd	52
45	Platform 5D-4-3rd-A	53
46	Platform 5D-4-3rd-A	54
47	Platform 5D-4-3rd-A	55
48	Platform 5D-4-2nd	58
49	Platform 5D-4-2nd	59
50	Platform 5D-4-2nd/1st	60
51	Platform 5D-4-2nd/1st	61
52	Structure 5D-22-3rd Substructure	62
53	Platform 5D-4-1st-C	64
54	Platform 5D-4-1st-C	65
55	Platform 5D-4-1st	66

Figures on CD-ROM

1	View of Central Tikal		8	Platform 5D-4-9th-B	
2	View of Tikal National Park		9	Platform 5D-4-9th	
3	View of Great Plaza, Tikal, AD 2000		10	Platform 5D-4-9th	
4	Author (1965) on Structure 5D-22		11	Platform 5D-4-8th-D	
5	Platform 5D-4-10th-A		11a	Platform 5D-4-8th-D	
6	Platform 5D-4-10th-A		11b	Platform 5D-4-8th-D	
7	Platform 5D-4-9th-B		12	Platform 5D-4-8th-C	

12a	Platform 5D-4-8th-C	37	Platform 5D-4-4th-A
13	Platform 5D-4-8th-B	37a	Platform 5D-4-4th-A
14	Platform 5D-4-8th-A	37b	Platform 5D-4-4th-A
15	Structure 5D-Sub.1-1st	38	Structure 5D-22-3rd-E
16	Structure 5D-Sub.1-1st W stair-side mask	39	View of Str. 5D-22
17	Structure 5D-Sub.1-1st rear	40	Structure 5D-22-3rd mask
18	Platform 5D-4-8th-A	41	Structure 5D-22-3rd-D
19	Platform 5D-4-7th-C	42	Stair-block mask, Str. 5D-22-3rd
19a	Platform 5D-4-7th-C	43	Platform 5D-4-4th-A
20	Platform 5D-4-7th-C	44	Structure 5D-23-1st-B
20a	Platform 5D-4-7th-C	45	Structure 5D-23 view
21	Platform 5D-4-7th-A	46	Platform 5D-4-3rd
21a	Platform 5D-4-7th-A	46	Platform 5D-4-3rd
22	Platform 5D-4-7th-A	47	Platform 5D-4-3rd-A
22a	Platform 5D-4-7th-A	47a	Platform 5D-4-3rd-A
23	Platform 5D-4-7th-A	48	Platform 5D-4-3rd-A
23a	Platform 5D-4-7th-A	48a	Platform 5D-4-3rd-A
24	Platform 5D-4-7th-A	49	Structure 5D-26-1st view
24a	Platform 5D-4-7th-A	50	Platform 5D-4-3rd-A
25	Platform 5D-4-6th	50a	Platform 5D-4-3rd-A
26	Platform 5D-4-6th	51	Structure 5D-33-3rd W mask
27	Platform 5D-4-6th	52	Platform 5D-4-2nd
27a	Platform 5D-4-6th	52a	Platform 5D-4-2nd
27b	Platform 5D-4-6th	52b	Platform 5D-4-2nd
27c	Platform 5D-4-6th	53	Structure 5D-34-1st view
28	Platform 5D-4-6th	54	Platform 5D-4-2nd
28a	Platform 5D-4-6th	54a	Platform 5D-4-2nd
28b	Platform 5D-4-6th	55	Platform 5D-4-2nd/1st
28c	Platform 5D-4-6th	55a	Platform 5D-4-2nd/1st
29	Platform 5D-4-6th	56	Platform 5D-4-2nd/1st
29a	Platform 5D-4-6th	57	Structure 5D-22-1st middle room
30	Platform 5D-4-5th	58	Structure 5D-22-1st middle room
30a	Platform 5D-4-5th	59	Structure 5D-22-1st Ca. 185
30b	Platform 5D-4-5th	60	Structure 5D-22-1st axial bench
31	Platform 5D-4-5th	61	Platform 5D-4-1st-C
31a	Platform 5D-4-5th	62	Platform 5D-4-1st-C
32	Platform 5D-4-4th-B	63	Structure 5D-32-1st view
32a	Platform 5D-4-4th-B	64	Structure 5D-32-1st view
32b	Platform 5D-4-4th-B	65	Structure 5D-32-1st view
33	Platform 5D-4-4th-B/A	66	Platform 5D-4-1st
34	Platform 5D-4-4th-A	66a	Platform 5D-4-1st
35	Platform 5D-4-4th-A	66b	Platform 5D-4-1st
35a	Platform 5D-4-4th-A	66c	Platform 5D-4-1st
36	Platform 5D-4-4th-A	67	Structure 5D-33-1st view
36a	Platform 5D-4-4th-A	68	Structure 5D-33-1st view
36b	Platform 5D-4-4th-A		

North Acropolis Chronology

Date	Time Spans	Arch'l Episodes	Rulers	Ceramic Complexes	Culture Periods
900 AD	2	7	30 to end	Eznab	Terminal Classic
800	3	7	30 to end	Imix	Late Classic
800	4	7	26-29	Imix	Late Classic
700	5	7	21-25	Ik	Intermediate Classic
600	6	7	21-25	Ik	Intermediate Classic
500	6	7	19-20	Manik	Early Classic
400	7	7	15-18	Manik	Early Classic
300	8	6	1-14	Manik	Early Classic
200	9	5		Cimi	Late Pre-Classic
	10	5		Cauac	Late Pre-Classic
100	11	4		Cauac	Late Pre-Classic
0	12	4		Chuen	Late Pre-Classic
100	13	3		Chuen	Late Pre-Classic
200	14	2		Tzec	Late Pre-Classic
300	15	1		Eb	
400 BC	15	1		Eb	

Notes: For Time Spans see TR 14: Chart 1. For Culture Periods and Rulers see Sabloff 2003:xxiv. For Arch'l Episodes see Conclusions, this volume.

Abbreviations

Bu.	Burial
Ca.	Cache
E	East
Fig.	Figure
Fl.	Floor
m	meter
N	North
Plat.	Platform
P.D.	Problematic Deposit
S	South
Str.	Structure
TS	Time Span
TR.	Tikal Report
U.	Unit
W	West

Preface and Acknowledgments

The Tikal Project began as a collaborative enterprise between the University of Pennsylvania Museum of Archaeology and Anthropology, and the Government of Guatemala. Though initially planned for ten years, excavations ran from 1956 through 1970. The extension was lucky for me in that I did not join the project until 1965 (Plate 4), too late if the original schedule had been followed.

Teobert Maler (1911) and Alfred Tozzer (1911) had shown the wealth of well-preserved Maya architecture at Tikal. By the middle of the 20th century this material had become widely known (Spinden 1913; Totten 1926; Kelemen 1943; Morley and Brainerd 1946; Thompson 1955; Kubler 1962; Proskouriakoff 1963; Robertson 1963; Marquina 1964; Pollock 1965). These accounts of Tikal architecture lured me into stepping aside from architectural practice to learn more about this grand tradition. I initially intended only a temporary leave, but as it happened I never did get back to the office.

The publication plan set out in Tikal Report 12 (1982:55-63) calls for two kinds of publications. Primary reports present the processes of investigation and the discoveries made in individual operations. Secondary reports use these data to study particular artifact categories. TR.34A is one of these secondary reports focusing on architecture of the North Acropolis.

The North Acropolis excavation is one of many Tikal Project operations. Its findings are presented in TR.14 (Coe 1990). In TR.34A the TR.14 data are considered from the viewpoint of architectural designers. Emphasis falls on aspects of architectural form, planning, techniques of construction, implied functions, meaningfulness, and design alternatives available to the ancient Maya builders.

Although TR.34A introduces no new material it presents the TR.14 data in a different format. Color plates (on the CD ROM) and line figures in the text, are based on digitally constructed models. These depict the North Acropolis as it evolved from the Late Preclassic into the Late Early Classic Periods (roughly from 300 BC to AD 600). They were produced by plugging TR.14 data into the general-purpose modeling program form. Z produced by auto•des•sys inc. of Columbus, Ohio. The models enable us to see the structures as they were when first built, in mint condition with shiny burnished plaster and fresh paint.

Since no structure survived intact and many were only partially accessible, a certain amount of interpolation has been necessary. This has been done as parsimoniously as possible. Hypothetical extensions beyond TR.14 data are noted in the text.

The developmental sequence illustrated in the plates and figures closely follows TR.14 but departs from it in a few instances. I have inserted additional steps where stratigraphic evidence does not demonstrate sequence but where architectural form and acropolis character suggest possible sequences. In these cases my hypothetical orderings never violate stratigraphy. They concern structures standing on a common sustaining surface. Stratigraphy cannot sort them out sequentially. But at the same time there is no proof they were all built at once. Therefore I have felt free to suggest sequences that seem at least plausible where there is some reason to do so. For the hard evidence, TR.14 is the solid authority.

Much of my exposition concerns the factors, issues, beliefs and aspirations that directed design efforts. These are as subjective as my hypothetical sequences.

The issues they raise cannot be entirely settled here. They are my personal opinions, based at least on direct experience and years of reflection, but still ambivalent. Some are quite contrary to prevailing opinion. I hope they open up some avenues of thought or raise some lines of speculation that may eventually lead to more solid conclusions.

Color renderings of the models are on the CD that accompanies this volume. Line diagrams within the text are identical to most of these models, but are not rendered. They provide identification for the various structures and features that appear in the plates. This allows the plates to remain clean as simulations of actual views.

I have avoided the temptation to set the models in realistic contexts. They are presented in isolation rather than pictorially in a landscape for which I do not have firm data.

In addition to the CD views that correspond to text figures there are additional views showing the same version of the acropolis from different angles. These have the same designation as their associated text figures with appended "a," "b," "c," notations.

The text has benefited enormously from very careful reading by Chris Jones, Bill Haviland, Simon Martin, Norman Hammond, Anabel Ford, and in particular, Walda Metcalf. My best thanks to all.

H. Stanley Loten

Introduction

The archaeological site known today as Tikal is the relic of an ancient Maya urban center located in a region now known as El Petén (Figure 1). This northern Department of Guatemala borders on Mexico to the north and west, and Belize (formerly British Honduras) to the east. It lies at the southern base of the Yucatan Peninsula, a region of broken terrain not well suited for agriculture. Despite a challenging environment the ancient Maya flourished here from about 2000 BC (Martin and Grube 2000:8) to AD 900 and established numerous cities throughout the area.

With decline of Tikal, around the middle of the 9th century AD, the Petén gradually reverted to forest and swamp. Up to the middle of the 20th century this condition prevailed over nearly the whole region and is still the case immediately around the site (Plate 2). A Guatemalan National Park 24 kilometers square centered on Tikal has preserved this section of forest. Part of a World Heritage ecological conservancy, it is a wonderful, high, subtropical growth almost as impressive to many present-day visitors as the ruins themselves. Sadly, outside the park much of this land has been cleared for farming during the last half century. Intact forests still exist along the Mexican border but south of Tikal they have disappeared, replaced by hardscrabble subsistence farmland.

Material encountered beneath the North Acropolis demonstrates occupation at this locus as early as 800 BC (TR.14:Chart 1, 813-15) but does not provide architectural information (see Chapter 1). Substantial North Acropolis architecture begins about 350 BC and from this time onward construction seems more or less continuous.

From late Pre-Classic beginnings Tikal steadily urbanized and eventually exercised political authority on a regional basis. At its height, from the 7th through the 8th century AD, the city covered more than 120 sq. km and housed a population of at least 45,000 (Haviland 2003:129). The North Acropolis, the Great Plaza, the Central Acropolis, and other complexes linked to these by continuous paved surfaces, represent only the central zone of the city (Plate 1). This is the area present-day visitors normally access (Plate 3).

They experience a setting profoundly unlike the center that the ancient Maya of Tikal would have known. For example, the Great Plaza surface, now grass, was then polished white plaster. The structures around the plaza glistened with a plaster coat that had been either painted or burnished. Restored masonry surfaces, now mottled black, give an entirely false impression of the original character. Even on an overcast day such as that of Plate 3 the scene would have been quite bright, and in full sunlight, blinding. It is unlikely that there would have been so many trees so close to the plaza.

Population declined drastically around the middle of the 9th century AD. Elite classes may have hung on longest (Haviland, personal communication), but over a couple of centuries the city was completely abandoned. Until the mid-19th century Tikal lay essentially lost in the forest, its existence forgotten until the mid 19th century (Coe 1967:12-17).

My initiation into archaeological fieldwork took place in 1965 at Tikal on the North Acropolis with Coe's guidance (Plate 4). However, I did not spend much time there. Most of my Tikal Project investigations dealt with unexcavated structures standing in the forest on the fringe of the central zone and farther out (TR. 23A).

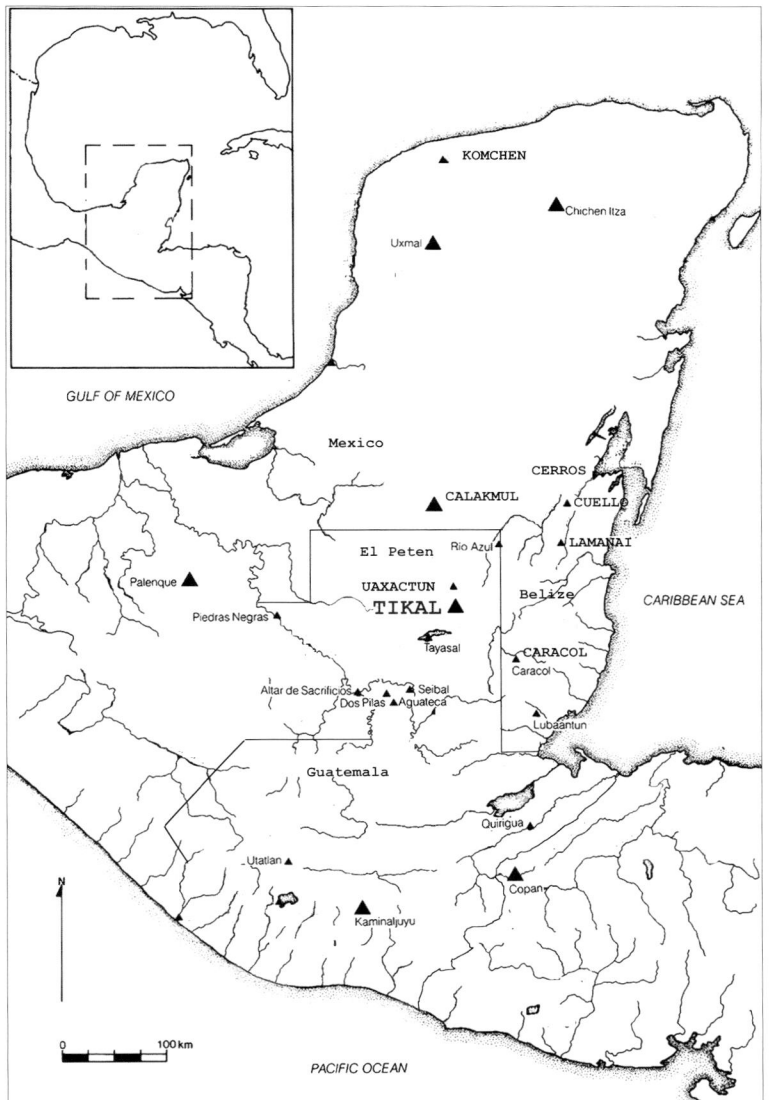

Figure 1. View of Central Tikal.

This volume, however, concerns architecture of the North Acropolis, one of the major agglomerations of monumental architecture at the center of the city. Figure 2 covers the central part of Tikal, the epicenter and its immediate surroundings. The urbanized area extends much farther in all directions.

The North Acropolis complex (inset in Figure 2) was investigated by means of a deep trench cut from the top surface down to bedrock and extended in lateral tunnels cut at various levels).

Figure 3, showing the main trench, but not the lateral tunnels, is a top view of the model (discussed below) for Plate 66. The cut does not look very impressive in this diagram but its true magnitude can be seen in TR.14:fig. 297. These excavations, while limited in the sense that not all parts of the fabric could be accessed, nevertheless resulted in a highly detailed account of North Acropolis architectural development presented in TR:14; the source of data for TR.34A.

Figure 4 is a drawing made manually by the author in 1966 based on an aerial photograph and best guesses as to the original appearance of the complex. It shows the North Acropolis from slightly west of north and above, a view not available to ancient Maya humans.

Supernatural allies of Tikal, and deceased ancestors, might have enjoyed this view. It points up the strong NS line formed by Str. 5D-22-1st (foreground), Str. 5D-33-1st (middle) and Great Temple V to left of the South Acropolis dimly depicted in the background. Significance of this direction is repeatedly evoked throughout the centuries-long architectural development described in chapters 1 through 10.

The foreground structure, 22-1st, looks to be the highest in this projection but that is only because it is closer to the viewer. Great Temple V is highest in the NS axial line followed by 33-1st. Great Temple I, to left of center is the highest structure depicted.

The full extent of sculptural elaboration suggested by this drawing is not included in the color plates (on the CD) mainly because most of this material suffered, collapse, erosion, and tree damage.

In Figure 2, Plate 1, and the *Frontispiece*, the North Acropolis can be seen at the center of the city, facing south on to the Great Plaza with Great Temples I and II positioned as though they were frontal adjuncts to it. The TR.11 map (Figure 1) shows terminal developments, much of which postdates the North Acropolis. Most of its growth took place through the Late Preclassic and Early Classic periods, that is, from the 4th century BC through the 7th century AD. This is the temporal span covered in the following chapters.

Following publication of the North Acropolis excavation report (TR.14 1990), I began to construct computer models of North Acropolis features using the quantitatively precise TR.14 data (see Preface). I had intended to use these models as illustrations in TR.34, the

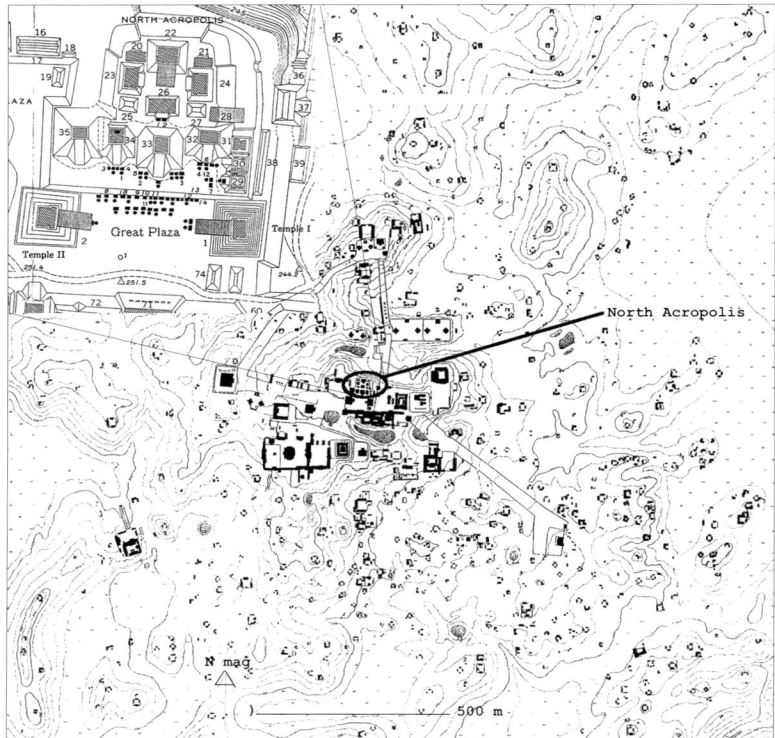

Figure 2. View of Tikal National Park.

volume that would bring together all the architectural material gathered in the many operations of the Tikal Project between 1956 and 1969. These plans changed once the North Acropolis models were completed. A decision was made to publish TR.34A and TR.34B separately. The latter volume draws on the whole inventory of Tikal Project architecture while the former concerns only one complex.

The models provide three-dimensional views of the buildings that supplement the plans, sections and details in TR.14 and provide a different kind of understanding. They enable us to see the architecture as fully intact, subject of course to the inherent limitations of archaeological data. Hopefully, they show the buildings as conceived by their ancient Maya designers. This view is not available to us today except in reconstructions that necessarily include some hypothetical aspects. With this caveat they enable us to appreciate the architecture qualitatively and I consider that this affects our interpretation of it.

In TR.14 the various features of the North Acropolis are formally designated as numbered platforms, structures, terraces and units. The main body sustaining summit features is designated as Platform 5D-4, 5D being the map square containing the North Acropolis (TR.11). Its major developmental stages are numbered as 1st through 10th, (latest to earliest). Platform 5D-4-1st is the surface feature, the partially collapsed ruin that was initially encountered and mapped. That is, it was the first version of the North Acropolis to be seen. Earlier versions, then, are numbered counting backward, in order of their construction prior to "1st." This ordering is termed an "architectural development" (Appendix II; TR.5:9).

Ten composite versions were identified (TR.14:Chart 1). As components of these ten acropoleis some fifty-two individual structures have been designated. Those initially visible on the surface, and invisible predecessors of surface structures, have "5D" numbers; those uncovered during excavations have "5D-Sub." numbers only if unrelated to surface structures. "Unit" numbers identify three hundred and fifty-one features such as stairs, patches of floor and problematic lumps of masonry. In the following chapters I have retained these designations so reference can be made back to TR.14, the basis for the present work. I have tried to minimize repetition of TR.14 data, though some duplication has been unavoidable.

A problem is that TR.14 does not provide formal designations for the different acropolis stages that can be recognized. Figure numbers (TR.14:fig. 6a-l) are the sole designators attached to the 12 developmentally distinct entities defined in TR.14. As labels for the 34 different versions of the acropolis that I have modeled, I use the TR.14 platform numbers. In TR.14 these refer specifically to lower parts of the acropolis. I use them for convenience, to avoid setting out yet another series of designations, and because while the series illustrated in TR.14:fig. 6 adhere strictly to stratigraphic controls some of my illustrations propose additional hypothetical stages as noted above (Preface). However, I have been careful to ensure that none of these violate stratigraphic evidence.

The following chapters are organized by developmental Platform 5D-4 designations, that is, 10th, 9th, 8th etc., following TR.14, beginning with the earliest, Platform 5D-4-10th and proceeding to the latest, Platform 5D-4-1st. Most of the views shown in the line figures and color plates (the latter on the CD) illustrate the whole acropolis. My assumption is that the ancient designers thought in terms of this whole. Therefore,

I have tried to interpret their motives and intentions through the impression that the whole acropolis provides. Certain interpretive insights are gained only from a view of the whole, as it was when first built, with freshly polished plaster and bright, new paint. This view is not the one we see today when visiting Tikal with its restored structures (Plate 3). To be sure they deliver a very powerful impression but still lack the original plaster finish and painted color.

Despite dark gray and black stonework the Great Plaza still projects a strong sense of monumentality. When the surrounding structures were new and shiny it must have been overwhelming. I suspect it was intended to be frightening as well.

The developmental sequence depicted in the outline figures and the color plates (on the CD) traces a continuous process of modification leading always toward an increase in monumentality until a final maximum was achieved (Chapter 7). After this point there was further development but no more increase in monumentality within the North Acropolis itself. In later years the Great Plaza became a great deal more impressive with construction of Temples I and II. During these Late Classic years the North Acropolis saw no more development. Therefore I have ended my commentary at this point, near the end of the 7th century AD. Subsequent trajectories of Tikal architecture are followed in TR.34B using more objective criteria of evidence and a much wider sample.

TR.34A addresses issues that were certainly not absent in TR.14 but given its focus on excavation and detailed description of findings, could not be greatly developed. In any case, the present work presents my own views for what they may be worth. Interpretation of architecture as evidence for intentions and motivations is a necessarily subjective enterprise and I am sure another investigator would come up with quite different readings.

In the following paragraphs I have tried to expose my biases as far as I am aware of them and indeed the chapters that follow present them fully; I have not tried to quash them; they are, after all, if not the substance, then the theme of this work. TR.14 presents the North Acropolis objectively; TR.34A re-presents it as a particular view of ancient monumental architecture designed to provide a setting for ritual function, and as landform transformed to encourage supernatural connections.

I subscribe to the modernist view that function determines architectural form but only partially. Even when functional criteria are deeply implicated in decisions made by designers significant aspects of form remain to be determined by other factors. In a work such

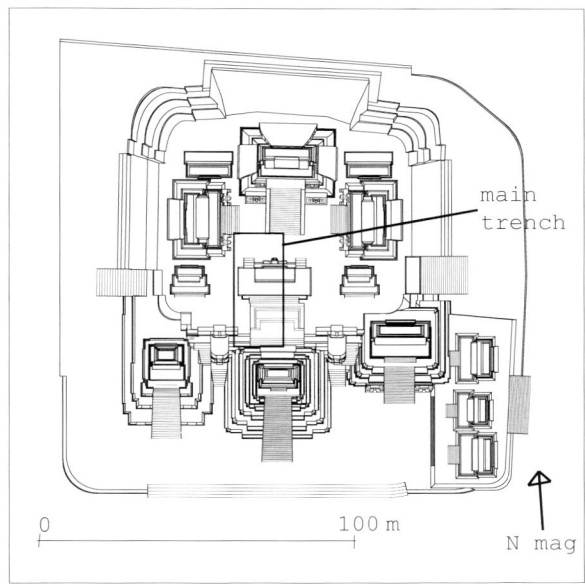

Figure 3. View of Great Plaza, Tikal, AD 2000.

as Tikal's North Acropolis, nurtured over many centuries, profound cultural and ideological values surely must have played a significant role. My objective in pursuing this work is to consider these factors although I may be able to do no more than guess about them.

Since this is a work of interpretation, not an objective account of findings, I feel obligated to explain the underlying assumptions that color my views. Marshall Becker (1992) proposes that "many Maya burials may have been viewed by their makers as offerings to the temples covering them rather than that the temples served as monuments to the people interred beneath them." His point is that although we understand caches as offerings intended to establish links with supernatural powers we tend to see burials in a different light. He points to the possibility of a strong conceptual overlap between the two.

Works of ancient architecture, particularly monumental ritual architecture, raise a similar problem. We tend to see them as settings for ritual or as self-aggrandizing works of the wealthy and powerful. The ceremonies conducted in and around certain structures are readily understandable as intended to forge links with supernatural powers but the structures themselves are generally not seen this way. I feel there may be an overlap between architecture and ritual that is similar to the overlap Becker outlines between burials and caches.

Such a conceptual overlap is almost inevitable in cultures dominated by the kind of natural science

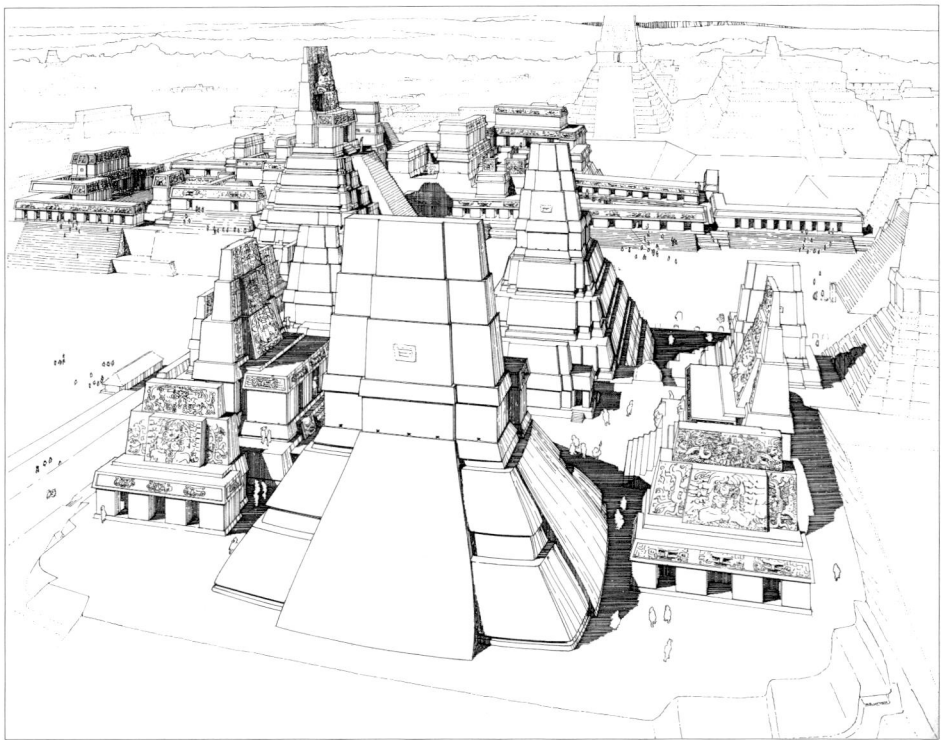

Figure 4. Author (1965) on Structure 5D-22.

known as animism. In this view of life the forces that cause things to move are understood as acting deliberately and intentionally. It follows, then, that mediation with such forces seems not merely possible, but mandatory.

Polities at the state level, in these societies, have an obligation to intervene with nonmaterial forces for the good of their members. At the same time rulers claim an ability to do this and they use it to bolster their authority and status. They can mobilize the full resources of the state to these ends. Hence we see large-scale projects such as the North Acropolis at Tikal in many ancient societies.

The most succinct statement that I know of describing the animistic outlook concerns ancient Egypt and the Nile. "When the river does not rise, it has refused to rise" (Frankfort et al. 1945:15). In this philosophy the river seems to have taken against the Egyptians. Clearly they need to do something about this if prosperity is to be restored.

The ancient Maya worldview (Freidel, Schele, and Parker 1993; Mock 1998) was essentially similar though developed very differently. So it is reasonable to expect that ancient Maya and ancient Egyptians held similar views though independently derived. If the rains have not come as expected, or if a battle has been lost, there must be a reason for this withdrawal of supernatural cooperation. No effort aimed at regaining supernatural support seems too great. Extremes of expense, effort and sacrifice seem appropriate.

Exactly how such beliefs influenced architectural design in any particular instance such as the North Acropolis at Tikal is hard to say with much certainty. Ample texts from Tikal (TR.33A 1982; Martin and Grube 2000; Martin 2003) throw some light on this matter but seven centuries of abandonment before European arrival mean that contact period documents are lacking. Centers such as Utatlán in the highlands of Guatemala (Carmack 1981), which were active in the sixteenth century, provide such documents and show how profoundly their absence impedes our understanding of Tikal material.

The central plaza at Utatlán parallels the Great Plaza at Tikal in one respect; a relatively tall structure stands on the east and a much lower one on the west (Carmack 1981: fig. 9.1) just as Temples I and II are positioned on the Great Plaza at Tikal. Temple I stands above the trees right of center in Plate 1 with Temple II opposite on the left.

Structures on the north and south sides of the Utatlán plaza, on the other hand, are not at all similar to those in comparable positions at Tikal. The north Utatlán structure occupying a position equivalent to that of the North Acropolis at Tikal is the Cawek lineage Big House. This presumably served social and political purposes rather than ritual observance. The south structure is a complex in the position occupied by the social/political Central Acropolis at Tikal (Harrison 1999:183-87). That is, north and south sides of the central two plazas appear to be reversed, functionally, between Tikal and Utatlán.

Despite these differences, a gap of some seven centuries, and a different Maya community, Carmack's research at Utatlán offers some clues to the way that ancient Tikaleños may have seen the epicenter of their city. For example, "..lords who had fought in battle had to be ceremonially purified outside the town before they could enter.." (Carmack 1981:183). I wonder if similar strictures may have been followed at Tikal.

The parts of central Tikal connected by plaster pavement, that is, the Tikal epicenter, in effect constitute a kind of town within the larger settlement. This might have been similar conceptually to the town of Utatlán for members of the elite class. If the above reference can be applied to this part of Tikal it must have been understood as quite distinct from the unmodified surface of the surrounding earth. My guess is that such distinction, if it did indeed exist, centered on presence, or potential presence, of supernaturals. Dealing with the most powerful supernaturals, by means of offerings, sacrifices, music, dance, and other rituals, was particularly the province of upper level elite Maya citizens, a dangerous business requiring careful preparation, purity of person, and professional expertise.

This service, provided by high-ranking individuals in ancient Maya society constituted the reciprocity that had to exist between elite and commoner classes (Pendergast 1992:77).

The architectural installation of the North Acropolis and the unbroken tissue of masonry building linked by paved surfaces provide part of the evidence for this social structure. Over time the pavement spread its tentacles quite far from the North Acropolis and may provide a hint that the ratio of elite to commoner increased somewhat both numerically and spatially through the Classic Period (Haviland and Moholy-Nagy 1992). Persistent heavy burning on plaster floor surfaces of the North Acropolis provides additional evidence that ritual activities were conducted at this locus (TR.14:935-39; Stuart 1998). Graffiti also support this inference (TR.31).

Commoners probably could come and go relatively freely since they did not interact at state levels with supernaturals, at least not to the same extent, or perhaps not with the same supernaturals (Haviland and Haviland 1995:295-309). Members of the elite class may have been able to move about somewhat freely while not immediately engaged in ritual activities or warfare. Injunctions regarding battle may have been necessary because of supernatural participation in military events. Carmack's observation cited above suggests that when elites left the epicenter, say for military action, or with intent to interact with supernaturals at some other locus, their purity would be violated.

If something like this obtained for the central area as a whole, similar injunctions must have been even more stringent for complexes like the North Acropolis. "Warriors could not go near them (the temples) without elaborate preparation. The regular and lay priests climbed the stairs to give offerings, but only after the required fasting and continence" (Carmack 1981:186, citing Villacorta 1962:356).

Warriors constituted one group within the elite class. All male members of the elite might have been expected to achieve some status such as warrior, priest, scribe or artisan. For them, as at Utatlán, approaching structures associated with supernaturals might have been difficult. In the midst of warfare they mingled with supernaturals, as shown by, for example, a mural painting on the south wall of the Upper Temple of the Jaguars at Chichén Itzá (Adela Breton 1989:fig. 19). Approaching a temple would imply a similar mingling, presumably requiring purification rituals. Even for fully professional priests, probably apprenticed from childhood, temples might not be approached casually.

From this we might infer that the North Acropolis was never a venue for sightseeing, strolling around, conversing, socializing or dwelling. It was probably never pleasant to mount the stairs up to the acropolis summit. The activities conducted there were probably of a highly skilled professional nature done in the utmost seriousness and with the greatest care and probably involving experience of pain.

"As residences of the deities, the Quiches' temples were houses of the gods" (Carmack 1981:186, citing Villacorta, 1962:333). This final citation from Carmack effectively summarizes the architectural significance of the North Acropolis, in my opinion, that is, assuming it has relevance to Tikal. If this contention is valid, as seems likely (Taube 1998), then the designers of North Acropolis architecture, not only of the structures on the acropolis, but the acropolis platform body and basal members, faced a most rigorous challenge. They had to imagine a fabric to attract supernaturals so they would choose to inhabit it or at least to be present there at times. My guess is that this stringent directive strongly influenced both design and development at the North Acropolis.

The professional priesthood, continually studying and developing new theological doctrines would have continuously evolved new conditions for attracting and retaining supernatural presence. Renewal of the temples would have been necessary to keep up with doctrinal progress. If individual temples related to particular supernaturals, then the process of renewal would have been piecemeal, as theological speculation reached new understandings of different supernatural entities.

This is precisely the type of developmental pattern displayed by the North Acropolis. The connection to rulership would have evolved as well, as political and social institutions also changed. On top of these factors calendric considerations probably exerted a powerful influence. It is, therefore, not surprising that architectural development in the North Acropolis proceeded along a lively path of near constant change and continuous reconstruction.

Our effort to understand the intensity of architectural investment in complexes like the North Acropolis is impeded by our view of the supernatural as unreal. Ancient societies, following animistic beliefs saw the supernatural as a seamless part of reality that could be manipulated for political and material ends just as well as anything else in their experience. Monumental architecture is one of the means available for this though rarely understood as such.

1

Platform 5D-4-10th

The earliest developmental stage that can be reconstructed at the North Acropolis locus is designated as Platform 5D-4-10th (TR.14:16-28; 813-16; fig. 4, 10, 14). It has two sub-stages. The earlier, 10th-B, includes architecture but in remnants too scanty for reconstruction and hence not illustrated here. This initial episode begins with primary occupation of the site in the 8th century BC on a low bedrock knoll (TR.14:fig. 4), the highest point in the area. This episode represents some five centuries of uncertain occupancy. The second, much shorter sub-stage, 10th-A (Plate 5, 6, Fig. 5), extends from 350 to 200 BC. Major changes introduced in this period are represented by structure fragments that were partially exposed at the very bottom of the excavation, right on bedrock.

The 10th-B material appears to have been either greatly disturbed by terminal demolition or secondarily re-deposited as trash scraped up from nearby areas and used as fill at the time of 10th-A development. This material includes domestic occupational midden trash (U. 223) as well as ritual items, including two burials (Bu. 120 and 121) and a human skull (PD. 83). A cryptic circular cut in bedrock, 0.65 m in diameter, lined with white plaster (U. 224A, TR. 14:20) looks like a sculptural feature, maybe an ear ornament, carved into the bedrock. If U. 224A really is the ear ornament portion of a largely obliterated rock sculpture residential occupation would seem improbable. If it is part of some utilitarian feature then domestic use might be indicated. Of course, there is no way to know when the feature was installed, and even if it is part of a sculptural work residential occupancy might have preceded it. If so, and if really figural, it would represent a dramatic change in locus function, and since ear ornaments are usually part of royal regalia, elite linkage to the North Acropolis may have begun at this very early date. On the other hand, subsequent developments are so modest in scale that either rulership was not involved, was still modest in scale and power, or the precise activities staged here did not call for monumentality.

At the end of the first developmental stage, (Platform 5D-4-10th-B), ca. 350 BC, the bedrock knoll was cut down and leveled for new construction (Platform 5D-4-10th-A). This process effectively destroyed evidence of earlier construction. Either there was none or leveled surfaces were not called for. This new foundation work of cutting and filling, seems to have been preparatory to construction of 10th-A features which, though modest in scale and seen only partially, nevertheless provide the earliest surviving architectural developments encountered in the North Acropolis excavation.

Figure 5 and Plate 5 provide a conjectural reconstruction of Structure 5D-Sub.14-2nd-B, the first of the 10th-A constructions. I have assumed a grassy surface around it in Plate 5 simply because in the climate of Tikal any open space quickly acquires vegetation. The contours used in Plate 5 are those provided in TR.14: fig. 4. They describe only the low knoll itself, not the ridge that it sits on 55-60 m above surrounding land on the E where the Bajo Santa Fe stretches almost to the horizon.

By any measure, Sr. 5D-Sub.14-2nd is quite modest in scale, only about 4 m in diameter (U. 71) and of uncertain original height. I show it reconstructed arbitrarily to 1 m. The curved masonry face of U. 71, exposed in the excavation, could be either the rounded end of a house platform or about one quarter of the circular platform illustrated. No plaster had survived *in*

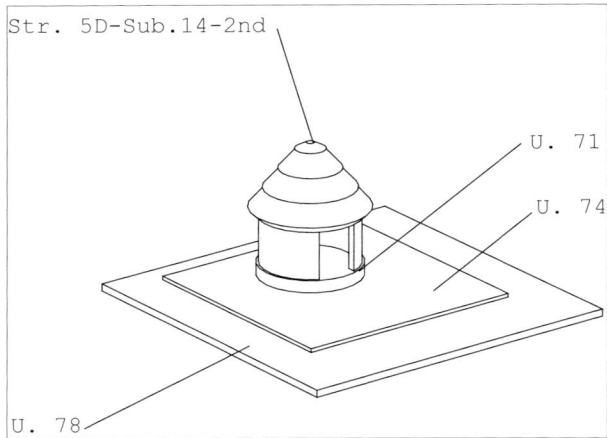

Figure 5. Platform 5D-4-10th-A.

ing material included chunks of red-painted plaster (TR.14:202). On that slender basis I show a circular building with red painted walls and a thatched roof on a low red-painted building platform (U. 71).

The unplastered sustaining surface (U. 74) extended beyond the trench so that its overall form is unknown though clearly not circular. Something like a basal platform is illustrated as arbitrarily squared pavement U. 74, in Figure 5 and Plate 5. The lower surface (U. 78) might have been much more extensive, perhaps a plaza floor. Only the part within the trench was exposed, and was seen to be unplastered. Its informal, dark earth surface implies that it may never have possessed the sort of distinct edges illustrated above and may not have been precisely leveled over its whole extent.

If the circular form were definitely known it could be taken to indicate ritual function (cf.Powis 1996; Pollock 1936; Kowalski et al. 1996), though on a very modest scale. At this time, the early 3rd century BC, some of the largest structures ever built by the ancient Maya were either already in existence or very soon to be built not far from Tikal (El Mirador, Matheny 1980; Lamanai, Pendergast 1981). At Tikal the Mundo Perdido complex was already much more substantial (Laporte and Fialko 1995:41-49). If Platform 5D-4-10th-A sustained a ritual structure it may have functioned primarily for priestly activities with little or weak connection to legitimacy of rulership.

Structure 5D-Sub.14-1st replaced 5D-Sub.14-2nd after it had been almost totally demolished. It has a rectangular plan at sub-structure level and therefore, if there was a building, it too was probably rectangular. Due to ancient demolition, nothing is known of it. As reconstructed in Plate 6, it strongly resembles a very ordinary, even modest, dwelling. That this form necessarily implies a residential function, however, is debatable. Symbolic house forms are well known in ancient Maya architecture and visual art (Houston 1998:349-52). To argue for a continuing ritual function it is necessary to assume that here domestic architectural form fulfilled a parallel role to that of the much earlier, and highly problematic, bedrock feature (U. 224A), referred to above. I assume a feature such as a mask would have been part of a ritual setting.

That ritual activities would benefit from a "home" for supernatural beings is not difficult to accept. A house form might have seemed a logical way to express this architectonically. No associated artifacts and deposits (TR.14:26-29) support residential function while on the other hand massive demolition of earlier installations, leveling of bedrock, and considerable burning on 5D-4-10th-A surfaces suggest some kind of corporate enterprise with ritual aspects.

Though modestly scaled and unimpressive in form, Plat. 5D-10th-A continued in use for more than a century. The platform sustaining it was modified twice (Fl. 17 and Fl. 16) and served as a setting for activities that included burning, found over much of the limited exposed area, and therefore possibly quite extensive. Burning suggests ritual activity but the possibility that the house simply burned down cannot be dismissed without more extensive survey of the surface. The full size of the

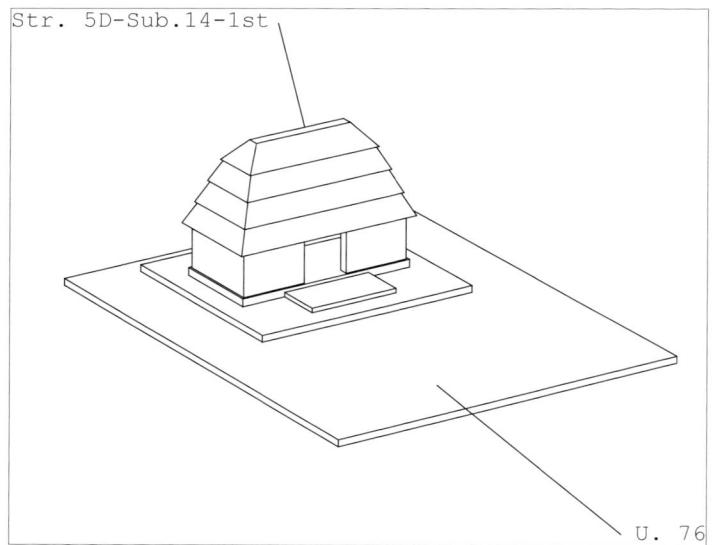

Figure 6. Platform 5D-4-10th-A.

paved surface on which these activities took place is unknown; larger than that shown in Plate 6, but whether a little larger or a lot larger remains indeterminate.

Prudence Rice (2006:91, 166) proposes that Tikal served several times as the "seat of the *may*" (13 k'atuns, 3,380 days, 256 years, that forms the basis of Maya ritual practice and the T'zolk'in divinational calendar). One of these seating dates is 334 BC, near the time of extreme re-modelling of the site on which Plat. 5D-4-10th-A was built. She speculates that the Mundo Perdido quarter would have been the ceremonial centre at this time since much more substantial architecture had already been built there (Laporte 2003). While the North Acropolis site may have been relatively undeveloped up to this time a new status for Tikal might have stimulated general upgrading throughout the central zone. Indeed, radical remodeling of an archaic institution may constitute evidence for the *may* seating, although this may never be certain. About five centuries later, ca. AD 200, another North Acropolis episode looks suspiciously like a special event (Figure 35, Plate 33). It follows another possible *may* seating at AD 179 (Rice 2006:91) by a near twenty-year interval roughly similar to that separating Plat. 5D-4-10th-A from the 334 BC seating mentioned above. Special ceremonies relating to the *may* burden might be involved in both cases.

2

Platform 5D-4-9th

Approximately at the beginning of the 2nd century BC architectural development took on a completely different trajectory (TR.14:30-40; 816-17). Features of Plat. 5D-Sub. 10th-A disappeared beneath an enormously larger installation (Plate 7) that functioned for another full century (TR.14:Chart 1).

Such massive replacement, completely concealing all earlier work, happened rarely over the course of North Acropolis evolution. Platform 5D-4-10th-B destroyed all earlier fabrics. Platform 5D-4-10th-A completely mantled 10th-B. Platform 5D-4-9th totally submerged 10th-A. But in developments subsequent to 9th, no single renewal project completely covered up all earlier features. Of course, the earlier fabrics are relatively small and easily covered whereas later ones, being larger, present more of a problem. But other factors suggest a different interpretation.

Both 10th-A and 9th seem to represent radical rethinking of architectural formats. Because of the drastic nature of change, these first two developmental stages suggest some kind of profound institutional evolution. If the primary function was indeed ritual, then perhaps changes were taking place in the premises and mythology underlying ritual practice. Subsequently, that is after 9th, architectural development proceeded in a more piecemeal fashion, more like fine-tuning than reconfiguring although some of these amounted to the most massive of all single developmental stages. Designers of 9th had evidently hit upon an architectural format that remained valid ever after. Aspects of 9th can be detected in all subsequent developments despite very great alterations both in overall character, in details, and in dimensions. A more evolved version appears at Uaxactun, Group H, South Plaza Estadio 3 (Valdes 1989:613). At the same time, ritual practice may have settled into the course followed through the Late Preclassic and Early Classic Periods.

Inflated scale and transformative architectural character suggest that the North Acropolis had suddenly acquired much greater status within the Tikal polity. A tenuous link to the office of rulership can be now identified (discussed below), as at Group E, Uaxactun (Hendon 1999:116). The shift in scale implies not only access to power and the resources necessary for large-scale construction but may also reflect a new role for the North Acropolis in relation to the office of ruler (Ahau). Whoever had previously used the site may now have acquired greater political authority. Enigmatic and fragmentary U. 224A (Chapter 1) may reflect ritual usage of some kind previously established; conflation of ritual with rulership may explain this abrupt shift in the trajectory of architectural development.

Platform 5D-4-9th-B (Fig. 7 and Plate 7) illustrates an entity not understandable until years after the excavations. The strongly unified architectural character it projects is partly due to assumptions employed in my reconstruction of it. A feature of this kind encountered on the surface would simply be designated as one "Structure" (see TR.5:6; TR.12:47). But, due to the piecemeal discovery of different parts at different times, deep within the acropolis excavation, various designations were employed as indicated in Figure 7.

For example in TR.14, the part labeled as the "acropolis" is Plat. 5D-4 U. 82 sustained by two lower platforms, U. 96 and U. 305 (Terrace South, see below and equivalent to a later feature designated North Terrace). As illustrated in Figure 7 and Plate 7 these appear simply as substructure platforms apparently sustaining the

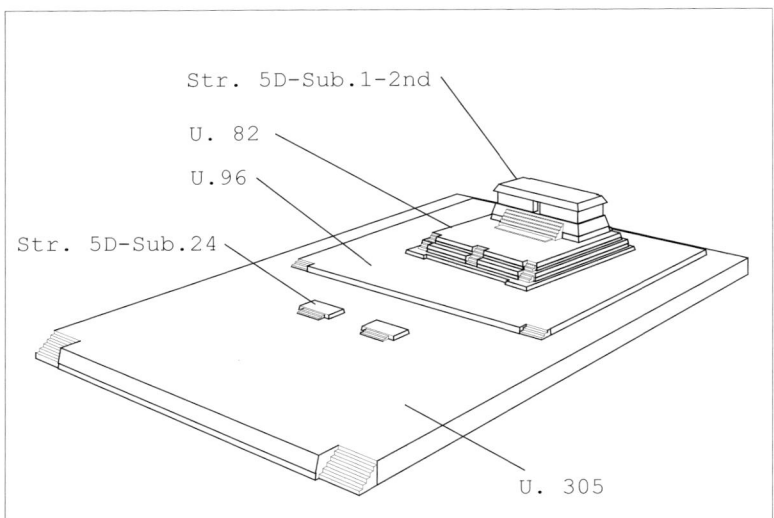

Figure 7. Platform 5D-4-9th-B.

(largely demolished) fabric of Str. 5D-Sub.1-2nd. If my reconstruction can be accepted, this ensemble might properly be referred to as the "first" North Acropolis. To recognize this formally, however, would entail a series of new designations. The inevitable confusion seems unwarranted.

Architectural features of 9th-B (TR.14:fig. 6a, 9a, 15-19) include Str. 5D-Sub.1-2nd, Terrace South (U. 305), Str. 5D-Sub.24 and its assumed eastern counterpart, U. 96, and (acropolis) U. 82.

Unit 305 was labeled "Terrace South" in TR.14 partly because of its uncertain form, with no paved top surface intact, and partly because of a suspicion that it had only three sides and backed into the bedrock slope rising to the north (TR.14:32). However, when I reconstructed a paved top surface located at the base level of U. 96, it just skimmed over the bedrock contours. I continued it further north as shown in Figure 7 and Plate 7 even though excavations found no trace of its presence there. As thus reconstructed it fills the role of a basal platform, a standard element in Maya monumental architecture (cf. Loten and Pendergast 1984:4; TR.12:47) though so extensive that it may have been a precursor to the Great Plaza.

By contrast, Plat. 5D-4 U. 96 does not fit any established Tikal Project architectural category except "supplementary platform". It is a low platform immediately above U. 305 (Terrace South) and it sustains U. 82 (Acropolis Platform). In TR.34B (in preparation) intermediate platform categories are set up, numbered ordinally from bottom to top, to establish a designation system able to accommodate any form of structure. In this system Terrace South is a First Supplementary Platform, U. 96 a Second Supplementary Platform, and U. 82 a third Supplementary Platform. These terms indicate only their position within the larger architectural whole and imply nothing about their formal properties. The First Supplementary Platform, in this case, is effectively a basal platform and the Third Supplementary Platform is identified in TR 14 as the "acropolis platform". But no other term has been applied to U. 96, the 9th-B Second Supplementary Platform.

This annoying re-labeling of features, with its attendant potential for confusion, frees the term "acropolis" to designate the architectural whole, and, of course, depends for its validity on my assumption that this entity was indeed designed as a whole. Plate 7 seems to me to suggest this, but the impression follows rather strongly on my own reconstruction.

The Plate 7 quadrangular First Supplementary Platform format with essentially level plastered upper surface presents an extrapolation far beyond evidence actually seen (TR.14:fig. 6a). No trace of an upper surface of this sort had survived. No E and W facings were detected. The entire rear portion had been removed anciently. However, presence of an apron molding on the S face (U. 110) seems to imply a more complete entity than the three-sided, unpaved feature reported in TR.14 in strict compliance with the evidence actually seen. If there really was a paved, level upper surface it had either eroded or been cut down to about half its original height along an irregular slope bearing a thin layer of black gumbo suggestive of ancient vegetation and topsoil (TR.14:32).

It seems unlikely that the terrace face beneath such a surface would have possessed an apron molding, or that Str. 5D-Sub.1-2nd would have been as Coe remarks "surrounded by dirt and seasonal mud." For these reasons I have restored a horizontal finish that results in a much larger platform than is suggested in TR.14.

If this reconstruction can be accepted the North Acropolis had gone at one stroke from modest to monumental. The fabric now looks like a single architectural composition comprising a basal platform, two intermediate supplementary platforms, one summit feature (Str. 5D-Sub.1-2nd), and two frontal features (Str. 5D-Sub.24 and its assumed E counterpart). This format embodies a triadic organization potentially loaded with symbolic content. One suggestion is that triadic compositions refer to the three hearth stones of creation (Sharer 1994:513-55; Freidel, Schele and parker 1993:65-67; Schele 1976; Hansen 1998:77-81).

The proportions that result from carrying the basal platform north of the building are rare in Maya architecture, an observation that might throw this reconstruction into question. Maximal dimensions more commonly run laterally, from side to side, perpendicular to frontal orientations rather than from front to rear as in this case. In my defense I cite similar proportions for the more completely known Second Supplementary Platform, though less extreme (TR.14:fig. 6a). and in the succeeding acropolis, 8th. In this latter case the issue of frontality is complicated by exclusively side access (TR.14:fig. 6b).

An even more unusual property of this basal platform is absence of a front axial stair. The succeeding acropolis (8th, Chapter 3), also displays this feature, but higher up, on the acropolis platform. From this I infer that some issue of symbolism was involved, probably to do with the NS direction frequently associated with rulers and deceased ancestors (Ashmore 1991:202; Coggins 19980:729; McAnany 1998:272). Absence of a stair where one would normally be expected could represent intentional emphasis on the directional axis in terms of its embodied meaning. Acropolis users, most likely overlapping categories of elites, rulers and ritual specialists, could not occupy the axial line until they reached the Second Supplementary platform leading directly to the summit level. Here the weight of symbolic meaning would be that much heavier for being inaccessible at the lower levels.

Plate 8 and Figure 8 show the rear axial outsets on Str. 5D-Sub.1-2nd building platform and Second Supplementary Platform where they are known to have been present. Hypothetical outsets are shown on the building and roof, parts that had been demolished anciently.

These outsets seem to exist only to emphasize the NS direction. It is difficult to imagine any other role that they might have played. As purely symbolic elements, they imply that expression of this axis was a conscious design consideration, probably related to the handling of axial and non-axial stairs as discussed

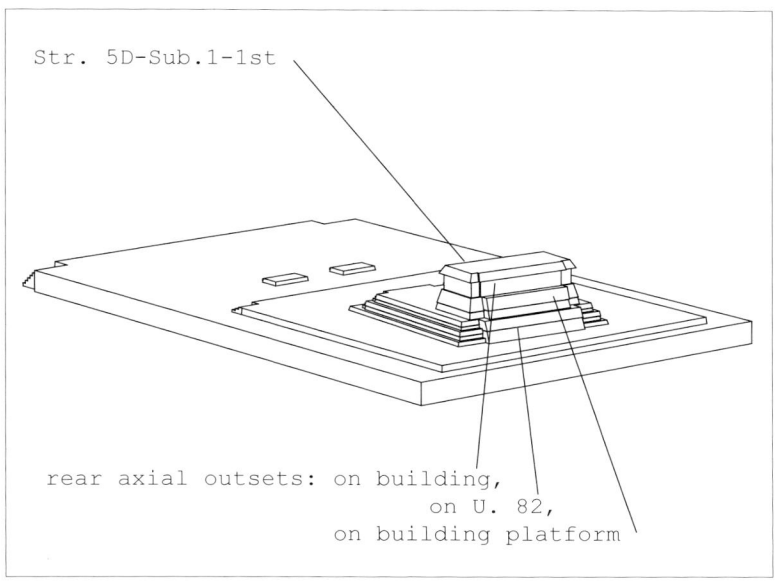

Figure 8. Platform 5D-4-9th-B.

above (more about non-axial stairs below). Such outsets might be considered as merely decorative elements, since no practical function is obvious. This is an etic evaluation. From the ancient Maya viewpoint, necessarily hypothetical, outsets might have been installed for the "practical" purpose of increasing the ability of the acropolis to attract certain supernatural beings, since directionality was inherent in their make-up (cf. Thompson 1950:223-24; Bassie-Sweet 1996:195-97).

I would extend this observation to suggest that presence of rear axial outsets might be a diagnostic feature of temples. The term "temple" is widely used with little precise meaning and even less certainty as to function (but see Becker 2003). Satterthwaite (1943) proposed as a short definition: (a) "structure believed to have been designed for public practice of religious rites and ceremonies", and referred to his earlier publication (1937) of a list of temple traits.

Although monumental structures are often referred to as public art, some temples may have been used exclusively by professional ritual specialists in ways that could not really be considered public. Furthermore, they may have taken many different forms. While traits such as presence of rear axial outsets and the others listed by Satterthwaite may identify some temples they probably would not apply universally.

Lateral stairs, that is, stairs within the front facade but flanking the axial stair, in both the basal platform and the second and third supplementary platforms may reflect both symbolic associations of E and W direc-

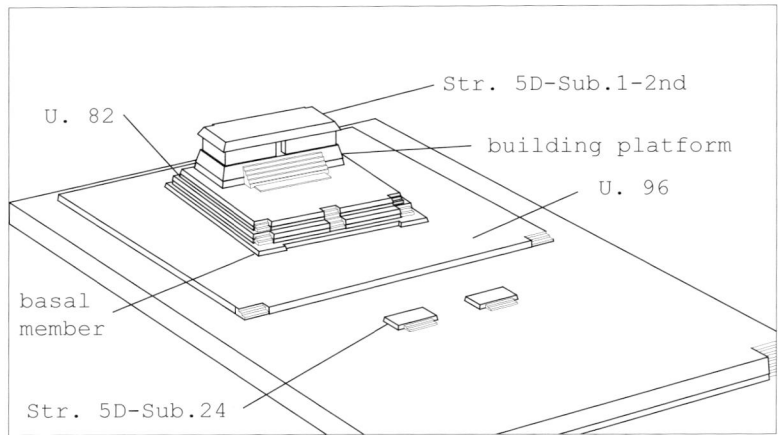

Figure 9. Platform 5D-4-9th.

tions and processional events incorporating movement in these directions. In the subsequent 8th Platform, side stairs were the only means of summit access, and then were dropped in later developments (7th through 5th) only to reappear even more prominently in the final stages (4th-1st).

Plate 9 and Figure 9 provide a closer look at the Third Supplementary Platform and Str. 5D-Sub.1-2nd. The apparent shift in orientation between platform and structure on the one hand, and lower parts (U. 96 and U. 305) evident here and in Plate 7, reflects absence of data pertaining to E and W faces of the latter features. These faces were not reached by the series of lateral tunnels that extended out from the main trench (TR. 14:fig.3).

Existence of Sub.24 (see also Plate 9) is certain but it had been demolished right down to base level leaving a simple rectangular plan outline on the U. 305 surface as the only sign of its former presence. Thatch roof on poles is purely hypothetical though such features do appear later (cf. Plates 18-23). Its undesignated eastern equivalent is assumed on the basis of symmetry and later practice. Lateral stairs placed at the E and W corners are known for the Second Supplementary Platform and are assumed for the lower ones on the basis of known absence on the NS axis. An axial stair at Third Supplementary Platform level is known, and is fully inset. This is an attribute of early architecture that contrasts with outset stairs on later works.

The two terraces of the Third Supplementary Platform have apron moldings formed largely of stucco with only slight working of the facing stones (an "apron molding" is a terrace profile formed by projecting an upper portion of the terrace face out beyond the lower portion (Loten and Pendergast 1984:3, fig. 1; see also Appendix II). Very shallow projection of the apron and absence of corbels (stones cantilevered out to carry the apron) or minimal corbelling are properties associated with early work, but not consistently maintained in this instance. Aprons on U. 110 and the rear axial outset are set on a projecting corbelled course in the manner uniformly adopted in later construction. This either reflects conceptual distinction between terraces and outsets, or, more likely in my opinion, different work crews doing things slightly differently on different parts of the complex.

Apron moldings recorded on the E facing terraces of the Third Supplementary Platform differ in details of construction from those on the S facing terraces (TR.14:35-36). I interpret this to mean that different crews were at work simultaneously on these separate faces, as noted above for the U. 110 apron. Observations concerning core assembly (TR.14:33) provide additional evidence for multiple work crews. It seems evident, even at this early date that a highly organized construction industry existed at Tikal. The increased scale of 9th over 10th in the North Acropolis was nothing new to these workers. Perhaps they had come from the Mundo Perdido project (Laporte 2003), or the South Acropolis (where early developments might well exist beneath later construction) or from one of several neighboring polities such as El Mirador.

A different sort of issue arises from the modest height of the Third Supplementary Platform (acropolis in TR.14), rising scarcely more that 2 m above its basal member, a height easily spanned by a single terrace. For such modest height neither structural nor construction considerations seem to call for division into two terraces. A specific number of terraces may have been induced by ideological considerations rather than structural exigencies. Terraces provide visually distinct layers or tiers that could be regarded as the parts of the fabric that specific mythological entities would inhabit. We have no direct evidence for such associations of architectural form in the Maya context but analogous findings are reported for the Aztec Templo Mayor (Van Zantwijk 1981:fig.2). From documentary sources Van Zantwijk found different supernatural beings associated with different terraces without any corresponding change in terrace form. The Third Supplementary Platform of Str. 5D-4-9th at Tikal could have been designed to satisfy a similar condition. Further, apron moldings might be accounted for by the same argument; they divide terraces into vertically separated zones so that a greater number of mythological characters could be accommodated.

Third Supplementary Platform terracing discussed above stands on a low basal member with forward projecting wings at its S corners (Plate 9). These stubby projections establish a very shallow U shape across the platform front. This seems to be nothing more than a formal gesture probably intended to enhance symmetry.

Although one cannot claim that symmetry by itself creates monumentality, it does contribute to this effect when the quality is present. This observation raises a difficult subject that requires much greater expatiation than would be appropriate here (see discussion in Introduction). Here I offer my own opinion that monumentality arises from the character of the parts and their compositional arrangement, or order. Scale and symmetry are key factors but are neither necessary nor sufficient to guarantee a monumental effect. My impression is that the 9th platform probably did achieve monumentality in the sense that it was capable of exerting an impressive effect that could be felt by observers and users. Subsequent changes systematically increase this effect up to a maximal point (Plates 55 and 61) after which frontal developments tend to diminish it, at least from the Great Plaza.

Existence of a Third Supplementary Platform basal member, too low to be rated as a terrace, raises a different kind of issue. Its presence implies a conceptual break with lower sustaining features. Physically it sustains the two upper terraces while visually appearing to mark some kind of distinction between them and the lower units, as a basal element setting up a new upper body. Possibly the Third Supplementary Platform held specific symbolic associations not shared by the lower parts. It may be appropriate, then, that In TR.14 this part is designated as the "acropolis" (TR.14: fig. 6a). On the other hand, the term "acropolis" may be unfortunate, with its old world connotations, and if used at all seems more appropriate for the whole complex pile. The distinction it implies, on the other hand, may be entirely accurate. For example, the acropolis platform might have been designed so that

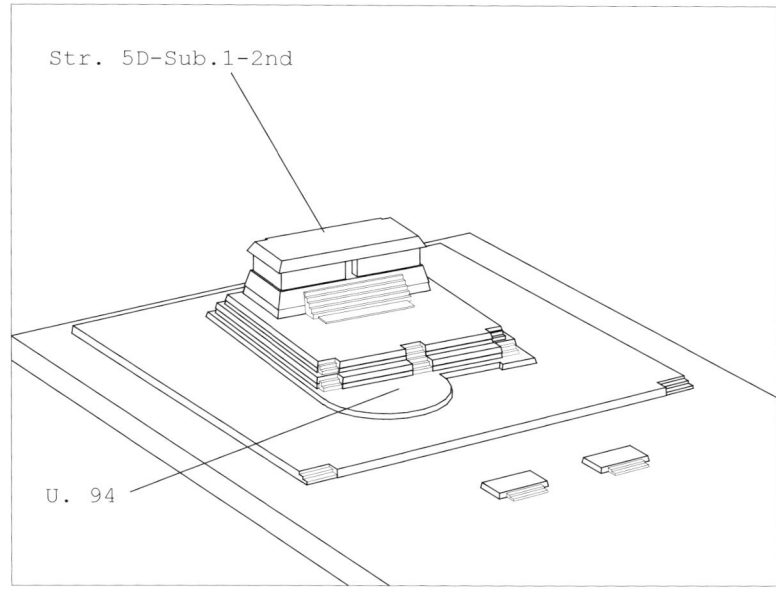

Figure 10. Platform 5D-4-9th-B.

ritual specialists could regard it as a particular zone within a supernatural landscape, the tiered "heaven" or perhaps underworld of ancient Maya mythology (Leon-Portilla 1988:135-43). Later, when the Great Plaza had been installed, the whole acropolis came to project a "north" association connected with rulership and, perhaps, celestial beings. This view obviously can be applied equally to all the North Acropolis substructure platforms built after the installation of the Great Plaza, and I will refrain from repeating this particular way of interpreting them in each of the following chapters.

Here, though, since this is where the matter arises for the first time, I think it appropriate to state clearly my view that to us architectural forms are merely symbolic. The ancient Maya, by contrast, might have understood them in quite different terms. They could regard the design of structures for ritual purposes as either dictated by supernatural beings, or permitted by them, since they understood all undertakings this way (Tedlock 1985:62; Carrasco 1990:92-123; Leon-Portilla 1988:91-98; Gossen 1986; Freidel, Schele, and Parker 1995:29-58; Thompson 1970:165-70; Mock 1998). In the ancient Maya animistic worldview it would follow that the human-made structure could be seen as formed by the will of supernaturals and, literally, as a portion of the supernatural realm projecting into the ordinary world of direct experience. Dangerous forces would be active there, and only well trained professional ritual specialists could safely use the premises. At this early date such functionaries may have been essentially priest/shamans, but later, during the Classic Period they may have been state officials, members of the elite, and rulers. Architectural development of the acropolis may well document a process whereby a shamanic site gradually morphed into a state enterprise with all the resources of a state available for its amplification and elaboration.

Because of ancient demolition, Str. 5D-Sub.1-2nd building platform height is estimated and all details of the building are hypothetical. I have illustrated a beam-and-mortar roof rather than thatch because of the likelihood of a rear axial outset, something not easily accommodated in thatch. The stair seems wide enough for more than one doorway but in the absence of data I have shown only a single opening although this would mean a rather dim interior.

Hypothetically, and not based on evidence, the building looks very like a residential unit, a simple rectangular plan with one central doorway. One cannot rule out the possibility that its function was indeed residential, as at Uaxactun (Hendon 1999:101), although no artifacts or special deposits support this view. Scale and complexity of the Plat. 5D-4-9th fabric suggest that if residence was part of the function it must have been a high-level elite individual or family. There is, of course, the possibility that residence was temporary and linked to major ceremonial rituals, perhaps for the purpose of fasting and seclusion.

Comparison with other works of comparable date may support a ritual interpretation. Late Preclassic Structure 350 at Cuello (Gerhart and Hammond 1991:113; Gerhart 1988) stands at one end of an open rectangular platform, and is clearly of ceremonial type. This arrangement, quite similar to Structure 450 at Komchen, Yucatan, provides another example (Ringle and Andrews 1988).

As a purely subjective response, no doubt deeply dyed with ethnocentric bias, I find it difficult to imagine this installation as a palace, with residence and reception as prime functions, although I suspect certain offices of rulership probably were performed here. Finally, there is the possibility, mentioned earlier, that residential form was employed to provide a "home" for supernatural or mythological characters even though these beings might be expected to inhabit the solid fabric rather than the rooms. A house form might still answer for this purpose.

Near the end of its career, that is to say approximately 100 BC (TR.14:Chart 1) a minor but puzzling addition, illustrated in Plate 10 and Figure 10, was made at the front base of the Third Supplementary Platform. This took the form of a low semicircular platform (TR.14:fig. 6a, U. 94) the same height as the basal member. The curious aspect of this, aside from circular geometry is its offset position W of the central axis. Given the concern for symmetry discussed above such a position surely must have been intentional. Placement on the W side of the axis suggests use for activities related to such things as death, sunset, dance, or simply offerings made in the W direction. The circular form certainly implies a ritual function of some kind, and the brief duration of this feature suggests a single event.

As mentioned earlier, Platforms 5D-4-10th and 9th completely obliterated all features of earlier works on the site. They represent an early pattern of development. A new course emphasizing partial replacement emerged after 9th and prevailed over the ensuing five or six centuries. In these later developments some parts of older fabrics always remained in use unchanged while others were replaced, or radically remodeled. This may reflect the scale that the complex had by now attained, making total replacement too demanding. But there are instances of very substantial additions (Fig. 26.5) in which earlier features still persist. Therefore I suspect doctrinal matters may have dictated this new departure. The following chapters describe these different patterns of development, all, despite very different formal characters, flowing from Plat. 5D-4-9th.

3

Platform 5D-4-8th

At this point (TR.14:40-56, 817-20) North Acropolis development gets more complicated. Obliteration of some previous features now accompanies preservation of others. A simple succession of one acropolis replacing another no longer applies. Plate 11 and Figure 11 illustrate the initial (8th-D) version of Plat. 5D-4-8th built perhaps in 156 BC, roughly 7.10.0.0.0.

This is date C of the Temple of the Inscriptions (Jones 1977:53-55). Its presence in this centuries later text implies something special and memorable. The same implication flows from the architectural development.

All parts of 9th not completely demolished have been concealed beneath new construction except for the dominant summit feature, Str. 5D-Sub.1-2nd; it alone survives from the previous fabric. The new acropolis summit surface, Fl. 13, was installed around it and presumably it continued in use for another (roughly) twenty years when it was cut down to Fl. 13 level and replaced by Str. 5D-Sub.1-1st.

Within the North Acropolis Platform 5D-4-8th-D seems to indicate something like a cultural horizon. From this point forward it appears the North Acropolis remained essentially the same in basic concept and function even though on-going social, political and intellectual processes either required or provoked transformations of the fabric. Surprising departures in architectural form explored novel morphologies but probably not because of new ownership or new functional programs. The continuing search may have been motivated by desire to display more dramatically the beliefs served by acropolis functions and to bolster the commitment those functions demanded.

This might reflect propagandistic/political agendas, but could also arise from essentially eschatological considerations. The two categories are not mutually exclusive. As previously discussed, in ancient Maya (animistic) natural philosophy more dramatic forms could produce better results in material things like victory in battle, success in trade, good crops, healthy offspring, long life, and general prosperity by pleasing the forces of the universe localized at Tikal that would then help them realize these desirable outcomes.

The ancient Maya undoubtedly considered that offerings and rituals were essential to these ends and that an appropriate setting for their performance could increase the probability of gaining support of these forces, critical, in their view, to success of any endeavor.

The acropolis illustrated in Plate 11 and Figure 11 appears to have expanded enormously to E and W, at least in the lower components (U. 111D). This may be slightly misleading in that E and W faces of equivalent 9th units were not encountered in the excavations. Increased amount of lower substructure build-up is already starting to appear at the E edge. The complex is expanding beyond the original bedrock knoll. This increases dramatically in subsequent developments.

Unit 59 is a strip of paving anticipating the Great Plaza but apparently not carried very far to the S (TR.14:166). The extent shown in Plate 11 is conjectural and minimal. The assumption is that the area later occupied by the Great Plaza was largely unpaved at this time though possibly somewhat leveled artificially. Unit 59 seems to represent a very tentative recognition that something more formal in front of the acropolis might be called for. The number of participants in certain ceremonies may have been increasing perhaps due to enhanced North Acropolis status, ability to command

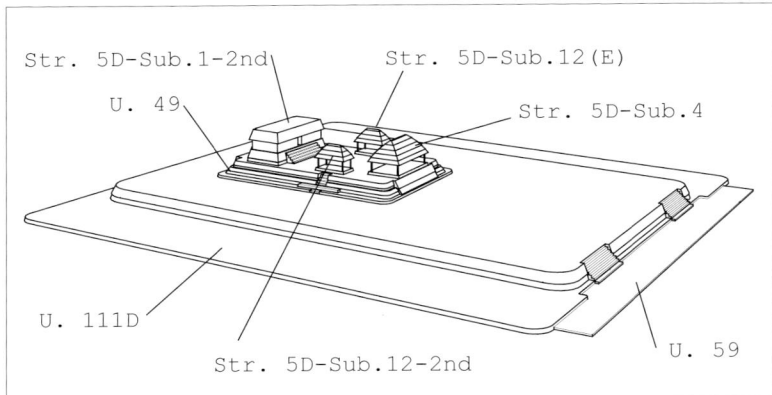

Figure 11. Platform 5D-4-8th-D.

attendance, or simply increasing urban population.

Arrangement of lower platform bodies, below summit level, follows the preceding acropolis to the extent that there are again three of them; a basal platform, or First Supplementary Platform (U. 111D), Second Supplementary Platform (Terrace South surfaced by U. 49 pavement), and Third Supplementary, or "acropolis" Platform (U. 232/83/and 64A terracing. But the setup is very different (discussed further below).

On the summit, Str. 5D-Sub.1-2nd continues in use and indeed it was only due to the thickness of Fl. 13 that any of it survived to show it had ever existed. The quadrangular arrangement of summit features formed by Sub.1-2nd, Sub.12-2nd, its E counterpart (assumed for symmetry), and Sub.4 is a major innovation. Although abandoned early on in 8th this quadrangular format possessed powerful associations and it reappears later (Plate 35).

Quadrangular summit compositions prevail through the final stages of North Acropolis development all the way to terminal abandonment. Such arrangements are, of course, endemic to ancient Maya monumental architecture and appear at a very large number of different sites in all temporal periods. They embody ancient Maya metaphysics. The cosmos was seen as four sided. North may equate with "up," the celestial realm, and South with "down," the underworld. Forces of nature were similarly envisaged. Quadrangular architectural compositions like this could reflect such ideas.

The 260 T'zolk'in days could lie behind this arrangement. The T'zolk'in divides into four sets of 65 days, each with 5 sets of the 13 numerical coefficients. Rice obliquely implies that each quarter may have been associated with a cardinal direction (Rice 2004:71). By rotating ceremonies around the quadrangle this subdivision of the T'zolk'in could be incorporated into ritual observances.

If Str. 5D-Sub.12-2nd did indeed have an eastern counterpart a triadic composition is present with Sub.1-2nd as its dominant central feature. Triadic arrangements carry as much iconographic burden (three hearthstones of creation) as does the quadrangle. The major mythic connection is with the beginning of the current era retroactively established as 3114 BC.

I show Str. 5D-Sub.12-2nd, its assumed eastern counterpart, and Str. 5D-Sub.4 as open pavilions of pole and thatch. This is entirely conjectural. No upper parts had survived to give any clue to superstructure form. Absence of stair projections suggests that substructures were low.

In TR.14 Str. 5D-Sub.4 is profiled conjecturally as higher than I illustrate (TR.14:fig. 44) and assumed to face S. This raises a problem in that it stands right on the edge of the axial outset in the south façade, so that a stair would have no landing. The low form illustrated in Plate 11 and Figure 11 avoids this problem.

Perhaps the most intriguing innovation to arise in 8th is exclusive summit access via stairs on E and W sides. This may not have been such a radical shift in its day, in that twinned frontal stairs at the lateral corners of 9th already indicate concern for EW directional aspects of ritual performance. However, it may reveal presence of doctrinal divisions among the authorities controlling acropolis development and use. Perhaps a faction particularly interested in EW rituals achieved dominance at this time.

The Third Supplementary Platform, referred to as the acropolis platform in TR.14, repeats the earlier (9th-B) formation comprising two terraces with apron moldings standing on a basal member. At the same time other aspects of this platform are radically changed. The NS direction is now emphasized by outsets on both north and S faces. The axial front stair is eliminated. Platform corners are rounded.

Both acropolis platform terraces stand on a low member that acts as a base, visually, and I suspect, conceptually, separating them from Terrace South. Designation of Terrace South as a feature distinct from, but sustaining, the acropolis recognizes this. My guess is that some ceremonial participants might have been allowed on to Terrace South but not any higher, while other were relegated to the lower E and W features (U. 111D).

The Second Supplementary Platform (Terrace South) extends southward to just in front of Plat. 5D-4-

9th-B U.305 (Plate 7). Its single terrace has an apron molding, rounded corners, and twinned stairs set within the front façade flanking the axial line but not at the extreme E and W edges as previously seen in 9th-B. It rests on a very low basal element (U. 111D) extending EW and U-shaped across the S front. This U shape is like the basal member of the 9th-B acropolis platform (U. 82), best seen in Plate 9. Its purpose seems to be that of strengthening the sense of symmetry around the NS axial line, locus of Bu. 164, and perhaps counterbalancing the EW emphasis of the U. 111D features by reasserting importance of the NS direction. East and W U. 111D projections provide paved areas facing toward the acropolis stairs. These surfaces seem like early versions of the (not yet formalized) Great Plaza, places where, as mentioned above, some members of the community could witness at least some aspects of ritual events on the acropolis, particularly processions mounting the stairs, or perhaps events staged directly on them. The U. 111D features act visually as a first intermediate platform sustaining Terrace South.

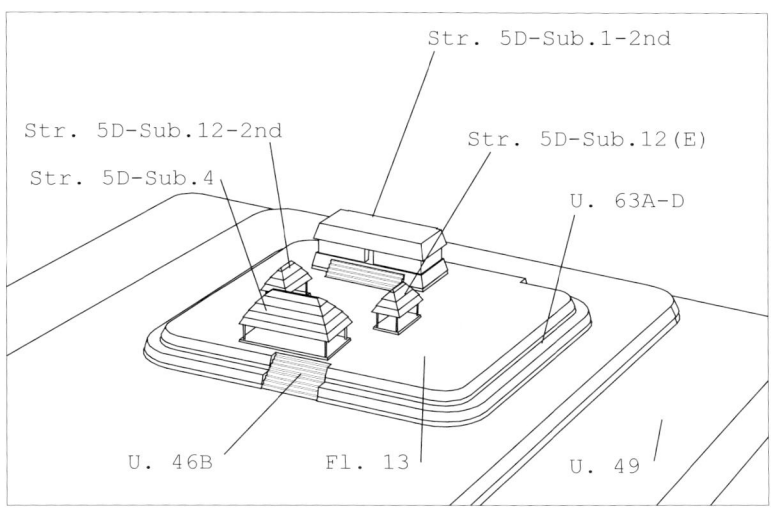

Figure 12. Platform 5D-4-8th-C.

Although quadrangular arrangements are known in residential contexts the level of formality evident here, at the summit, suggests either ritual use or a very special kind of residence. Persistent on-floor burning (TR.14:Table 5) may reflect ritual use although both cooking and terminal destruction of buildings could be represented. Lateral (EW) spread of U. 111D basal features suggests provision for an audience too numerous or not sufficiently purified to be on the acropolis. Ritual functioning is implied. Later development of the Great Plaza may represent expansion of this aspect of North Acropolis function.

Leaving the summit quadrangle intact, the acropolis platform is now completely remodeled, no higher, but much wider, and expanded eastward (Plate 12). This new platform introduces plan geometry typical of all later development in that its maximum dimension extends from side to side rather than from front to rear. Rounded corners are assumed but the two terraces with apron moldings (U. 63 A-D), and the new central stair (U. 46B) are known. The unbalanced condition illustrated in Plate 12, with its very evident asymmetry, probably did not prevail for very long but did exist briefly. Presumably the decision to build W-facing Str. 5D-Sub.9 assumed to be more substantial in scale and elaboration than earlier summit features, on the E side of the summit (see below), had already been made and this development provides for it. At the same time, changes in the make-up of the acropolis platform raise some intriguing points.

The acropolis platform is now simplified to only two terraces; the 8th-D basal member has been eliminated. If that basal member had the kind of significance I have proposed for Platform 5D-4-8th-D (above), then a shift in understanding of the whole set of platforms must have taken place. In effect Terrace South is now part of the "acropolis" and appears to stand on a new basal unit (U. 111D) pertaining to the whole complex rather than specific to the acropolis platform body. If the different platform bodies each held specific associations in ancient Maya eschatology, there may have been some change in these beliefs.

Structure 5D-Sub.1-2nd, Sub.12-2nd, its assumed eastern counterpart, and Sub.4 all remained intact while these changes were made. Presumably, the summit quadrangle continued to function while construction was underway and, to judge from the way the new axial stair on Acropolis Axis B (TR.14:fig. 5) came up to Str. 5D-Sub.4 (TR.14:fig. 44) for a (probably short) time after construction had been completed.

With Sub.1-2nd still extant and the new acropolis platform in place with an axial front stair and a (retained) rear axial outset, the NS axis now clearly dominates. Developments leading up to this point and following afterward suggest a pattern of alternating emphases switching from NS to EW and back again, as though user groups were taking turns controlling development, or perhaps, changes were being made in response to calendric factors calling for these differing directional emphases.

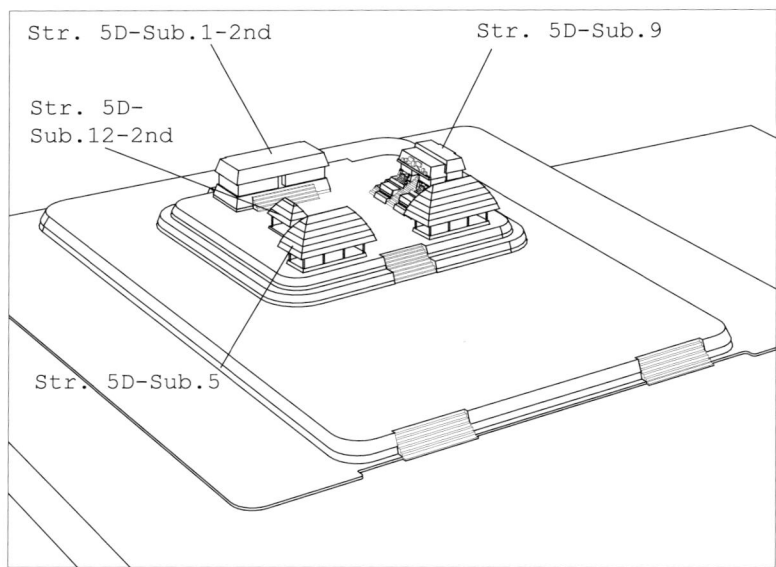

Figure 13. Platform 5D-4-8th-B.

For example, during one particular period, a K'atun perhaps, NS forces might have been considered in control of events (cf. Haviland 1992:74-79), so that NS emphasis would contribute most effectively to optimal results, while in another calendric period EW forces might be ascendant. These and other factors might affect the duration of individual structures, for example 5D-Sub.1-2nd stood for more than a century and must have functioned in at least five different K'atuns during the run-up to the arrival of Baktun 8 while other features on the summit were replaced.

The Plate 13 (Figure 13) sequence of events is unclear. Structure 5D-Sub.9 could either precede or follow Sub.5 and its (assumed) eastern counterpart though it seems likely any interval between them was quite brief. Venerable Str. 5D-Sub.1-2nd was still standing when Fl. 13 was laid (TR.14:209) and therefore could have continued in use while Str. 5D-Sub.9 and Sub.5 were being built. I have assumed that if there ever was an eastern equivalent to Str. 5D-Sub.12-2nd it would have been removed for construction of Sub.9. The summit illustrated in Plate 13 probably enjoyed only a very short duration although many of its features continued in use more than a century and through the first four or five K'atuns of Baktun 8.

If the symmetrical arrangement of Str. 5D-Sub.5 on the W side of the axial line balanced by an assumed equivalent structure to its E is correct the intention must have been that of firmly marking the new axis, several meters E of the previous one. Discrepancy between Sub.1-2nd and the axial stair of the acropolis platform clearly reveals the extent of this displacement.

Architectural form of Sub.5 is largely unknown. Almost every speck of its material had been removed for Str. 5D-Sub.3-F (Plate 18) and its existence is indicated by a couple of scribe lines in the floor surface supporting it (U. 42, an extension of Fl. 13 carried over the few remaining bits of Sub.4). The form shown, then, is hypothetical.

A similar state of minimal evidence applies to Str. 5D-Sub.9. Only a few basal features were exposed in excavations. The parts of features actually seen appeared similar to analogous ones on the more completely investigated Sub.1-1st (Plate 14) and for this reason Sub.9 has been reconstructed identically in all respects. This, of course, raises a procedural issue as well as an architectural one. In general, reconstructions beyond evidence are not based on forms of other structures since this introduces an obvious analytic glitch. The architectural issue, illustrated in Plate 14 is posed by presence to two identical structures in different orientations; Sub.1-1st aligned NS, and Sub.9. Identical structures in the same orientation appear later in the sequence (Plate 43) though, again, the E feature is less thoroughly examined than the W one. In the case of Sub.9 evidence available implies similarity to Sub.1-1st but the degree of uncertainty is such that no great argument can be developed around it.

The summit composition illustrated in Plate 14 and Figure 14 may well be the arrangement envisaged when the 8th-C acropolis platform was installed only a few years earlier. I have assumed that Str. 5D-Sub.1-1st was the last of the new features to be put in place. Stratigraphic evidence does not provide a clear sequence since all four bear the same relationship to Fl. 13. The arrangement looks odd and inconsistent in that strong symmetry set up by Sub.5 features is then destroyed by the rest of the summit. Asymmetry of Sub.9 and Sub-12-2nd seems to be certain since whatever may have been the form of Sub.9 it is clearly much larger. To that extent the unbalanced character of this long-lasting acropolis summit must be acknowledged. Possibly the EW/NS eschatological interests discussed earlier may be still at play here. In any case, however, the new axial line (TR.14 Axis B) is certainly made evident by the position of Sub.1-1st.

My conclusion that Sub.1-1st follows Sub.9 is based on alignments of terraces in the front part of its substructure. This matter is further developed below (Plate 15). Here I just mention that the front part of the substructure seems directed slightly toward the SW not parallel to the rear terraces. This frontal divergence is barely visible in Figure 15 and Plate 15 but quite clear in the TR.14 1:100 plans (TR.14:Fig. 21). I suspect that Sub.9 was already either under construction or entirely in place when these Sub.1-1st frontal terraces were laid out. Their westward deflection is obvious enough to suggest intentional planning and opens up the NE corner of the summit quadrangle. The evidence we have, however, supports either this reconstruction or one in which structures 5D-Sub.1.1st and 5D-Sub.9 are built simultaneously.

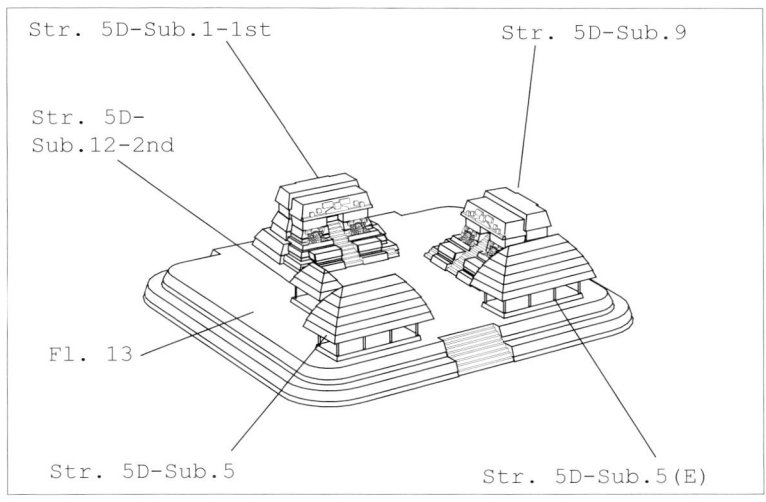

Figure 14. Platform 5D-4-8th-A.

As mentioned above, the rather strange composition formed by presumed identical structures Sub.1-1st and Sub.9 is partly artificial since few details of Sub.9 are available. The problematic aspect of it, for me, is that if Sub.1-1st is the dominant feature, on the axis, its status does not appear to have been expressed architecturally. A similar condition can be seen in later developments (Plates 25 and 26) during transitional stages. Otherwise, summit compositions that functioned for more substantial periods always presented a single dominant feature at the N end of the NS axis, larger than other summit features. It seems likely to me that these N structures held special significance of central importance to the role the North Acropolis played in the life of Tikal. Therefore I feel dubious about reality of the Figure 13 and Plate 13 with no architectural distinction between the N and E features.

Plate 15 and Figure 15 provide close-up views of Sub.1-1st as seen from the SE quarter. It has been described as "one of the most remarkable early buildings of the Americas" (Coe 1965:11). The roof, upper zones and upper parts of the building walls had been dismantled (TR.14:210-16) but lower parts are relatively well preserved except for the demolished rear walls. Only a few patches of heavily weathered exterior plaster survived.

Although the Tikal Project inventory of structures does not provide any comparable early works apart from almost totally demolished Str. 5D-Sub.1-2nd, it seems likely that Sub.1-1st followed a well established formula for ritually specialized monumental architecture. As Plate 15 shows, there are two major parts, a rearward body and a frontal body. Both divide horizontally into three parts; lower substructure, pseudo building platform (see Appendix II, "Platform" article) and building. Presence/absence of a roof comb is not known, but a large amount of modeled stucco debris perhaps indicates its presence. All the parts of the frontal body are set one step below their rearward counterparts. All sub-components are confined within horizontal divisions, except the rear axial outset, which extends vertically from the base level of the rearward terracing to the base of the building rear wall. The entire substructure was assembled and plastered prior to construction of building walls. Frontally, substructure height is almost exactly one third of the width at base level, a ratio much higher than the value found in dwellings (Haviland 1985). This ratio will be investigated more comprehensively in TR.34B.

The lower substructure of the frontal body has large outsets flanking the axial stair so that it appears inset even at base level. The stair is divided into two flights; one in the lower platform, the other in the Building Platform. This upper flight is so deeply inset that its landing emerges well within the front room between jambs that project into the room space; a rare feature in Tikal architecture.

Two additional stairs ascend the lower platform on the outer edges of the outsets. These recall lateral stairs on acropolis and basal platform units of earlier fabrics and may indicate that functions of such stairs and basal units, eliminated earlier had been reinstated in Sub.1-1st.

Division into frontal and rearward bodies parallels division of the acropolis platform into two terraces. Similar reasoning may have determined morphology

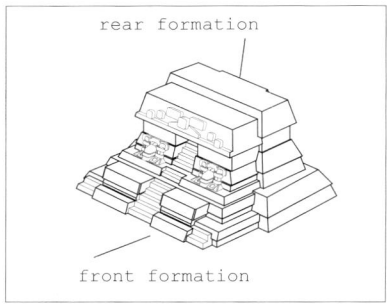

Figure 15. Structure 5D-Sub.1-1st.

in both cases. That is, concern to provide for a specific number of supernatural entities. Presumably they were expected to inhabit different parts of the fabric. Forming it in the appropriate number of distinct bodies would allow for this.

The different entities involved might not have been entirely different, but could have been dualistic aspects of some larger supernatural body. Dualism was a deeply ingrained feature of ancient Maya natural philosophy, as for example a living ruler linked to a deceased ancestor (Carrasco 1990:40; McAnany 1998:273). Many other examples of dualistic concepts in Mesoamerican thinking could be cited (cf. León-Portilla 1963:80-103).

Architectural attributes of Sub.1-1st are treated more comprehensively in TR.34B. I single it out for individual attention here (Plate 15 and Figure 15) because it seems to me a key diagnostic feature for North Acropolis interpretation. Questions of function, royal residence, sacerdotal complex, setting for sacrificial ceremony, or some combination of all three with perhaps other functions thrown in as well, will probably always remain open. My bias leans toward ceremonial activities with connections to rulership. The shift eastward from the earlier axis might reflect a dynastic change.

Str. 5D-Sub.1-1st looks to me like the kind of architecture that might have served such purposes. I think it presents formal properties, traits, or attributes diagnostic of "temple" architecture (see discussion in Chapter 2). Attributes of Sub.1-1st that look to me like "temple" traits include bifurcated substructure with distinct front and rear formations, particular type of mask panels flanking the stair, vertical proportions of height in relation to width side to side (aspect ratio 1:1.9), rear axial outset, and interior axial recesses. Abundant evidence of burning on floor surfaces in and around the structure may be a "temple" indicator but burn marks appear on residential floor surfaces also.

Presence of offerings (caches) would greatly strengthen "temple" interpretation but Sub.1-1st fabric failed to produce any and the attributes listed above must stand as the evidence for this category of function.

Distinct frontal and rearward substructure bodies differing in height, width, terrace formation, and sculptural treatment seems to me one of the strongest attributes pointing to "temple" function. Observations presented in Chapter 2 concerning division of the acropolis platform into two terraces would apply equally to these substructure bodies. Similar reasoning may have determined morphology in both cases. The rear body might associate with one set of supernatural forces and the front body to another.

On a simpler level of interpretation, the rear room of the building might have housed certain articles or served certain functions, while the front room accommodated different ones. Consideration of the mask panels, discussed below, suggests nocturnal functioning for the front part of the structure. Perhaps the rear room was used in daytime.

Mesoamerican interest in dualistic aspects of supernatural forces, cited above present another line of speculation. The dyadic form of Sub.1-1st potentially embodies such esoteric ideas in an immediately obvious and impressive way. Professional ritual specialists would certainly see these forms. The lay population might see them from a distance. Concurrence by commoners would have been essential to the emergence of a polity in which authority derived at least in part from these activities.

The designation "Sub.1-1st" reflects its position directly replacing the almost totally demolished Sub.1-2nd and apparently representing some kind of conceptual continuity between the two structures (see Introduction, Appendix II, and TR.5:9 for discussion of the Architecture Development designation).

The later fabric, "1st," is seen as a reconstitution of the earlier "2nd" because of its position (similarity in form would be helpful but 2nd had been almost entirely removed). If conceptual continuity seemed lacking the later structure (1st) would have been assigned another number in the "5D-Sub." series. From this viewpoint one can reflect back on Sub.1-2nd, which did not possess enough surviving features to show what sort of architectural character and form it possessed.

Either Sub.1-2nd was indeed unadorned and formally simple, as shown in Plates 7-12, or it had features similar to Sub.1-1st that were all destroyed or left traces that lay beyond the reach of the excavations. In any case 1st is certainly larger than 2nd and very likely more richly elaborated and articulated. These changes may have been made to show meanings already implicit in 2nd despite its apparently residential format. At the same time replacement of 2nd with a larger fabric might have been intended to increase the effect of monumentality and more effectively dominate the acropolis complex, including extensive Terrace South expanse (Plate 16).

On the frontal Building Platform, large masks flank the axial stair. Although poorly preserved they have been understood as jaguar references (TR.14:213). Plate 16 shows a reconstruction of the W mask based on TR.14:fig. 23 and 24. When Str. 5D-Sub.1-1st was partially demolished, roughly a century and a half after its initial construction, for major increase in acropolis height (Plate 26), these masks were partially defaced. Large chunks of modeled stucco, knocked off but remaining nearby, were recovered in the excavation. The stone armature that had held them, still in place, shows the rough mask shape. Polychrome detailing, illustrated in TR.14:fig. 23 and 24) is omitted from Plate 16.

Sculptural treatment, not previously in evidence at this locus, though not necessarily absent earlier, raises a different kind of question concerning fundamental intentions. It is tempting, from a twentieth century secular viewpoint, to treat this as mere decoration, a display of power, status and wealth. But this could be quite wrong. If my fundamental assumptions concerning design intentions in the North Acropolis are correct, even approximately, then features such as these masks were calculated to increase functional effectiveness by strengthening the likelihood that supernaturals would choose to be present, that they would accept the offerings made to them, and that they would be inclined to support Tikal enterprises. In this sense the masks could be considered as endowed with power.

Roughly contemporary with Str. 5D-Sub.1-1st (Late Preclassic) in the southern lowland region, jaguar imagery appears at El Mirador on Structure 34 (Hansen 1984), on the Tigre pyramid (Matheny 1987), at Cerros on Structure 29B (Freidel and Schele 1988:fig. 2-6, and at Uaxactun Group H Valdes 1989: fig. 6-10).

In subsequent years at Tikal jaguar imagery shows up on Stela 4 (TR.33A:fig. 5), Str. 5D-22-3rd (TR.14: fig. 97, 2), Str. 5C-4:Li.2. (TR.33A:fig. 73), Str. 5D-1:Li 3 (TR.33 A:fig. 70), a Manik Complex vessel from Bu. 22 in Str. 5D-26-1st (TR.25:fig. 22), a Bu. 190 Imix Complex plate in Late Classic Str. 7F-30 (TR.25: fig. 81), and most spectacularly on Str. 5D-3:Li. 2 (TR.33A:fig. 72). The latter image is perhaps the most telling, even though far removed in time from Str. 5D-Sub.1-1st. It shows a Terminal Classic Tikal ruler wearing jaguar skins and a jaguar headdress. Jaguar imagery has long been associated with the night sun (cf. Thompson 1960:134) although more recent studies question this (personal communication C. Jones).

The jaguar image carved into the wood of Lintel 3, Str. 5D-1 (Temple I) looms behind the renowned ruler Jasaw Chan K'awiil and is accompanied by texts citing his victory over the rival center of Calakmul (Schele

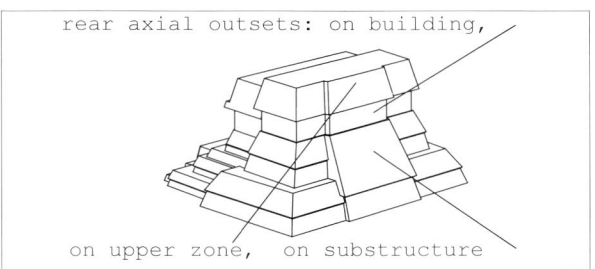

Figure 16. Structure 5D-Sub.1-1st rear façade.

and Freidel 1990: 211). According to these authors the jaguar image depicts a war palanquin captured in battle. To temple users the image might call forth the force, power, or being(s) responsible for that victory. Its presence would evoke those particular supernatural entities for their continued support in other Tikal enterprises.

Significantly this and other similar images at Tikal are within the buildings. They would not be visible to the populace at large. Perhaps their power was such that only professionals could behold them.

In subsequent Str. 5C-4 (Temple IV):Li. 2 a human figure stands in similar posture behind a seated ruler and wears the cruller eye ornament of number seven and the jaguar. The same cruller appears on the carved stair-block of centuries earlier Str. 5D-22-3rd, at that time the dominant north feature of the North Acropolis. The Temple IV figure has been identified by Simon Martin (1996) as a Naranjo war palanquin captured in AD 744 by the son of Jasaw Chan K'awiil.

In Olmec contexts (M. Coe 1989:73), on artifacts other than buildings, mesoamerican Jaguar imagery appears much earlier than anything currently known at Tikal. Such images are enigmatic compared with the Late Classic and Terminal Classic Tikal examples cited above but seem related to both rulership and shamanism. Architectural development of the North Acropolis from Preclassic into Early Classic may recapitulate a transition from shamanistic to dynastic function although these are not distinct categories in that rulers may well have functioned shamanistically.

Iconographic studies of jaguar imagery, linking feline features with such things as the number seven, the watery underworld, shamanism, and rulership, naturally focus on symbolism. But the ancient makers of figurines, sculptures, and architectural features may have had more directly pragmatic issues in mind.

Production of figural imagery is a kind of naming and from within the shamanic worldview naming things calls them into being. Therefore, placing jaguar images on North Acropolis buildings may be a way of calling to non-material jaguar counterparts for practi-

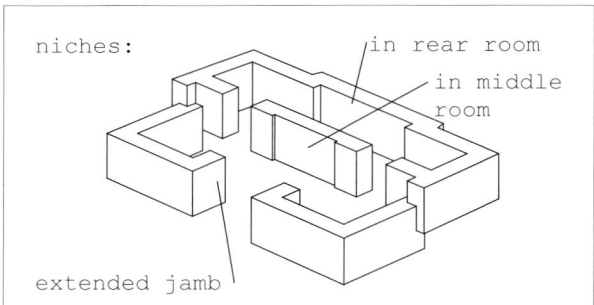

Figure 17. Structure 5D-Sub.1-1st building walls.

cal, pragmatic, materialist purposes, such as victories over powerful rivals like Calakmul and Naranjo.

Anyone mounting the axial stair of Str. 5D-Sub.1-1st would enter the space of the masks and might be reminded that entering the building meant confronting dangerous forces that might easily be offended. Therefore I would infer that users of this structure were high-level, experienced and trained, professional ritual specialists, technicians skilled in dealing with unstable forces that could as easily wreak enormous damage as grant spectacular profit. In later centuries it is clear that rulers often occupied these positions in Mesoamerican society (Chase and Chase 1992:3-17).

Here, at this early date, the role of rulers is less obvious, but some of the intense on-floor burning within the building, particularly in the W half of the front room, may result from rulers acting for the general benefit of the emerging state. Haviland and Moholy-Nagy (1992:57), citing North Acropolis tombs, point to precisely this period, the 1st century BC as the time when a Tikal elite establishment can be identified archaeologically.

In Plate 17 and Figure 16 Str. 5D-Sub.1-1st is seen from the NE quarter. As mentioned earlier, the entire rear wall of the building had been demolished but its base lines could be seen in the plastered top of the Building Platform (TR.14:212). From these, and other surviving details, it is clear that the rear axial outset reflects interior axial recesses in the rear walls of both the front and rear rooms (Figure 17).

These recesses (TR.14:fig. 21) seem too shallow to have served any physical purpose. They appear to be aspects of form that carry the NS directional emphasis of the structure right through the building, not only as exterior display. As interior features that would be seen exclusively by ritual specialists, and perhaps a few other individuals, these cannot be considered to represent rhetorical elements of merely symbolic significance. My guess is that these are particularly clear examples of morphology aimed at securing benevolent supernatural influence by embodiment of a directional orientation presumably associated with certain supernatural entities.

At substructure level the rear axial outset, rising unbroken to the building walls, may indicate that, despite its morphological divisions, this part of the structure had a single identity perhaps associated with a supernatural force larger than those of its parts. That is, some over-arching association may have subsumed the various entities connected with the many different parts so clearly articulated. In this sense the whole substructure might properly be regarded as a Building Platform despite the fact that, from the front (Plate 14), there appears to be a very distinct separation between an upper body and a lower body. This may merely hint at the complexity of natural philosophy embodied in this and many other Maya structures built to serve ritual specialist functions.

Some time within the last quarter of the 1st century BC (TR.14:Chart 1), the twin structures that had been flanking the axial acropolis stair were demolished completely (at least on the W side). Only differential burning and layout scars remain as testimony to their previous existence. They were replaced (Figure 19) by a new structure Sub.3-F (TR.14:fig. 37) placed squarely at the head of the stair, asserting the new N-S axis (Axis B) and sustained by Fl. U. 41, an auxiliary floor that blends into old Fl. 13 further N. Old structures Sub.12-2nd, Sub.1-1st and Sub.9 remained in use. Either simultaneously with Sub.3-F or only slightly later, Str. 5D-Sub.11 appeared on the SW corner of the summit (Plate 19). I have opted to show Sub.11 as a separate addition, in contrast with Coe's sequence, on the grounds that it is united with Fl. 12 (TR.14:fig. 33b), and that this floor abuts Sub.3-F (TR.14: Fig. 44).

Plate 18 illustrates Sub.3-F with a beam-and-mortar roof although it could as well have had a thatch roof. The substructure is divided into lower frontal and higher rear bodies, but there is no corresponding shift in the plan lines of the building walls indicated by floor turns and some wall fragments that were within the trench (TR.14:248-51). Therefore there are no awkward corners to complicate thatching. Nevertheless I have opted for beam-and-mortar because of the presence of a rear axial outset (further discussed below) in the N wall. A beam-and-mortar roof could have repeated the outset at the upper level. A thatch roof might not have done so.

The Sub.3-F substructure, low compared to Sub.1-1st, incorporates several similar features. It too has a rear axial outset echoed in the rear room by an axial recess similar to those of Sub.1-1st and presumably similar in significance. My guess is that these rear axial recesses mark the NS axis within the rooms so that this focus of architectural form, and also perhaps of ritual action, is not obscured internally. The front axial stair is deeply inset and projects well into the interior. Masks, barely preserved, probably bearing ear ornaments, flank the stair.

Exterior outsets on Sub.3-F and Sub.1-1st carry the NS axial line of the acropolis beyond the confines of the structures, or at least beyond the limits of their rear rooms so as to indicate that the axial line does not terminate in either feature. The reason for this may be that the axial line was not seen by the ancient designers merely as an organizing device for architectural composition but as a real line of some kind, perhaps a locus of force, energy, or an aspect of the identity of the non-material beings including deceased rulers, addressed via ritual actions.

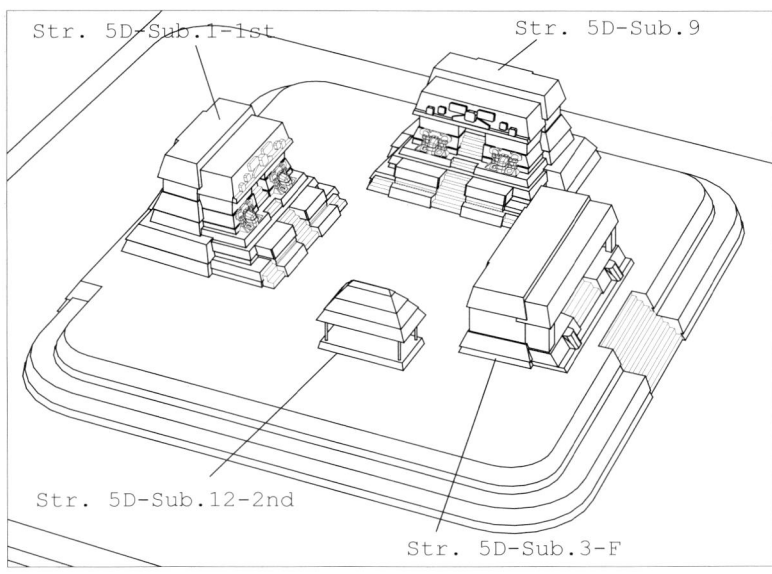

Figure 18. Platform 5D-4-8th-A.

The front room of Str. 5D-Sub.3-F has an opening almost 12 m wide, too wide to be considered as a doorway. Directly behind it, giving into the rear room is another huge opening, almost 9 m wide. No evidence of intermediate support is visible within these openings. How they were spanned is problematic. I have simply shown the frontal opening with no intermediate support and left the problem hanging.

Formality generated by replacement of Sub.5 with Sub.3-F shows up asymmetry of the acropolis summit compound with greater clarity. Although only limited excavations probed the W side of the summit at this level, it seems very unlikely that there could have been another structure of comparable dimension to balance Sub.9. Asymmetry appears conspicuously, much later, in the contrast between Great Temples I and II.

The assumption of identical form in structures 5D-Sub.1-1st and 5D-Sub.9 is not far-fetched. Duplication of architectural form, though infrequent at Tikal, is seen at the Seven Temples complex (Coe 1967:88-9), in twin structures 3D-41 and 3D-42 in the North Group (TR.23A:7, fig. 3), in the Twin Pyramid complexes (Coe 1967:84-85) and may be suspected in Str. 5D-90 and 91 (TR.11:Great Plaza sheet). Duplicate structures are assumed earlier on the North Acropolis in Plat. 5D-4-9th-B (Plate 7), Plat. 5D-4-8th-D (Plate 11) and Plat. 5D-4-8th-B&C (Plate 12). As mentioned above twinned structures may embody some aspect of dualistic ideology. A major structure on the E would not be surprising given the importance accorded this direction in ancient Maya thought (Paxton 2001:17). But for this very reason it seems improbable that such a fabric would have the same features as one facing S. However, such appears to have been the case at this time. The notorious complexity of ancient Maya ritual calculations (Love 1992:205-16) may have identified a rare conjunction for which this unlikely formula was required. There is also the suspicion noted above that the authorities operating the North Acropolis may have included rival sub-groups aligned to NS and EW. Seemingly strange appearance of identical structures in complementary positions may have resulted from a temporary unification of the two.

The wide central doorway of Sub.3-F, mentioned above, resembles an open porch. This may be seen as a precursor to the multi-doorway systems later employed to open up front rooms. In this case, considering its location at the head of the stair, the front room could have served very effectively as a setting for dramatic presentation of richly costumed individuals displaying emblems and symbols of rank, status, and supernatural affiliations. The arrangement would have served admirably as a stage where the claims of legitimacy based on those badges and symbols could have been most effectively made. The rear room, then, might have been where the multitude of insignia needed for such displays were stored.

The structure faces S toward the area soon to be formalized as the Great Plaza, and backs on to the summit space enclosed by Str. 5D-Sub.1-1st and Str. 5D-Sub.9. Thus it can be regarded as an entrance or portal structure, although lacking doorways in the rear. That is, one could not pass through the building to enter the summit precinct. An entry sequence might have entailed entering the building, exiting via the same front portal, and then passing around it either to E or to W. As a result, entry to the summit would have been on the diagonal rather than on the NS axial line. The intercardinal direction of the diagonal might have held ideological significance that justified this arrangement.

4

Platform 5D-4-7th

The architectural developmental designated 7th in TR.14 functioned through the 1st three quarters of the 1st century AD. It incorporates a major design adjustment-either elimination or radical transformation of the old basal platform body. The Great Plaza might answer the second alternative but since it engages other features it requires its own platform designation, Plat. 5D-1 (TR.14: 164-95).

Early in the 1st century AD momentous development took place, not so much on the acropolis as in front of it and somewhat around it (TR.14:56-68 and 820-24). These years saw the first version of the Great Plaza (only partially visible in Plates 18-22) a massive construction project deploying a huge volume of material to provide a paved plaza surface that could accommodate large assemblies.

With this large expanse of polished white plaster in front and at least partly around the acropolis the level of solar glare during daytime would have made users extremely uncomfortable when the construction was newly completed. After weathering, this effect would no doubt diminish. Whether glare was intended or accidental is moot. The plaza space probably was set up so that large numbers of people could either participate or witness events staged on the acropolis. However, ceremonies performed during daytime in sunny weather would have been very difficult to observe through blinding glare. The ample hats worn by the two protagonists on Altar V (Jones and Satterthwaite 1982:fig. 23) may have been really needed. These characters may be depicted in the Twin Pyramid enclosure, but the glare effect of the Great Plaza might have called for similarly protective headgear.

Intense glare in the plaza, or in a complex such as a Twin Pyramid Group, might have been understood as proximal presence of the supernatural force (or forces) remotely resident in the sun. Ritual activity on the acropolis might have been designed to procure this immediate and dangerous presence. The glare factor must have been present to a lesser extent in earlier versions of the acropolis and Great Plaza builders could have anticipated its effect. Red painted structures would have reduced the glare effect although the color red, with its connotations of blood, probably possessed its own compelling reasons for use.

Preceding acropolis fabrics (Plates 7-17) had possessed expansive lower platform members with extensive paved surface areas. The Great Plaza might have been undertaken as an extension of these bodies, to accommodate much greater numbers, and to greatly increase the effect of monumentality projected by the acropolis. In the final stage of development during the Late Classic Period, the Great Plaza projected a somewhat reduced presence, a mere surface linking the North Acropolis and the Central Acropolis. So it appears today with its edges obscured (Plate 3).

Initially it stood out as a distinct volume rising above adjacent contours. It could be seen as a platform linked frontally to the North Acropolis. It would have been experienced as an acropolis body, and maybe was designed as such. It would have appeared as a basal platform apparently sustaining the North Acropolis. In this light the old basal platform maybe was never eliminated but rather expanded.

In any case, the North Acropolis itself now presented a simpler appearance, the Great Plaza (Plat. 5D-1) apparently (but not actually) sustaining a nearly square intermediate platform (Plat. 5D-4-8th) on its own basal

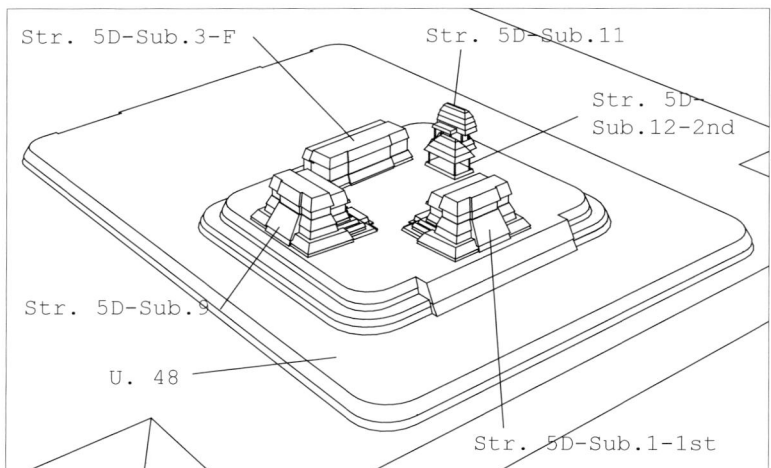

Figure 19. Platform 5D-4-7th-C.

element (Terrace South) initially sustaining a summit complex of four structures (Str. 5D-Sub.1-1st, Str. 5D-Sub.9, Str. 5D-Sub.3-F, and Str. 5D-Sub.12-2nd).

Friedel and Schele interpret major paved Plaza surfaces as symbolic primordial seas (Friedel, Schele and Parker 1993:138-43) and as portals to the underworld (Schele and Friedel 1990:425 n.4). This view strongly supports the interpretation I offer throughout these pages. Such installations are often referred to as "sacred spaces." This term seems weak to me. If Schele and Freidel are correct, places like the Great Plaza and North Acropolis were not merely "sacred" to the ancient Maya but were power places. They were literally "supernatural". This is not to deny symbolic reference to primordial seas, or celestial bodies. The symbolism is germane but may not convey the fundamental reality as the ancient Maya may have seen it. A single step from "this world" earth and grass to "other world" polished plaster may have been a step into supernatural presence made convincing partly by solar glare. It seems likely to me that few Tikal citizens would have taken casual walks through the Great Plaza.

The acropolis illustrated in Plate 19 (Figure 19) as 7th corresponds to TR.14: fig. 6d but omits Sub.12-1st and Sub.10-2nd, which appear in Plate 20. This precise arrangement, that is, without Sub.12-1st and Sub.10-2nd, functioned for only a few years (TR.14:Chart 1) at the beginning of Fl. 12 use (10 BC-AD 25). A Great Plaza pavement is now in place, Plat. 5D-1-4th-B, but its extents are uncertain and shown here hypothetically as a vaguely defined flat surface with non-specific edges.

Unit 48 is a remake of the feature identified in TR.14 as "Terrace South" expanded easterly to re-center the acropolis, which had become noticeably unbalanced on the preceding terrace. With this development, architectural composition has simplified in lower parts at the same time that summit arrangements are becoming more complex. Now there are only two major platform bodies and, although not visible in Plate 19, Terrace South could easily be understood as the acropolis basal platform as can be seen in Figure 20.

The two-terrace "acropolis" platform, designated in earlier acropoleis as Third Supplementary Platform (TR.14 U.63), now could be reclassified as a "First Supplementary platform," sustained on a basal platform (TR.14:U. 48-Terrace South). It continued into 7th unchanged except for a new axial stair with stair-side outsets and a new upper surface, Fl. 12. Presence or absence of masks on the stair-side outsets could not be determined.

Renewal of the acropolis at this time may have been stimulated by death of a prominent individual interred in Burial 166 beneath new Str. 5D-Sub.11 on the SW corner of the summit. The ruler in office at this time might be none other than the "Founder" Yax Ehb' Xook,

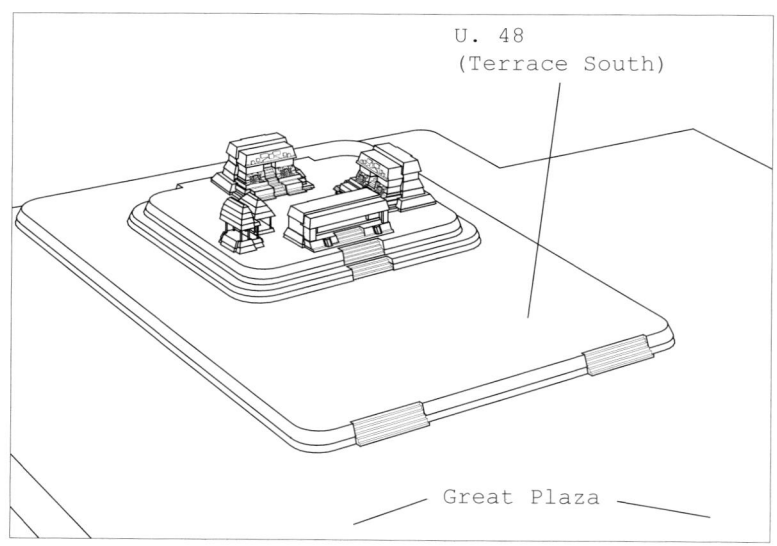

Figure 20. Platform 5D-4-7th-C: view from SW.

(Schele 1992:138). His tomb might be Bu. 85 (Martin and Grube 2000:26). The individual in Bu. 167 (TR.14:230-33) would be another possible candidate.

Structure 5D-Sub.11 (TR.14:235-44; fig. 33-35) was built integrally with Fl. 12 and therefore installation of Bu. 166 must have preceded the acropolis renewal. Position and orientation (burial head-to-N, structure facing E, unusual at Tikal) suggest highest rank and mural paintings in the tomb certainly support this assessment. Venerated ancestors at Tikal were often interred in this position (Becker 1971:2003).

The tomb provides the earliest known vaulting at the North Acropolis locus. Walls below the vault spring are painted orange-red, elaborated with intricate black line figures that, although fragmentary through flaking, depict mythical beings or supernaturals, including females (the two bodies in Bu, 166 are both female). From this one might suppose that the occupants of the tomb were ritual specialists whose task in life was to engage with the beings depicted on the walls. Such individuals could equally have fulfilled a rulership role.

The open pavilion form assumed for Sub.11, with thatched roof supported on poles, is hinted at by floor conditions, but no post-holes were actually seen (TR.14:236). Red paint now appears on the substructure after a long absence. Exfoliated fragments of red-painted plaster had been found in core material surrounding largely demolished Str. 5D-Sub.14-2nd (Plate 5). Red paint makes a more substantial presence on Str.

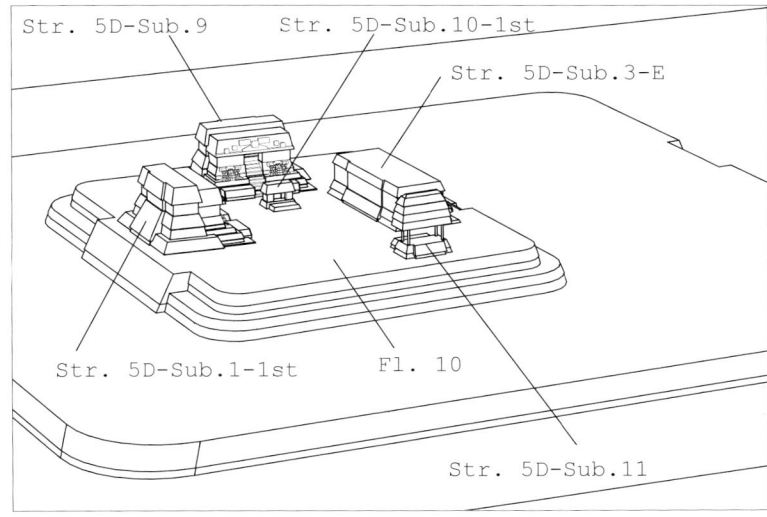

Figure 22. Platform 5D-4-7th-A.

5D-Sub.3-F as a second coat on the initial white coat (TR.14:251) Plate 19. This might have coincided with installation of Sub.11.

Two small structures, 5D-Sub.10-2nd and 5D-Sub.12-1st, and major structure 5D-Sub.3-E were all built on Fl. 12 during the middle years of Platform 5D-4-7th, that is, around the mid-point of the 1st century AD (Plate 20).

Structure 5D-Sub.3-E is a re-do of "F" with larger masks badly preserved and almost no surviving superstructure evidence. Frontal masks have traces of red paint but the structure as a whole may have been left unpainted as illustrated in Plate 20. It is most unfortunate that mask preservation was not better since this seems to have been the only real change that was made and might have shed at least a little light on the puzzling series of rapid renewals made in this particular structure.

Although designated as Sub.12-1st because of its location directly above Sub.12-2nd, the N facing later feature does not appear to be a renewal of the (probably) E facing earlier one. It has a higher rear body and a lower frontal body, a format that probably signifies ritual function. Its position, crammed into, actually overlapping, the NE corner of Sub.11, seems very odd, as though responsive to some pressure to keep the W side of the summit free of structures, suggesting that the view to the W horizon had some importance. Its plan proportions, shallow front-to-rear relative to width side-to-side suggest that it may have supported a superstructure since

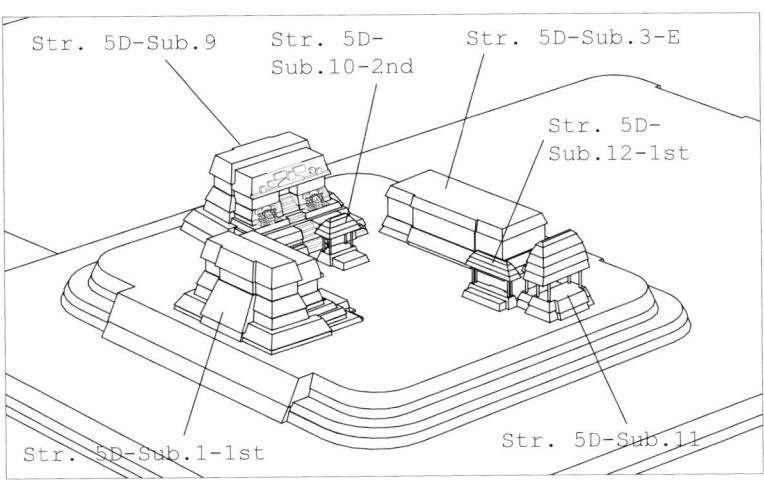

Figure 21. Platform 5D-4-7th-C.

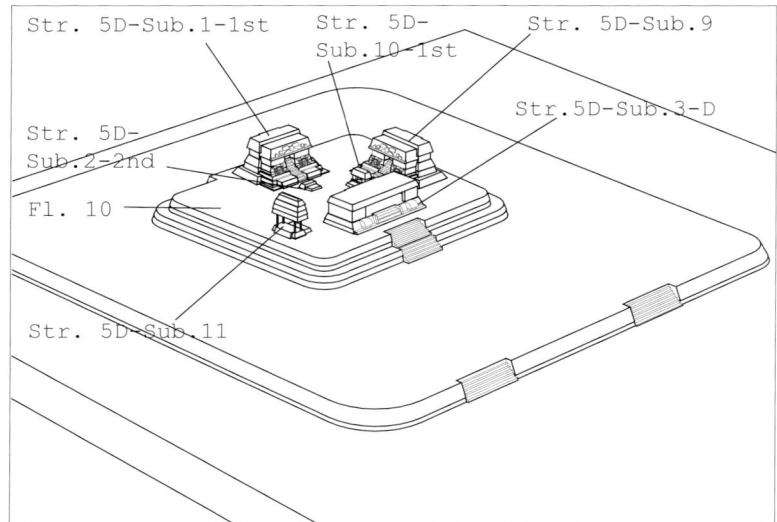

Figure 23. Platform 5D-4-7th-A.

superstructures generally have similarly rectangular proportions. In the absence of surviving evidence Plate 20 shows an imaginary superstructure similar to those illustrated in Plates 12, 13, and 17.

The third small summit addition is Sub.10-2nd built on Fl. 12, and therefore later than Sub.12-1st built at the same time as Fl. 12. Sub.10-2nd facing W, stands at the foot of the Sub.9 stair. It has a rear body and a frontal body, and a rear axial outset, like Sub.12-1st, and like Sub.12-1st its superstructure, if there had been one, had been totally removed by ancient demolition. Hence there is little that can be said about it except that its placement is remarkable, completely blocking the Sub.9 stair. With Sub.10-2nd in place users would have had to clamber over either the N or S rear corner of Sub.10-2nd to get a foot onto the Sub.9 stair. Presence of a superstructure would have made this even more awkward yet its successor, Sub.10-1st, implies that a 2nd superstructure very likely existed.

Toward the end of the lifetime of 7th, some time between AD 50 and 75, another remarkable interment (Bu. 167, TR.14:230-33) either stimulated or was associated with acropolis renewal (Plate 21). At this time Terrace South was greatly expanded to reach nearly square proportions. A new upper surface, Fl. 10 caps the summit, lapping around the base of Sub.1-1st, Sub.9 and Sub.3-E, and riding over the demolished stump of Sub.12-1st. The acropolis platform received a new set of facings with apron moldings and a new axial stair, without stair-side outsets. The ruler later cited as the dynastic "Founder," Yax Ebh' Xook, might have been in office when this work was done.

The interment, Bu. 167 (TR.14:230-33) may have been that of a nuclear family; a male, a female, and an infant. They were placed in a roughly finished mud plastered vaulted chamber cut through the basal bodies of demolished Sub.10-2nd at the base of the Sub.9 stair. Above it, a superstructure was erected, probably vaulted but upper parts had been demolished in later developments. Its outer wall surfaces displayed mural paintings across the rear façade, that is, facing Sub.9. The vaulted room and its position at the foot of a stair, suggest a "shrine" function, no doubt related to the occupants of the tomb below. Haviland suggests (personal communication) that the royal family may have been murdered to clear the way for the new dynasty founded by Yax Ebh' Xook

The murals depict standing human figures with grotesque faces framed by elaborate scroll elements that descend from a sky band. The imagery has been interpreted as ancestor referencing (Schele and Freidel 1990:131-33). The ancestors most likely to have been interred in the North Acropolis would have been deceased rulers (McAnany 1995:52), close relatives of deceased rulers, or prominent ritual specialists. Grotesque visages might depict ritual performers in a trance state or perhaps the very ancestors of the persons in BU. 167 in their deceased roles as supernatural beings.

Stylistically similar murals have been discovered recently at the site of San Bartolo, about 35 km NE of Tikal (Saturno et al. 2005). These murals are dated to some time in the 1st century BC, somewhat earlier than Sub.10-1st. Here, the scroll images are interpreted as representing breath rather than blood.

Another set of human figures standing amid scrolls appears at Uaxactun, Group H, Structure Sub. 10 (Schele and Freidel 1990:137-39, citing Valdez 1987). Schele and Friedel interpret the scrolls as either smoke or blood and identify the figures as rulers.

Structure 5D-Sub.10-1st, placed at the foot of the Sub.9 stair presents an architectural conundrum that reappears later on, even more prominently, with 33-3rd, 2nd, and 1st. Although designated as a separate "structure," Sub.10-1st (and 2nd, for that matter) could equally be regarded as a component body of Sub.9, similar to the stairway shrine on Str. 5E-38, just E of the Central Acropolis (TR.11, Great Plaza sheet). As such, the Sub.10 elements provide a third division of space, after the two rooms at the summit. Sub.10 stands below room 1 of Sub.9 just as that room stands below room 2. The three entities could be understood as a single connected series similar to the three rooms found in later ritual structures.

Marks of intense burning within Sub.10 demonstrate that its minute interior space was heavily used. Ritual conducted here could relate either to the tomb below the building, to W facing Sub.9 behind it, or both.

Sub.10 could be regarded as a shrine room, an integral part of Sub.9 but set low down for the conduct of certain rituals, or for the use of certain officiants, not granted access to the upper rooms. Presumably such usage would have been addressed to supernaturals, including deceased ancestors that were associated with the EW directional focus.

Size and complexity of the North Acropolis, even at this early date, imply existence of a large body of ritual specialists serving a variety of ceremonial programs. All sorts of scenarios can be imagined. Tikaleños not admissible to the acropolis might have been able to commission services on their behalf conducted by relatively minor officiants, shamans, or even apprentices, who could use installations such as the Sub.10 structures.

Becker (1992:185-96) has proposed a hypothesis linking burials to caches as deposits intended to facilitate interactions with supernatural forces. Structures 5D-Sub.10-1st and Sub.9 might be examples of architecture designed specifically for the kind of function Becker alludes to.

As one of the final developments in Platform 5D-4-7th, perhaps a little before AD 75, yet another elite burial was installed on the acropolis, this time on the central axis and at the foot of its dominant feature, Structure 5D-Sub.1-1st (Plate 22). This is Bu.85 cut through Fl.10 and capped by Str. 5D-Sub.2-2nd (TR.14:217-20; Coe and McGinn 1963:29-32).

Architectural features seen previously in Sub.11, Sub.12-1st and 2nd, and Sub.10-1st and 2nd, reappears in Sub.2-2nd, except for apparent absence of a building. These include a rear body with rear axial outset preceded by a slightly lower front body, with apron moldings on both parts. Sub.11, with a somewhat higher substructure, additionally has a small projecting stair. Otherwise, except for small variations in dimension these structures are essentially identical, and due to

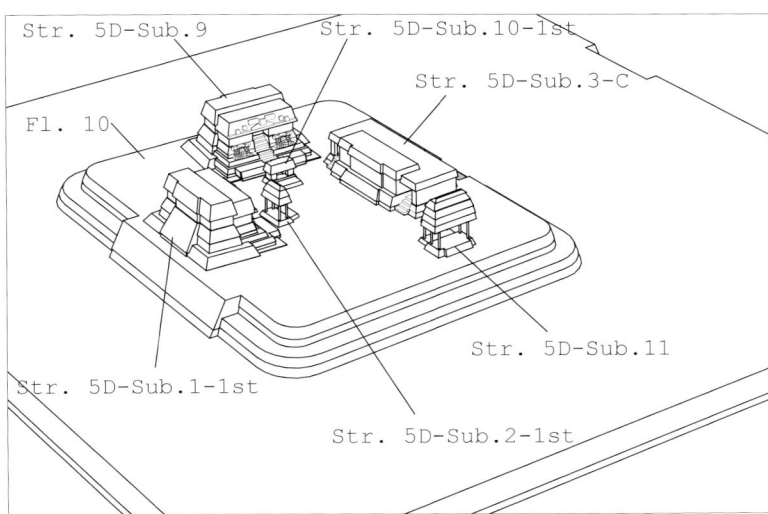

Figure 24. Platform 5D-4-7th-A.

their diminutive stature it seems inescapable that apron moldings, present on all, served no structural purpose but must have been entirely iconographic features.

A rich collection of artifacts accompanied the individual interred in Bu.85, including a blood letting instrument (sting-ray spine), high office emblem (perforated spondylus shell) and a serpentine mask that may have replaced the head, which, together with the thigh bones, had been removed prior to burial. These funerary details strongly suggest that this tomb provides the earliest persuasive evidence for burial of rulers in the acropolis.

Location of Sub.2-2nd on the central axis and proximal to Sub.1-1st further supports the above interpretation. Small scale may at first seem a counterindication, but this is mitigated by proximity to the north axial architectural feature of the acropolis. Sub.2-2nd is not quite as tightly bound to Sub.1-1st as Sub.10 is to Sub.9, but still it sits right at the base of the stair only about 0.5 m in front of the bottom riser, and could easily have been perceived as a component part of Sub.1-1st. It might have been used for rituals addressed to the deceased ruler as distinct from rituals conducted higher up in the Sub.1-1st superstructure.

Martin and Grube (2000:26) suggest that this c. AD 90 tomb might contain the remains of Yax Ebh' Xook, cited in later inscriptions as the founder of Tikal's ruling dynasty. Dating of Bu.85 appears consistent with a possible death date of "the Founder" (Haviland, personal communication). In the Late Classic texts Yax Ebh' Xook must have been a semi-legendary ancestor whose name had survived in oral history as well as in carved texts. Whether or not he was buried under Sub.2-2nd, his name must have been connected with some kind

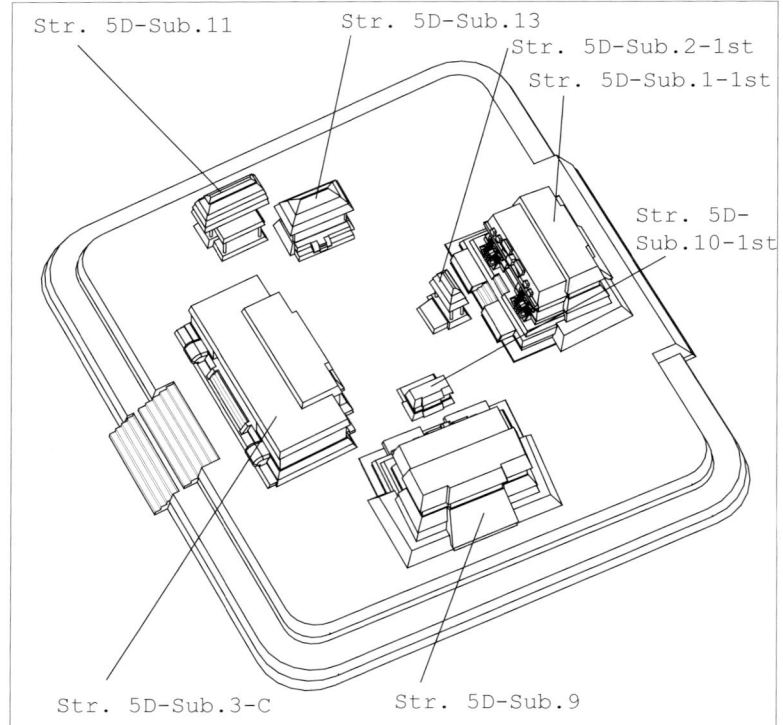

Figure 25. Platform 5D-4-7th-A.

of high point in the early history of Tikal. Subsequent acropolis developments (see Chapter 5) may further validate Martin and Grube's suggestion.

In the terminal stage of Plat. 5D-4-7th-A developments, during decades approaching AD 75, Sub.2-1st and Sub.3-C were built, both standing on Fl. 10 (Plate 23 and Figure 24). Presumably they were not constructed at precisely the same time, but any time lapse between them could not have been very great.

Str. 5D-Sub.3-C is the fourth reconstruction of this facility at the head of the acropolis stair over a span hardly more than fifty years, and the first to make a significant architectural change that went beyond frontal mask revisions. Twin stairs are introduced in the rear façade flanking a rear room of greatly reduced lateral extent, raised one step above the front room, which now extends laterally around it on E and W. Plate 23 shows the rear façade with the stairs and doorway openings, the latter assumed on the basis of Sub.3-B. All "C" level building details had been obliterated in "B" construction.

Rear stairs providing for through circulation confirm architectural classification suspected earlier. Sub.3-C now can be catalogued unequivocally as a "portal" structure, although functional implications remain debatable. Portal structures (reviewed in TR.34B) are understood as primarily intended to control entry into compounds, patios, plazas or groups. The assumption is that persons entering the North Acropolis summit would necessarily pass through the portal structure where they would be admitted, or denied entry, or perhaps purified.

Because of its position at the head of the acropolis stair a second quite different function for Sub.3-C might have been involved. Ritual specialists, including high-ranking elite individuals, active on the acropolis, would be able to enter Sub.3-C from the rear and appear dramatically in the wide front opening. Costumed with the extravagant regalia illustrated in ancient Maya sculpture and painting, they would make a most spectacular sight at a suitably prominent position, readily visible from the Great Plaza. Indeed, installation of the Great Plaza may have been precisely for this purpose and similar performances might have taken place earlier using the earlier versions of Sub.3. The revision illustrated in Plate 23 might have been undertaken in order to provide a more effective theatrical setting for such a ceremonial presentation. The fact that the summit precinct could be entered without passing through Sub.3-C further attests to some function other than, or as well as, entry control.

Structure 5D-Sub.2-1st was built to replace Sub.2nd over the important burial BU 85. Its surviving upper details (TR.14:fig. 27) include post-holes positioned where supports for a thatch roof would occur, although there was some uncertainty concerning whether the holes were primary or secondary (TR.14:222). Alternatively, these holes might indicate banner poles. These would be removed and reinstalled on the occasions of particular ceremonial events. Plate 23, however, illustrates a thatch roof as the simplest hypothesis. No offerings or burials were found in association with Sub.2-1st, so the renewal seems to have been essentially self-validating. That is, the architectural renewal might have been a kind of offering, expressing reverence for the individual in the previously installed tomb. Burning on the entirely removed upper surface of Sub.2-2nd might have disfigured the structure enough to stimulate its renewal on simple maintenance grounds.

Also on Fl.10, later than Sub-10-1st, but in no known sequence with Sub.2-1st and Sub.3-C (and therefore no more appropriate in Plate 24 than in Plate

23), Sr. 5D-Sub.13 finally came to occupy the W side of the summit compound, a position that had been kept open for some time previously (Plate 24). Only its front face was cleared in the excavations (TR.14:fig. 36) so its complete architectural form is highly speculative.

Without knowledge of tomb presence or absence in Sub.13, motives for this addition remain obscure. Some exigency may have impelled construction, but at the same time it seems there was a long held desire to keep the W side open. Significance attached to Sub.9 perhaps obviated anything E facing of similar magnitude. Later developments (Plates 35-66) show this reservation as temporally limited. That is, a balanced EW arrangement eventually came into existence. Therefore, the unbalanced condition prevailing during most of 7th, and still obtaining with diminutive Sub.13 in place, may have been connected with a particular time period.

The issue raised here is the famous "Maya obsession with time," sometimes expressed as Maya worship of time. The divinatory calendar of 260 days (T'zolk'in) very clearly set out the proposition that effects of supernatural forces impinged on human affairs in predictable ways at specific times (León-Portilla 1988:91-112). The date-reaching mechanism in the Venus Table of the Dresden Codex (Closs 1977:89-99) allowed Maya ritual specialists to predict Venus effects on specific T'zolk'in days; that is, the focus was on the time-relation of the effect. It is not surprising that calendric factors might have influenced North Acropolis architectural development, nor that such design directives can rarely be detected.

5

Platform 5D-4-6th

Up to this point the acropolis had developed essentially horizontally. Although more than 40 m across the front, the two-terrace acropolis platform rose only about 4 m above the basal platform surface (Terrace South in TR.14), an aspect ratio of approximately 1:11. Now, in the third quarter of the 1st century AD something stimulated a radical adjustment in these proportions (TR.14:68-78, 824-26).

On the same basal platform a vertically conceived complex began to develop (TR.14:68-78). A new political reality might lie behind this, or perhaps it was no more than a response to the presence of the Great Plaza, which may have dwarfed the old acropolis somewhat so that greater height was needed to regain the former condition of physical dominance and commanding presence. In either case the ability to undertake such a huge enterprise stands as evidence of robust economic health and confidence that the investment would pay off. This latter point may bear on tentative assignment of Bu. 85 to Yax Ehb' Xook (Martin and Grube 2000:26; Martin 2003:5-9; Schele and Freidel 1990:133, 140) and discussion above). If a powerful ruler had won major victories and/or Tikal had enjoyed unusual success in some way, then investment in a more architecturally powerful acropolis might have appeared opportune, particularly after his death. I imagine the argument advanced for this would contend that a powerful deceased ruler would be an effective advocate for Tikal interests and therefore extraordinary efforts to secure this support would be justified regardless of the expense.

The new acropolis bulk is at the same time extended farther N so that plan proportions revert to an earlier ratio with front-to-rear dimension greater than side-to-side.

Intention to build vertically is evident in the first body of core material laid down over the old acropolis summit. Plate 25 (Figure 26) illustrates this material (topped by Plat. 5D-4 U. 91B), placed around still standing Sub.1-1st and Sub.9. Structure 5D-Sub.3-B is designed to meet this presumably temporary level. The U. 91B rough surface coincides with the base of masks on Sub.1-1st, and presumably also on Sub.9. They remained visible while this surface was in use. Presumably they were still relevant to the activities served.

The old acropolis terracing, U. 60, and the old summit surface, remained exposed across the front, and the old axial stair continued in use. Although less than two meters high the new distally concentrated material was placed with great care in core units built for stability (TR.14:69). Such treatment, seen later in the substructure of 33-1st, followed a structural design strategy employed for high, pyramidal bodies. In tall substructures this served to avoid accumulation of lateral stresses so that retaining walls at the outer faces would not be required. Here such a factor would not be at issue. Core units of this construction probably reflect organization of the building industry rather than structural strategy.

For some reason there was a pause in construction marked by U. 91B, a layer of black muck (TR.14:69, fig. 10). A roughly horizontal layer of mortar running through substructure core might be expected at a terrace level, and indeed this might be the case here. But U. 91B appears to be more than just a terrace level carried through the core body although no signs of activity such as burning were seen in the axial area sampled by the excavation. It seems clear that Sub.1-1st and Sub.9 were still intact at this point. Therefore the possibility exists that some ritual activity using these structures

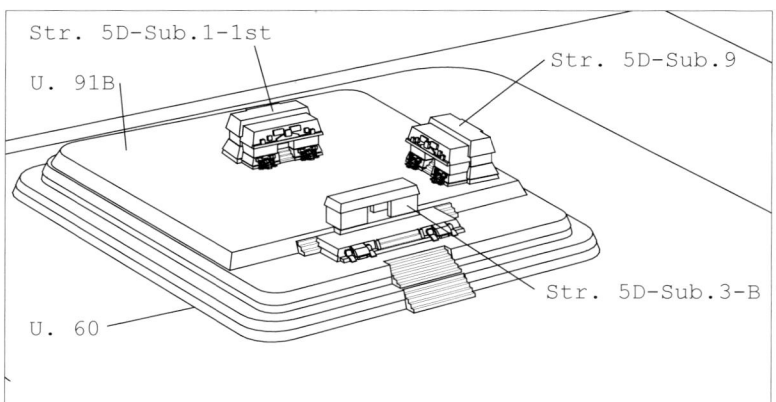

Figure 26. Platform 5D-4-6th.

was to be conducted despite the major construction project then underway. One possibility might be the de-commissioning of the old summit structures, which must have been venerable fabrics long considered inherently powerful. To partially demolish and bury these structures, as was about to be done, might have required special observances to deflect possible harmful effects, perhaps to reassure the workmen so that they would agree to do the work, and perhaps to protect them from harm. Erecting ritual structures such as Sub.1-1st and Sub.9 might have been relatively safe procedures, but dismantling them may have been regarded as inherently dangerous if supernatural forces remained in residence or hovered nearby. In any case, for at least a brief span near the end of the 1st century AD the acropolis must have appeared as shown in Plate 25.

The decision to retain and renew Sub.3, Sub.3-B (TR.14:fig. 41), while radically increasing the acropolis height may have been contentious in that retaining Sub.3 constrained the S edge of the new raised fabric. Either Sub.3 possessed an intrinsic value, or the U. 91B event rated a portal structure. An alternative possibility is that Sub.3 users held enough power to prevent demolition of their structure but not enough to stop it from being radically diminished by the new development immediately behind it. A third speculation is that Sub.3-B was a stop-gap intended to function only for a short time while U. 91B surface was in use and therefore its reduction was tolerated. The previous building was removed and a new single rear room built with aligned front and rear doorways (TR.14:fig. 41) for access to the stair (U. 68) rising up behind it. The area previously occupied by the front room was left open. The result is the curious partly open arrangement illustrated in Plate 25. Flanking stairs attached to the Sub.3 substructure permit lateral access to the main stair, while a third access pathway, perhaps first in status, proceeds across the now open frontal stage of Sub.3-B and directly through the single, rear-placed room, onto the main stair. At this point Sub.3 has become little more than a portal arch with flanking stairs that perhaps recapitulate an earlier arrangement allowing for summit access either through Str. 5D-Sub.3 or by-passing it.

Immediately following whatever event had transpired on U. 91B, and assembly of the new acropolis core body rising five meters above the previous acropolis summit there was another relatively brief interlude illustrated in Plate 26. A rough floor surface, U. 40, caps this work and on it a circular structure, Str. 5D-Sub.6, was erected. It is painted red together with the surrounding summit surface. Plate 26 illustrates red paint on a rough surface, further mottled by mud (TR.14:261-63). Roughness of the U.40 surface implies that Sr. 5D-Sub.6 was designed for a single event and the acropolis illustrated in Plate 26 probably did not endure for very long.

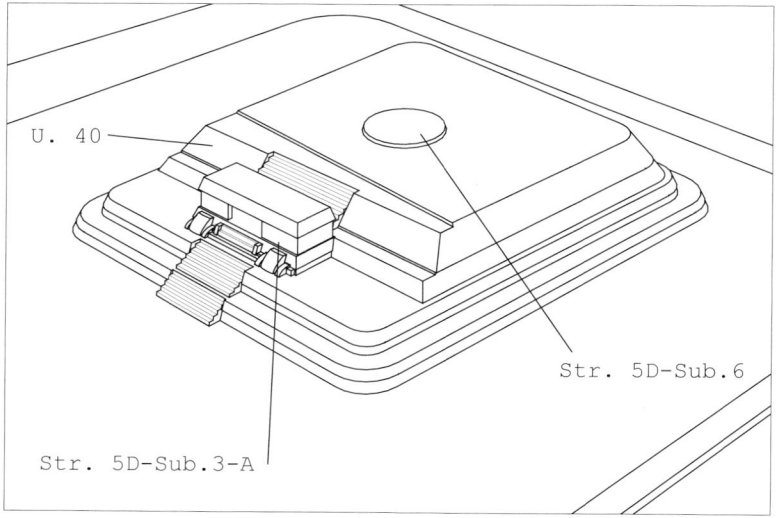

Figure 27. Platform 5D-4-6th.

Circular Str. 5D-Sub.6 recalls earlier features on the acropolis Sub.14-B and U. 94 (plates 5 and 10). The Sub.6 topping had been removed and hence presence of a superstructure is uncertain. I show it without one but have no basis for doing so. At much later dates circular geometries are associated with specific deities (Sabloff 1973:128), but whether these apply to Protoclassic Tikal is not clear. Circular structures have long been linked with Quetzalcoatl in his aspect as the wind (Pollock 1936:161). In any case, Sub.6 existed as the focal ritual structure on the newly elevated acropolis summit long enough for supporting structures to be built (see below). Perhaps this was its role; to provide for ritual activities while the structures that eventually occupied the new summit were under construction.

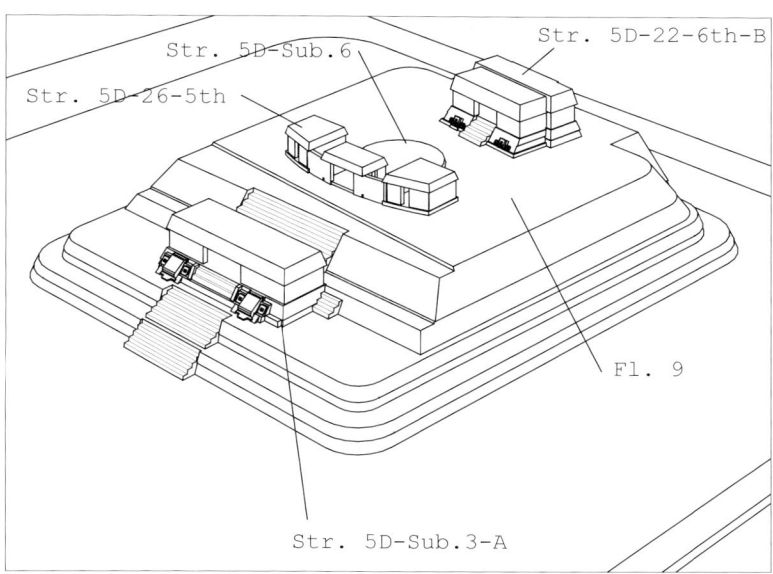

Figure 28. Platform 5D-4-6th.

The new high acropolis platform illustrated in Plate 25 suffers, in reconstruction, from lack of knowledge concerning the E and W terrace facings (TR.14:73). These were never encountered in the excavations, and they may have been demolished in the course of later construction. Therefore, apparent absence of an ordered series of terraces rising to the summit cannot be taken as ancient design decisions. I was tempted to apply terracing for Plate 25, but decided to stick with the forms indicated in TR.14 (TR.14:fig. 6f).

Having established the new, elevated acropolis, workers proceeded to demolish Sub.3-B and replace it with a final version, Str. 5D-Sub.3-A (Plate 27). This new building reverts to the earlier two-room plan but with axial circulation through to the stair immediately behind it (TR.14:fig. 42). Presence of Sub.3-A at the base of this high stair must have caused problems during the rainy season. Water would have cascaded down the stair and into the rear room. To avoid this, the rear doorway was initially equipped with a raised sill and then later the whole interior floor level was raised one step.

With Sub.6 still in use, Sub.21 (E and W), 26-5th (TR.14:fig. 49), and 22-6th (TR.14:fig. 58) were installed at the summit (Plate 27). They probably were not all built at the same time but no sequence can be demonstrated stratigraphically.

Although designated as separate structures, because connections could not be physically established (TR.14:262), Sub.21 and 26-5th were probably parts of one work, a strangely original piece of Tikal architecture. It was built as a curving screen with rectangular rooms at each end. These two interiors were probably covered with beam and mortar roofs. The curving geometry may have been intended to connect this feature visually and probably also conceptually, with Sub.6. Equally there may have been a need to avoid any format that could be misunderstood as embodying EW associations. The intent seems to have been concealment of Sub.6 as though secret rites were being conducted there.

The designation 26-5th reflects the position of this feature directly beneath 5D-26-1st similarly located at the head of the main stair and assumed to be developmentally connected. But in terms of architectural form, 5th is utterly unlike 1st. That it was also conceptually distinct is not so clear. Both features acted as portals giving access to the acropolis summit but at the same time denying, or at least discouraging, the previous possibility of by-pass access. This question reappears with arrival of 26-4th (below).

During the period of Sub.6 use, but on Fl. 9, installed around it, 5D-22-6th-B was erected as the N axial feature (TR.14:333-39; fig. 6f, 10, 58), presumably intended to be clearly seen as the dominant focal element of the acropolis in terms of its position on N end of the axial line. Importance attached to it may be indicated by conservative treatment of architectural form. The rear room, for example, has a shallow niche corresponding to the external rear axial outset on the central axis, like that of Sub.1-1st. Walls of the building are thin and probably could not support vaults. A beam-and mortar roof is assumed. The partly inset stair rises to a landing within the front axial doorway, similar to Str. 5D-Sub.1-1st but

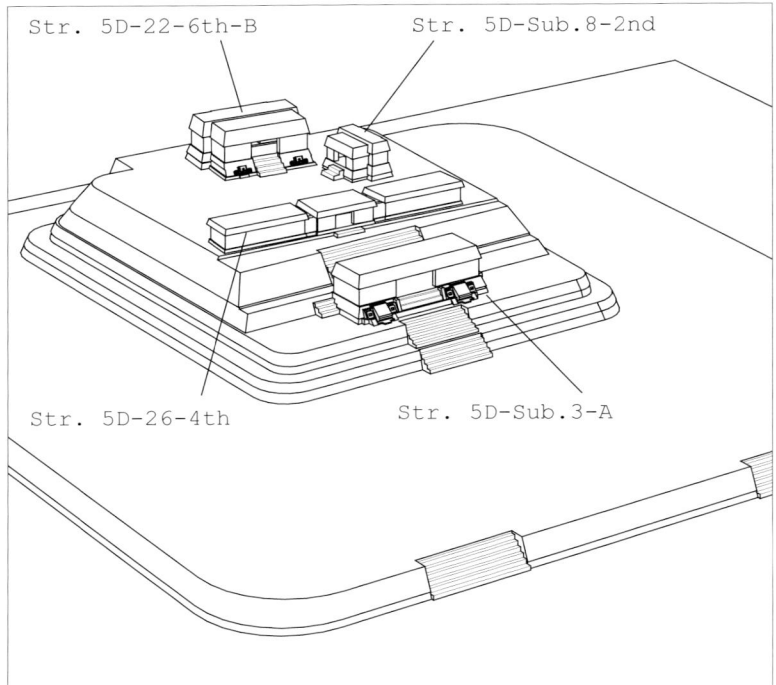

Figure 29. Platform 5D-4-6th.

not quite so far in. The substructure is composed of two bodies, a higher rear body and a lower, narrower front body. Masks flank the axial stair.

The west mask (TR.14:fig. 60c) features a large head, humanoid above the cheeks and grotesque below with plant tendrils issuing from the mouth. Large ear flares flank the head and beyond them other less well-preserved details fill the space. Many features recall Str. 5D-Sub.1-1st but these masks put greater emphasis on human rather than supernatural form. Apron moldings are even more archaic, at least in profile, similar to those of Platform 5D-4-9th though cut into projecting corbels rather than modeled in stucco. Some parts certainly, and possibly all parts were painted red, a venerable treatment probably applied to Str. 5D-Sub.14-2nd-B.

Since this structure lies above Str. 5D-Sub.1-1st it could have been seen as a later development of the earlier structure, particular in view of its conservative features. But it is so much smaller than Str. 5D-Sub.1-1st that the usual direction of architectural developments, larger over smaller, seems not to have been followed. A new series seems called for. Hence it has been designated as the first in the Str. 5D-22 series. The 5D-22 structures, 6th through 1st, came to dominate the north Acropolis. Structure 5D-22-6th, on the other hand is so small relative to the whole acropolis that it is hardly visible from the Great Plaza. For summit users of the acropolis it might have been the most important structure, but if so, this was not strongly expressed architecturally. Possibly the greater height that the acropolis platform had risen to by this time achieved such a monumental impact by itself that the north axial summit feature could be left at a modest scale. Still, it is the logical successor to Str. 5D-Sub.1-1st and the logical ancestor of the 5D-22 series.

A second line of argument follows from the combined character of Str. 5D-Sub.21 (E and W) and Str. 5D-26-5th which seem designed to screen summit features from general view while providing for entry and perhaps storage. The relatively small scale of 22-6th conforms to this condition. The structure would not have been very visible from locations S and E of the acropolis. It may be that motivation for elevating the acropolis was not merely a concern for power and dominance, but also for the arcane nature of specialist ritual activities, and desire to remove these from casual, uninitiated gaze. At the same time, if rulership was involved as earlier suggested by Bu. 85, this development may reflect increased distance between the office of ruler and the populace in general.

Floor 8, installed immediately prior to construction of Str. 5D-26-4th (Plate 28), added about 1 m to the total height of the acropolis now less than 2 m short of its final height.

The front (S) edge of the acropolis summit, at the head of the main stair, is set at a noticeable angle to adjacent acropolis features, several degrees S of E. This could hardly have been accidental and conforms with orientation of 26-4th. My guess is that this might have been a device to remove 26-4th from EW conceptual associations which had received explicit recognition with installation of Sub.8-2nd on the E side of the summit precinct. If 26-4th was a larger version of 26-5th, built for screening, storage and control of entry, features calculated to attract supernatural forces might have been inappropriate. It may have been essentially a support facility.

Significantly, with Sub.6 no longer extant, the curving geometry is discarded. This reinforces my earlier suggestion that 26-5th/Sub.21 had some kind of conceptual connection with Sub.6.

The open condition of the summit toward the W is somewhat uncertain as excavation probes did not fully reach this area. With this proviso the arrangement shown in Plate 28 tends to confirm earlier conjectures concerning intentional openness to the W.

From minimal exposures Sub.8-2nd (TR.14:267-68) appears to be a smaller version of 22-6th, with a fully outset stair, and presumably with two rooms but without stair-side masks. Plate 28 shows the terminal version of Sub.8-2nd. It had been originally finished with white plaster heavily marked by burning, mostly interior and in front. After the period of use indicated by the burning scars the structure was painted red and then demolished before any more burning had defaced the new finish.

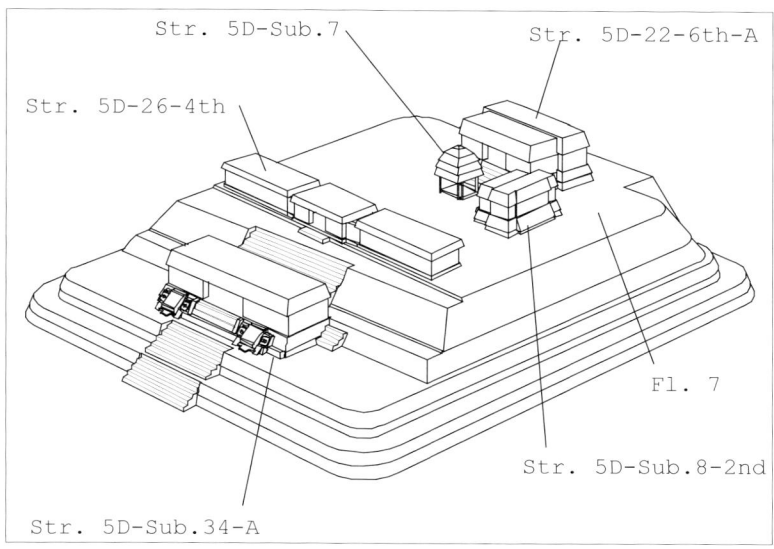

Figure 30. Platform 5D-4-6th.

Directly in front of 22-6th-A minimally scaled Str. 5D-Sub.7 (Plate 29 and Figure 30) reminiscent of earlier features frontally sited in relation to Str. 5D-Sub.1-1st and Sub.9 appeared on Fl.7 (TR.14:64-66). It would be hard to imagine anything smaller that could be classified as a structure. It has only one masonry body, a simple rectangle one step high, with rounded corners. A slightly larger rectangle formed by post holes set in Fl. 7 surrounds it, presumably to support a thatch roof though set like a shelter for the structure rather than part of it. Severe burning has deeply marked its surviving surfaces. As with parallel precedents this feature could perhaps be regarded as a secondary frontal appendage to the larger Str. 5D-22-6th-A. No burial or cache dedicatory to Str. 5D-Sub.7 was found.

Some time after construction of Sub.7 an interment, Bu. 125, was made on the NS axis of Str. 5D-22-6th-A in the narrow gap between Sub.7 and 22-6th (TR.14:335-37, 826, fig. 62). A cut was made through the 22-6th-A stair, through the rear part of Sub.7, and on down to the rear base of Sub.1-1st (TR.14:fig. 10). The single individual was tall (ca. 6 feet), even for the Tikal elite population (Haviland and Moholy-Nagy 1992:58).

The grave is roofed by beams rather than vault stones. Above it, six or seven layers of flint flakes were placed. There were no grave goods at all in the large chamber, but parts of perhaps four other individuals mingled with the "naked giant" (Haviland, personal communication) were placed above the tomb. There must have been something very special about this personage though the lack of grave goods suggests some sort of irregularity.

The interment was sealed at the level of Fl. 7 by a hard patch that ran over one of the now empty Sub.7 post holes. That is, the burial cut not only went through the tiny Sub.7 masonry platform, but also involved demolition of the pole and thatch roof above it. Heavy burning on red-painted Sub.7 came after sealing of BU. 125. The next stage of major acropolis development outlined in Chapter 7 may have stimulated this burial (cf. TR.14:819).

At some point during the use of Fl. 8 Str. 5D-22-6th was modified by addition of a new stair of expanded width that covered up, and thereby preserved, the masks previously prominent beside the old stair (TR.14:334; fig. 6g, 59). With these sculptural elements hidden beneath the new stair Str. 5D-22-6th-A must have appeared distinctly less ornate. An assumption of TR.14: fig. 59 is that a change from one doorway to three doorways prompted the wider stair. If this is correct then obliteration of the masks might have been a byproduct of the doorway modification. Pursuing this speculation further, loss of the masks was the price paid for installation of three doorways where previously there had been only one. Incidentally, this change probably would have involved extensive roof reconstruction at the same time. Such remodeling implies that the three-doorway issue was an important one, and indeed, triple doorways appear in many subsequent North Acropolis structures. From this we may possibly conclude that the three-doorway façade was conceived as another device calculated to increase links with supernatural powers. The triple doorway arrangement may have been initiated here, to replace the masks as a device for securing non-material support, either a more effective device, or one responding to innovation in ritual. Elaborately garbed individuals standing in the doorways, impersonating supernatural beings, might have been seen as a more effective way to gain their cooperation.

6

Platform 5D-4-5th

In the final quarter of the 2nd century AD acropolis authorities added a curiously irregular increment, U. 66, to the frontal zone of the summit (TR.14:78-85; 827-28). It provides greater height as seen from the Great Plaza (Plate 30) and covers up the stumps of partially demolished Str. 5D-26-4th that had previously screened the summit precinct from the plaza space. Unit 66 also performs a screening function for the summit patio in front of Str. 5D-22-6th-A and Str. 5D-Sub.8-2nd. Truncated features concealed within U. 66 core could easily have been demolished to the level of Fl. 7, a mere skin coat on Fl. 8. Therefore, I infer that parts of Str. 5D-26-4th were left standing precisely because some form of screening for the summit patio was still desired. At the same time U. 66 provides a frontal effect of greater height, and concomitant with that, a higher, more impressive, front axial stair (see Plate 31 below).

Figure 32 illustrates the very obvious eccentricity that had developed through successive expansions to the E twin stairs on the basal platform (Terrace South) are also now offset to match the axial line of the upper parts.

Atop U. 66, at the head of the monumental stair, 26-3rd took over the acropolis portal role previously filled by its 4th and 5th predecessors and the now eliminated sub.3 structures. In plan (TR.14:fig. 55) 26-3rd somewhat resembles Str.5D-Sub.3-B, but with a front room in place and probably vaulted (TR.14:fig. 56). Volumetrically 26-3rd retraces a format earlier employed by Sub.3-C and B. Its rear substructure member is very restricted and engulfed on three sides by the much broader frontal member reversing the long established format in which rearward members extended laterally beyond the frontal ones.

The new canon of three doorways appears on the front façade above a wide set of stairs broken by a projecting axial series of deeper treads. Two non-axial doorways open through the rear façade flanking the rearward body with its rear axial outset. This arrangement recalls an earlier speculation (Str. 5D-Sub.3-C) as to the primary direction of circulation served by the rear doorways. This might move either northward into the acropolis precinct or southward into 26-3rd to make a dramatic appearance at the head of the stair confronting the Great Plaza. This latter possibility may account for dual circulation pathways; one running through the structure and one bypassing it on both sides.

In the case of 26-3rd, the rear exits confronted a meter-high drop into the summit space accessed on the W by a most peculiarly configured stair, partly open and partly at the end of a deep slot (faintly visible in Plate 30 directly below 26-3rd) or E by a second more normal stair. The set of two stairs accessing the acropolis precinct seem to repeat the long established pattern of twinned stairs leading onto the acropolis basal platform (Plate 11 and Figure 32 U. 114B). If EW iconography was embodied in these stairs acropolis users might have chosen one or the other first to approach the acropolis from the plaza and second to enter or leave the summit precinct. Perhaps processions arriving or leaving proceeded in pairs.

One architectural effect of the paired stairs leading down from 26-3rd into the summit precinct may have been to disguise the axial offset that had developed, perhaps unintentionally, between 26-3rd, positioned at the head of the main acropolis stair and 22-6th at the N terminal position. Eastward expansion had generated

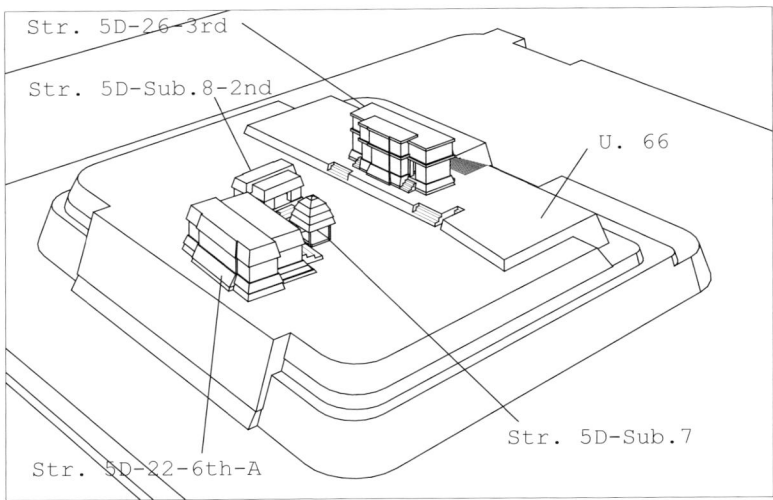

Figure 31. Platform 5D-4-5th.

a very noticeable divergence between the axial line of the S acropolis face and the older, more westerly axis still occupied by 22-6th. Presumably these two axes would have been regarded, from a conceptual point of view, as the same NS line and the dog-leg in it might have seemed merely a trifle embarrassing to philosophical purists. On the other hand, if the NS axis was deemed attractive to supernatural beings a broken axis might have seemed less so. A straightforward axial path of through circulation leading directly from 26-3rd into the acropolis precinct would have made this defect glaringly evident.

The summit space or patio is now relatively well defined, at least where U. 66 extends along its S edge. The N edge is bounded by 22-6th formed as an object occupying space rather than as a linear element designed to define an edge. A similar condition prevails on the E side with Sub.8-2nd. The W remains open, as it had been previously (plate 30) and at this level lack of an E-facing feature appears definite (TR.14:266). Before proceeding to Chapter 7, however, a brief look at the frontal aspect of Plat. 5D-4-6th is in order.

From this view (Plate 31 SW and Figure 33) we can appreciate the monumental impact of the new stair (U. 35). It cuts through terraces that extend across the S face but die on E and W faces. For example, the third frontal terrace turns into a sub-apron on W façade. The over-all visual effect is weaker than that produced by terracing carried consistently around the sub-structure. Although a significant proportion of architectural form illustrated here reflects lack of data rather than positive knowledge, this view effectively points up a generally respected principle of ancient Maya monumental architectural form. The normal, canonical, pattern was that of well-defined bodies formed either as morphologically complete entities within the larger whole or sufficiently complete to give an appearance of wholeness.

For example, the frontal bodies of Sub.1-1st (Plate 17) can easily be understood as the visible portions of three-dimensionally whole units supporting a single room. In Plate 31 the acropolis platform, although divided vertically into a number of layers, cannot be understood as a set of three-dimensionally complete entities. The effect of monumentality is diminished by this lack of formal clarity and the perception of layers, presumably each with symbolic associations, is relatively weak. This poorly resolved formal property is made even more strikingly evident by contrast with the visually strong effect of the axial stair. As mentioned earlier, desire for such a stair might have motivated the increase in acropolis height made at this time.

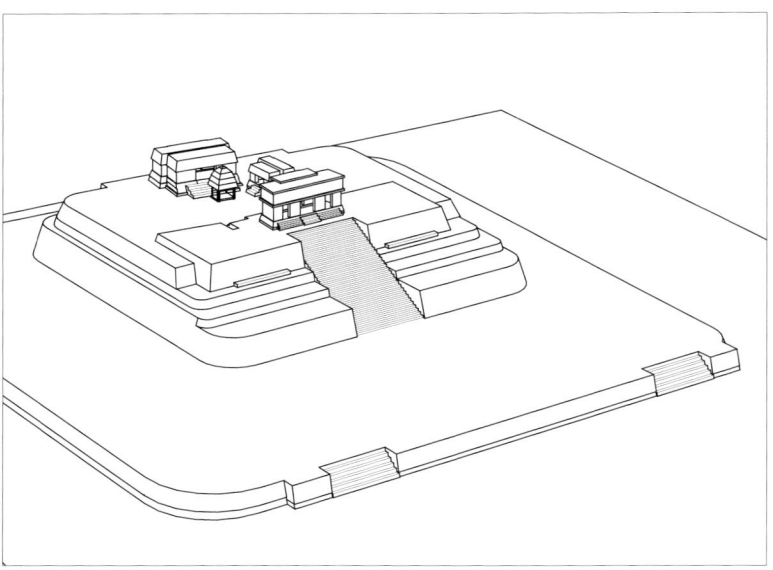

Figure 32. Platform 5D-4-5th.

Although the U. 35 stair represented a radical departure toward greater monumentality it was conservatively executed as an inset stair in the traditional manner common to the majority of earlier stairs on the acropolis. This can be seen equally on Str. 5C-54 (Laporte 2003:fig. 10.3). Previously, the main acropolis stair had risen from a cramped space immediately behind portal Str. 5D-Sub.3-A (Plate 29). This seemingly awkward arrangement had been present on Lamanai Str. N10-43 three or four centuries earlier (Pendergast 1981:fig. 13), and at Altun Ha (B-4 Pendergast 1982:fig. 47). Clearly it was not merely a Tikal experiment. Its abandonment parallels concealment of stair-side masks by Str. 5D-Sub.8-A and Str. 5D-22-6th-A. In both cases simpler arrangements replaced more elaborate earlier ones. Presumably the simpler set-up must have satisfied functional requirements. Perhaps ceremonies conducted on the new stair were deemed sufficiently effective and impressive to justify elimination of Str. 5D-Sub.3-A.

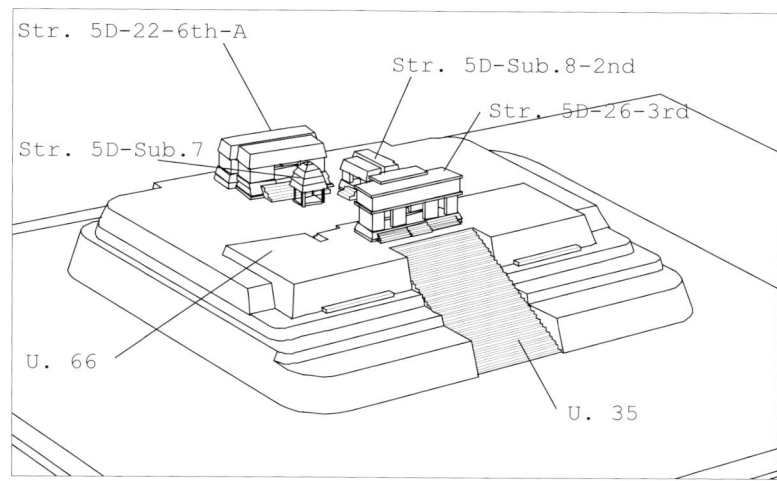

Figure 33. Platform 5D-4-5th.

7

Platform 5D-4-4th

The grand new stair installed with the final renovation of 5D-4-5th (Chapter 6) must have inspired North Acropolis authorities with a new sense of the value and impact that could be delivered by monumental architecture (TR.14:85-102, 828-32). With Platform 5D-4-4th they embarked on a renewal project more ambitious than any preceding projects. Coe (TR.14:918) suggests this development may have been triggered by Bu. 125.

In any case, they now complemented this impressive stair (U. 35) with a wholly new acropolis scaled to its level of grandeur. Expansion is easterly on a new and larger basal platform (Terrace South) accessed by a single, axially offset wide stair (U. 115). Structure 5D-26-3rd is the only feature, apart from the U. 35 stair, to survive intact from the earlier fabric. Structure 22-6th-A remains in use, but with its substructure almost completely buried. Every other earlier feature is completely obliterated by new construction from plaza level to the summit. The basal platform is greatly expanded in area but, as compared with the previous arrangement, the acropolis summit is enlarged even more. The transformed acropolis that emerged when the work of construction had been completed is so much broader that, as illustrated in Plate 33 and Figure 35 (below), it actually appears lower than the previous one.

Extensive demolition (TR.14:86) of the previous acropolis S front may have been done so that the great stair, saved from the pre-existing fabric, would not be too deeply inset. Nevertheless a deeper than usual inset resulted with facings left unfinished (TR.14:89). This seemingly temporary condition may indicate that further developments were already envisioned. Further indications supporting this supposition are considered below.

Plate 32 (Figure 34) is equivalent to TR.14:fig. 6h. This is a newly contrived, greatly enlarged acropolis, with an architecturally coherent overall character despite numerous aberrant features. A triadic theme can be detected among the major bodies: basal platform (Terrace South), acropolis platform, and summit complex, the latter formed by three summit structures. The acropolis platform, too, has three terraces, although they are not equal or even similar in dimension. The restricted area of the summit, surfaced by very well made Fl. 6 (TR.14:88), seems to have been calculated to provide for the group of three relatively small structures that loosely defined the upper precinct.

The potentially much greater area provided by the lower terracing seems designed for a set of much larger summit features that were not installed at this time. Perhaps a need for on-going ritual observances preserved 22-6th. Alternatively, Bu. 125, apparently made immediately prior to the development from 22-6th to 5th, might have continued to act as a ceremonial focus even though Sub.7, and nearly all the 22-6th substructure, had been obliterated by the build-up to Fl. 6. A calendric factor may have been invoked. The period immediately following 5th construction may have been deemed particularly auspicious for ritual activity relating to 22-6th and Bu. 125. The 5th-B acropolis (Plate 32) may have been left semi-finished pending completion of this calendric period, with further development anticipated once a new calendric period had arrived. Alternatively, there may have been a period of mourning, or perhaps a power struggle following the death of a dynamic ruler.

East and W façade details were not accessible, so the arrangement illustrated in Plate 33 may not be ac-

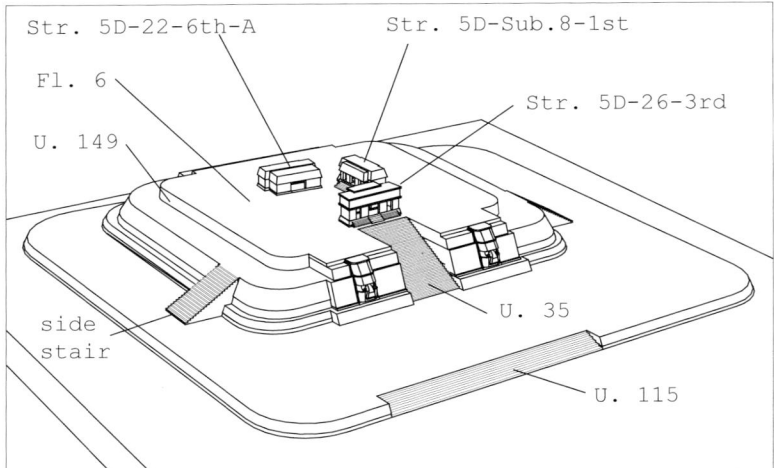

Figure 34. Platform 5D-4-4th-B.

curate, particularly with respect to the unusually high second terrace standing on a very low first terrace. But the upper member, represented by U. 149, was partially uncovered and its anomalous aspects ally it with the peculiar conditions flanking the U. 35 stair. Firstly its area is strangely curtailed, leaving a very wide terrace top surface separating it from the lower two members. Secondly the uneven character of its masonry facings suggests that perhaps this was never intended as a finished face; it does not have an apron molding. In TR.14, U. 149 is described as "shoddily faced" (TR.14:89). Therefore, in Plate 32 I have shown it unplastered, similar to the facings flanking the U. 35 stair.

The one new summit feature assembled on Fl. 6 is Str. 5D-Sub.8-1st (TR.14:fig. 64). Only frontal parts of Sub.8-1st were seen but it appeared to be a considerable expansion over Sub.8-2nd directly beneath, and a similar two member format is assumed. Evidence of considerable burning (TR.14:268-71) following renewal of stair plaster demonstrates that Sub.8-1st did indeed serve for a significant period of time prior to its eventual demolition. Curiously, although Sub.8-2nd had been painted red, 1st was finished in white, unpainted plaster.

After an interval of roughly four centuries the new acropolis platform is again equipped with stairs on its E and W sides (Plate 33). The previous set of side-façade stairs, on Platform 5D-4-8th-D (Plate 11), had provided access directly to the summit precinct and had been located close to the mid-point of each side. These new stairs are placed as close as possible to the S corners, where they would be visible from the Great Plaza. If visibility was an issue, something worth seeing must have taken place on the stairs. Processional events might answer, but if so, they were not destined for the acropolis summit. The new lateral stairs rose only to the top of the second terrace and from that level there was no way to get up to the summit short of using wooden ladders.

This condition parallels the stairs built into terraces of Str. 5D-1 (Great Temple I) and 5D-2 (Great Temple II). These stairs also rise only part way up the substructure and evidently provide access to terrace levels. They seem calculated for ceremonial performances in which substructure terraces were occupied by either participants or witnesses. A spectacular theatrical type of ceremony seems indicated. The stairs access an ample surface extending rearward right around the acropolis and providing plenty of space for an impressive assembly. Processional ceremonies could rise up on one side of the acropolis and descend via the other, leaving the basal platform and then returning to it again.

If this seems like a plausible explanation both for the side-façade stairs and the irregular upper terracing, it apparently had only temporary currency. The architectural development soon to follow provides for a quite different path leading from the side stairs to the summit level.

Evidence that at least some parts of the 4th-B platform were seen as a temporary or short term installations may be provided by U. 149, the aberrant facing on the upper terrace body, lacking an apron molding, and possibly never finished. This arrangement may have served a single event. The side stairs leading to the space left open by the U. 149 facing, may have been installed for just one performance. A calendric consideration may be involved. The intricate calculus of ancient Maya divination ritual could easily identify a short period, such as a particular K'atun ending, when a certain type of event was deemed appropriate and would not be repeated once the calendric moment had passed (Haviland 1992:76-79). However, this initial set of side stairs must have answered some longer-term need as well because the side stairs were repeatedly renewed in later developments.

At the same time that side stairs were installed on the acropolis, twinned stairs were eliminated from the renewed and enlarged basal platform (Terrace South in TR.14). In their place a single very much wider stair was installed (Plate 33). Oddly, however, this new stair is placed noticeably off-center to the W, roughly on the line of an older acropolis axis. The two events might easily be connected. Considerations calling for twin stairs at the basal level might have been now applied to the acropolis in the form of side stairs. However, apart from the off-center location, the broad single basal platform stair was not a short term expedient. This arrangement carried through to the final stage of acropolis development, along with continued installation and renewal of side stairs. The offset position relates to an earlier axial line perhaps still meaningful even though it had been superceded. Certainly, the ancient Maya who used the acropolis were keenly aware of axial lines and frequently placed caches and burials on them. Possibly there was a conceptual distinction between an upper axis and a lower one, although, if so, it did not persist through final developments.

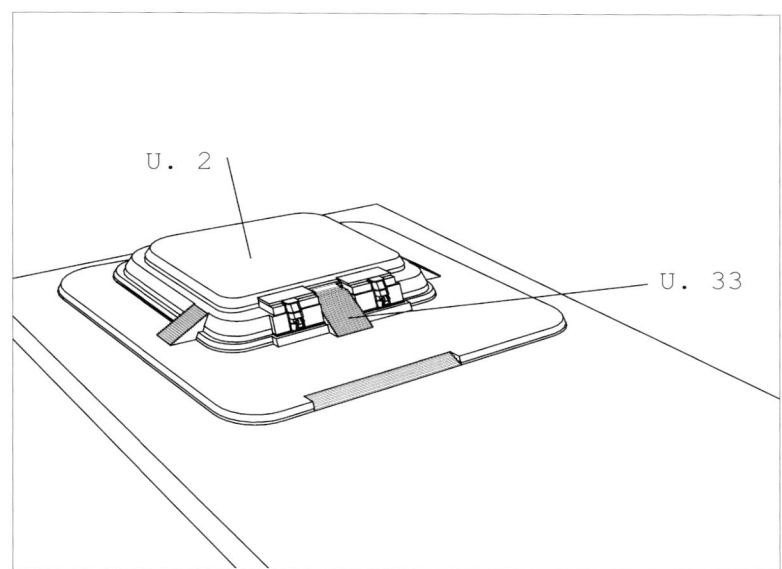

Figure 35. Platform 5D-4-4th-B/A.

Grasping at straws, the offset position of the new basal platform stair may have been determined by the position of 22-6th. This too is offset to the W. acropolis development had proceeded by way of more eastward than westward expansion. The new lower stair is centered farther W than the center of 22-6th and this position would have provided a somewhat better view of the modestly scaled north axial feature, to one side of 26-3rd, which otherwise blocked the view of 22-6th from the upper level axial line.

Notwithstanding all that has been discussed above concerning Platform 5D-4-4th-B, the most striking new aspect that it presented undoubtedly would have been the two enormous masks installed to flank impressive stair U.35 which had been carefully carried forward from the previous acropolis. These were built up using very large masonry units (TR.14:87), perhaps the largest individual stones employed in the entire acropolis history. Dominant features of these masks are very large humanoid heads, sadly, severely defaced in the course of later renovations.

Plate 33 illustrates these masks in rough outline only. No finish plaster had survived and all remnants of color had been stripped off. No doubt they were elaborated with intricate detail and polychrome rendering. They were scaled to the dimensions of the acropolis platform and my guess is that the identity they displayed was that of the acropolis, rather than any individual part such as 22-6th, or the recent anomalous interment Bu.125. This, of course, is no more that a personal supposition based on my belief that the terraces and fabric of the acropolis were regarded as a "home" that supernatural beings might choose to inhabit at certain times when ritual activities were underway. My hypothesis is that a great many supernatural entities might be conceptually linked to the various parts of the acropolis. The new and most impressive stair (U. 35) might easily be the acropolis part that certain beings or forces or entities identified by the masks might be expected to inhabit.

A possible scenario, in my imagination, is that once the great stair was built, its impressive impact might have convinced ritual specialists that some particularly powerful entity had chosen it. Then, under the belief that this potentially beneficial force was indeed accessible, it would make sense to undertake a massive renovation to consolidate this advantage. The masks would have made this conclusion conspicuously evident to all users of the Great Plaza, but this might have been a secondary consideration. The primary issue would have been that of securing presence of the supernatural force and therefore I would contend that the masks were installed for the benefit of this presence; that is, to further ensure likelihood of pleasing the supernatural client.

Representation of a human-like countenance may have been connected with the office of rulership. Rulers claimed descent from gods and gods sometimes appear in human form. A ruler, in office when the masks

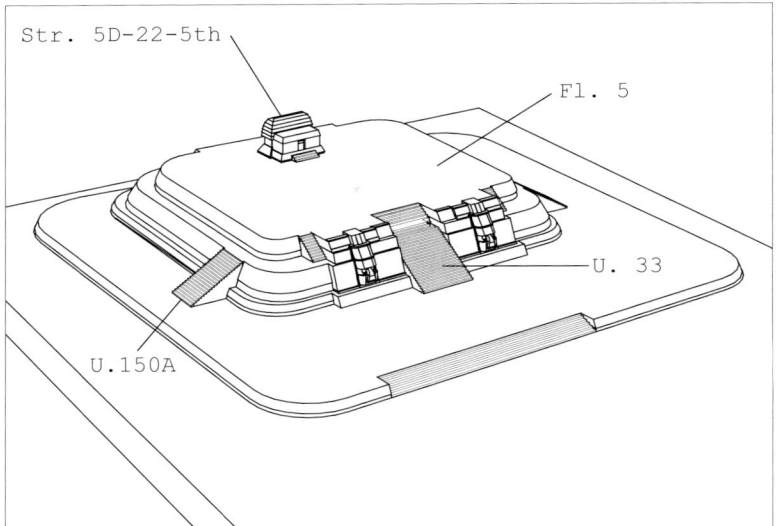

Figure 36. Platform 5D-4-4th-A.

were installed, may have been able to claim that it was not only the stair that induced the essential presence, but equally, the royal person who used the stair and who performed ritual acts on the acropolis. The human visage may have been devised to take advantage of this claim, assuming of course, that such claims were generally accepted as valid. Alternatively the same argument could be advanced for a deceased ruler as the human referent of the mask iconography.

Late in the 2nd century AD (TR.14:Chart 1) the apparently provisional upper acropolis arrangements of 4th-B began to be altered, initially as illustrated in Plate 33 (Figure 35) by an installation that was even more provisional and puzzling. A new wider stair was built (U. 33) up to the level of the stair-side mask tops where it ended on some kind of landing made unclear by later demolition. Above this stair, extending over the acropolis top, and covering the stumps of demolished summit features, a body of core material was built up, capped by U. 2, a layer of floor-body material, 0.80 m thick, lacking a smooth surface and not connected to any known terrace facings or summit structures. A few enigmatic depressions provided the only U. 2 features. Nevertheless, there seems to have been a definite pause in development at this point and the acropolis must have existed in this even more unfinished state for at least a short time. The limited U. 2 surface that was seen showed no sign of any kind of activity and the depressions noted in its surface might have resulted from core settling rather than on-floor use. I felt that this transitional stage was worth illustrating because it seemed to me to indicate an ongoing state of un-

certainty, or perhaps, very short term exigency, consistent with immediately preceding developments.

The time of these seemingly hesitant yet ambitious developments happened to fall close to the turn of the ninth K'atun (8.8.0.0.0: 199 AD, Sharer 1994: Table A.3). Although this date does not appear in the inscriptions the ancient Maya must have been aware of it. The turn of the K'atun may have been a factor unsettling ritual specialist users of the acropolis as they tried to interpret ambiguous signs concerning the fate of the newly seated K'atun and the direction that ceremonial activities should take. An alternative proposition is that acropolis architectural development was influenced by a variety of stimuli; some that endured for lengthy periods and others of very short duration. As discussed in Chapter 1, because of its date, this event may be connected with Tikal's role as seat of the *may* at this time (Rice 2003: 91, 166).

At last the acropolis formed by Platform 5D-4-4th-A, a fabric fated to endure through the 3rd and into the 4th century AD, was completed (Plate 34 and Figure 36), presumably in the form anticipated when 4th-B was begun. But indecisiveness in architectural matters had not been eliminated. What now followed could hardly have been much worse. A first rate beginning was followed by a third rate development. The frontal acropolis masks show that an understanding of architectural scale had existed at Tikal, but those responsible for 4th-A summit development managed to avoid any awareness of it.

Plate 34 illustrates the problem. The four summit structures that eventually appeared are all founded on Fl. 5, so any sequence between them is not evident in stratigraphy. But this lack of evidence for sequential development is not evidence for simultaneous development. Therefore, I have opted to pose a hypothetical sequence. If the N axial feature was the conceptually dominant element of the acropolis, as seems to be indicated by subsequent physical properties of 22-3rd-1st then perhaps 22-5th might have been installed first to minimize interruptions in the most essential acropolis functions. A modestly scaled structure could be completed relatively quickly while work continued in the other summit features that stand on the same floor (Fl. 5). The acropolis, then, would have appeared as shown in Plate 34 and Figure 36, at least for a time.

The new version of structure 22, 22-5th (TR.14:339-42), is located as far to the N as possible and shifted E to conform to the axial line of the frontal stair (U. 33). But, despite severely limited knowledge, it seems to have been scarcely larger than 22-6th, and may even have reverted back to the archaic single-doorway format last seen in Str. 5D-22-6th-B. The only evident progressive innovation is expanded width of the front room which may have been initially thatched (TR.14:340) although lateral projections of the rear room would have made thatching difficult. Walls are still so thin that roof type is uncertain but likely did not employ masonry vaulting. I have given it a thatched rear roof and a beam and mortar front roof in Plate 34 and Figure 36.

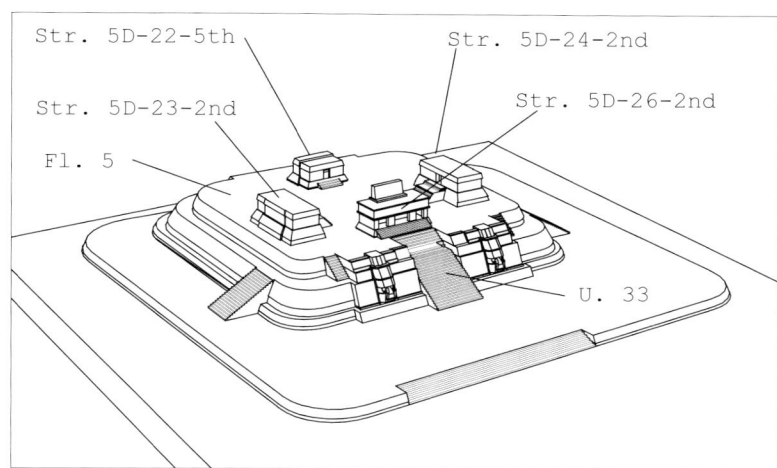

Figure 37. Platform 5D-4-4th-A.

Integral with completion of the 4th-A acropolis, a new frontal stair was installed, wider than the previous one, which had been carefully saved during 4th-B remodeling, and equipped with a landing just four steps below Fl. 5 level. This seems curious in view of the measures taken to preserve the earlier stair, but may be consistent with the view that the stair had acquired a special significance. The in-flight landing near the top might have provided a place for conspicuous ritual performance, a theatrical space confronting the Great Plaza. This may substantiate my earlier speculation concerning supernatural presence focused specifically on the stair and ritual activities staged there. Subsequent developments reinforce this supposition (Figure 44).

At the same time a new set of lateral stairs (U. 150) was installed flanking upper level additions to the mask assembly and leading up to the acropolis summit. This now allowed for summit access via the side-façade stairs, something not previously possible. Whatever role the 4th-B side stairs had served was now altered at least somewhat. Processional displays might still have been staged, but if so they now could have proceeded on up to the summit level. Several other interpretations also appear feasible. The new lateral stairs might have been merely adjunctive features allowing for access to the summit but separate from the side-stair events that could have continued as before. Then again, the new lateral system could have provided access to the summit during activities staged on the now amplified axial stair.

Structure 5D-22-5th standing at the N edge of the acropolis summit is dwarfed by the scale of the recently expanded fabric. This effect is particularly evident with 22-5th as the only summit feature, as shown in Plate 34. This possibility while not demonstrable, is not over-ruled by stratigraphic evidence either.

The new summit area, however, seems calculated either for a set of much larger features or for an expanded inner precinct. The developmental pattern suggests a change of plans, or perhaps conflicting views on how best to proceed. Increased importance of the frontal acropolis zone with its enormous masks and impressive stair may have temporarily eclipsed the summit as the prime focus for ritual theatre. Presence of the Great Plaza, already paved for some time, may have contributed to this. Ritual activities on the axial stair might have taken pressure off the summit complex so that relatively modest structures could serve their particular functions while other, perhaps more splashy, events were staged frontally.

Whatever may have been the sequence of construction on Fl. 5, its eventual outcome is an open-cornered quadrangular group of four structures around an inner precinct (Plate 35). Although this arrangement may represent a single developmental decision, there must have been some kind of sequence to the construction operations even if the time interval between structures may have been minimal.

The north member of this group, 22-5th, discussed previously (Plate 34), stands somewhat apart from the other three as though a space had been intentionally left for its future enlargement. This may or may not have been the case, but the implication accords with my earlier suggestion that 22-5th might have been deliberately undersized for expediency. I show it in Figure 37 with a beam and mortar roof simply because this is a possible

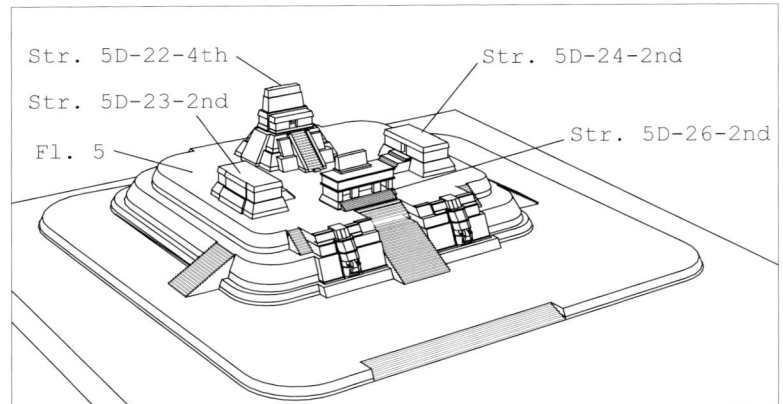

Figure 38. Platform 5D-4-4th-A.

interpretation of the surviving wall-level evidence.

Now standing at the head of the acropolis stair is 26-2nd (TR.14:286-8; fig. 72, 73) somewhat larger than 26-3rd but very similar in plan, its S façade taken up by three wide doorways. Although walls of the building are quite thin (ca 0.70 m) it may have been vaulted. Scaffolding holes at the base of the walls constitute the strongest evidence for this inference. Scaffolding in some form would have been needed for vault construction, partly to set up guidelines and partly to provide working platforms for the masons. Thatching can be done from ladders. Debris from the demolition of 26-2nd included modeled stucco (TR.14:287) probably from upper zone surfaces, additional evidence for either vaulting or beam-and-mortar roofing.

Rear doorways once again provide for through circulation from the acropolis stair into the summit precinct although at the same time it would have been quite easy to pass around 26-2nd and into the precinct via the open S corners. The previously proposed interpretation (Plate 23) that rear doorways provided entry from the upper precinct for performers who would appear above the Great Plaza in the three front doorways seems even more plausible given elaboration of the main stair.

As rendered in Plate 35, the outward form of 26-2nd is based on Coe's reconstruction of 26-1st (TR.14: fig. 77-79). I have not shown any sculptural treatment in the upper zones although, as noted above, modeled stucco fragments, with polychrome rendering, were recovered.

East and W sides of the quadrangle are now occupied by comparably scaled features, 23-2nd and 24-2nd (TR.14:417-33; fig. 123) finally breaking with a centuries old tradition that for some unknown reason kept the W side of the summit precinct relatively open. The W side feature, 5D-23, was comprehensively investigated in Tikal Project operations, but only a very small portion of 23-2nd was exposed. The E side of the acropolis was left for future study and an even smaller exposure of 24-2nd suggested that it was essentially a mirror image of 23, at least with respect to overall form and scale. Presence of single doorways in E and W structures is entirely hypothetical.

Plate 35 shows the initial arrangement prior to any modifications of the four summit features. At this time at least some part of the 23-2nd substructure was painted with an unidentified green pigment TR.14:418). I have taken the liberty of rendering the whole, very hypothetical superstructure green as well. This is unusual but not unique. Wauchope (1970) reports a green-painted version of the Awalix temple at Utatlan, also located on the W side of the complex (cited in Carmack 1981:272). Substructure masks have polychrome treatment that I have not attempted to illustrate. No superstructure details were accessible, and probably few would have survived subsequent modification.

A symmetrical open-cornered quadrangle enclosing a summit precinct had not been installed on the acropolis for nearly four centuries. The previous instance was 8th-D (Plate 11) early in the 1st century BC, which also had stairs on its E and W sides (side-stairs), as in Str. 5C-54 and in the twin pyramid complexes at Tikal. I imagine that doctrinal considerations would have been deeply involved in architectural compositions at the acropolis summit. As mentioned in connection with 8th-D, quadrangular arrangements, and four-sidedness were deeply ingrained in ancient Maya natural philosophy (Bassie-Sweet 1996:21-48; Ashmore 1992:173-84). Linda Schele proposes that this open-cornered configuration might be an architectural trope referring to extreme positions of the Milky Way during the solar year (Freidel, Schele and Parker 1993:59-122). The arrangement of four structures around an open space or patio is analogous to the glyphic organization of affixes around a central element (Thompson 1962:39-63). Glyphic writing may seem unrelated to architectural design but the people who wrote the codices very likely used ceremonial complexes and may even have designed them. If so, similar thinking would not be surprising.

Although the quadrangular plan may well be described as a "cosmic template" (Ashmore 1992:178) my guess is that the ancient Maya thought of it in concrete as well as abstract terms. I imagine that they conducted ritual activities oriented toward the four cardinal directions as they conceived of them. In other words the "cosmic template" may have been used for practical purposes.

Plate 36 and Figure 38 show the 4th-A acropolis with 23-2nd now painted red and 22-5th replaced by 22-4th. Very little is known of 4th but those features that were encountered suggest it was considerably larger than 5th (TR.14:342-48; fig. 92). The form conveyed in Plate 36 is mainly derived from much more completely known 22-3rd (Plate 37, below). Therefore some details may be incorrect. But in terms of overall acropolis architectural form the picture is probably valid. The N axial position of maximal power and significance is now visibly embodied in a structure larger and more imposing than any other on the acropolis. Sculptural elaboration, not suggested in Plate 6, probably would have added to this impression. Replacement of 22-5th with a much larger structure founded on the same floor (Fl. 5) may reinforce the impression, proffered above, that 5th was a temporary expedient run up quickly while larger construction projects to complete the acropolis summit were still under way.

The summit complex now presents a more balanced quadrangular set-up with E and W represented similarly in terms of architectural form. The earlier condition, with 23-2nd painted green, may have been doctrinally more correct in the sense that westward oriented ritual would likely not duplicate activities oriented toward the E. However, apparent similarity between 23 and 24 is largely assumed and may not have been as close as these illustrations suggest.

During the long tenure of Fl. 5, through the 3rd century AD and into the early 4th (TR.14:Chart 1) the entire suite of summit features was renewed and enlarged while all other parts of the acropolis continued substantially unchanged. Plate 37 presents an initial appearance with white plaster on 22-3rd making a dramatic contrast against the red paint of the other structures, 23-1st, 24-1st and 26-1st, all part of the same development.

The majestic architectural form of 22-3rd (TR.14:349-63) may have been initially developed in 4th but it was only with 3rd that excavation yielded the data necessary for a confident reconstruction.

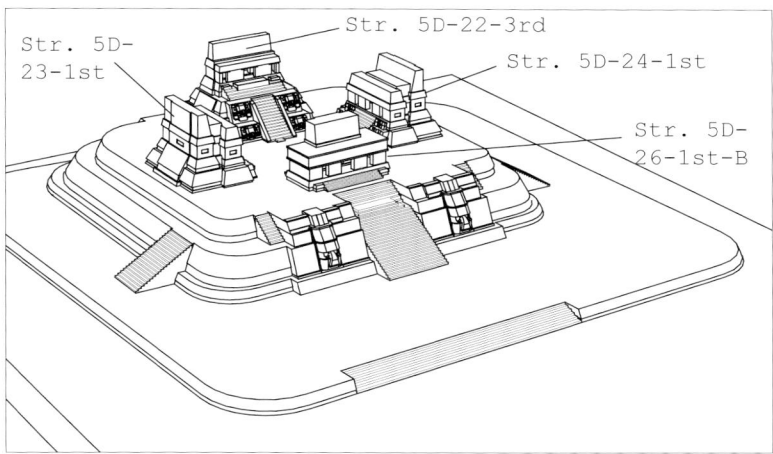

Figure 39. Platform 5D-4-4th-A.

Plate 37, primarily included to show the new set of summit features, illustrates 22-3rd from the rear NE corner. This view stresses the rear axial outset prominently topping off the vertical array of outsets rising from base level right up to the (hypothetical) roof comb through all component bodies of the acropolis. Also clearly visible from this angle is the open diagonal running from NE to SW. A similar diagonal opens from NW to SE. These voids add to the four-sidedness of the summit composition so that an eight-directional figure can be understood. Iconography of this arrangement is further considered ahead in relation to Plat. 5D-4-1st-C.

Whatever the ancient Maya may have intended by this compositional arrangement its visual effect was that of unifying the whole fabric so that it could be understood as one architectural entity organized around the north axial dominant feature. If a sense of architectural scale had been lacking earlier it had certainly been recovered by this time.

The impression of unity projected by elements of the N façade was not at all generated southward where observers in the plaza could appreciate it. Perhaps the view from N was meant for the benefit of non-human beings, deceased ancestors, and/or the forces of nature; there is no place for mere humans to appreciate it from closer than the North Group.

The pile-up of rear axial outsets results in a vertical culmination at the north that contrasts markedly with the horizontality of the façade fronting the plaza. Architectural character evident in Plate 37 suggests that the north façade may have been designed in relation to the 5th direction addressed by ancient Maya ritual specialists, the vertical, symbolized by the ceiba

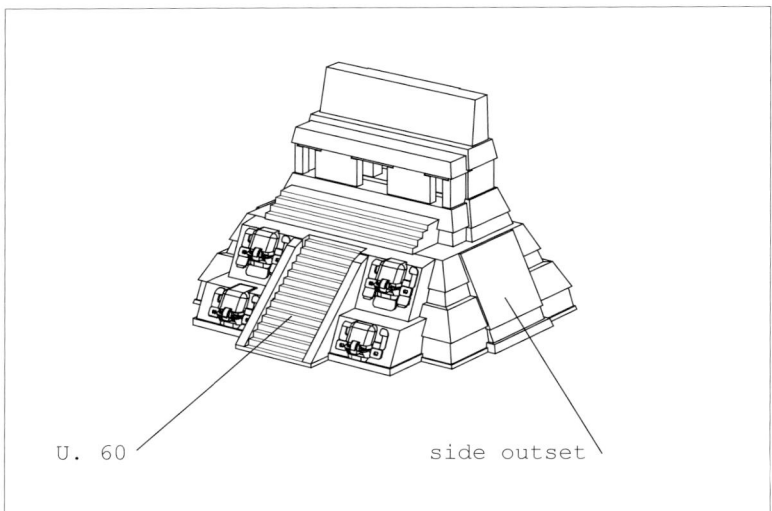

Figure 40. Structure 5D-22-3rd-E.

tree and by frequent association of "north" with "up". Initially, 22-3rd was left white, the direction often associated with north.

Platform 5D-4-4th supports the acropolis associated with the early years of the dynastic line established by Yax Ehb' Xook, possible occupant of Bu. 85 beneath Str. 5D-Sub.2-2nd, interred perhaps as early as AD 75. Names of the first nine rulers in the succession are unknown (Martin 2003:6-7) but since they span two and quarter centuries their tenures of office average twenty-five years. Ruler 11 was Siyaj Chan K'awiil I (Martin 2003:7), in office some time around AD 300, that is, toward the end of the 5D-4-4th development. He was followed in AD 317 by a ruler once thought to have been female, possibly representing a break in the lineage. More recently this seems doubtful (Martin 2003:9). Nevertheless, it may have been this ruler who presided over the final stage of Platform 5D-4-4th development.

The succession of rulers cited above roughly equates with tenures averaging around 25 years. This may indicate a period of stability and gradual growth. Platform 5D-4-4th development may reflect this. Most of the 5D-4-4th changes are concentrated on the summit structures and result in an increasingly coherent and impressive effect.

This raises the question of the relationship between rulers and major architectural projects. It remains unclear whether rulers commissioned such projects individually, or whether the projects were decided upon more or less collectively as corporate undertakings for the benefit of the community. Powerful rulers, suc-cessful in warfare and personally charismatic might have been thought to enjoy support of supernatural powers during their lifetimes. Structures associated with them after their death might have seemed likely to be effective for ceremonial activities and would justify major investment. From this point of view the 3rd century AD may have been a time of success for Tikal.

From a frontal view (Plate 38 and Figure 40) 22-3rd is revealed as having a simplified lower substructure consisting of a single, two-terrace, body extending from front to rear and elaborated with large side outsets vertically spanning both terraces. In Plate 39, a photo taken in 1963, the W side outset and two terraces of Str. 22-3rd appear as the left-most features of the substructure. The main corner, of three terraces, belongs to Str. 5D-22-2nd. The upper mask, partially still unexcavated, is on 22-3rd while the lower mask and stair are 22-1st features. Convex curving profiles typical of early terracing and aprons can be seen clearly.

A similar arrangement may have preceded this in 22-4th but the form would have been innovative in terms of North Acropolis architecture and was probably conceived to raise the level of this N axial feature both physically and conceptually. The side outsets in particular must have been iconographically potent elements invoking the EW directional aspects of supernatural beliefs that have been cited in numerous references above. In effect doctrinal issues embedded in the quadrangular planning of the acropolis summit are reiterated within the substructure of 22-3rd.

The greater size and height of the 22-3rd rear axial outset (see Plate 43) may have similarly stressed a hierarchical relationship between NS and the EW axes in architectural design. These aspects of form indicate that elevation of the building was not the only or perhaps even the primary purpose guiding design of a substructure component approaching pyramidal proportions. From them I infer that the substructure was expected to provide a "home" for supernatural beings just as much, and perhaps even more than, the building.

Because the frontal stair and lateral side outsets are nearly equal in magnitude a radial symmetry similar to arrangements seen in Str. 5C-54, and the EW platforms in the Twin Pyramid complexes at Tikal (Coe 1970:85) becomes evident. Structure 5C-54 is considered part of an "observatory" complex; that is, a set of structures concerned with movement of the sun. The quadrangular plan of the Twin Pyramid groups may have a similar import. The whole of the North Acropolis may have cosmic significance, as suggested above, but Str. 5D-22 may have condensed this into its own fabric almost as though it constituted a whole complex all by itself.

On this ideologically complex lower substructure stands a more or less conventional building platform with rear and frontal bodies in turn sustaining a traditional two-room tandem building almost certainly vaulted. The front room has three outer doorways in accordance with recently established conventions. Central doorway width greatly exceeds widths of lateral doorways placed remotely at the extreme edges of the façade. I suppose width of the axial doorway reflected position on the axial line, the locus of caches, burials and much burning. The axis may have been the locus of the most focused and proximal supernatural presence.

The front room is very narrow front-to-rear, its extremely reduced depth running counter to the more common tendency for front room width to exceed that of other rooms in the same building. This may have been a compromise solution so that outdoor space could be provided immediately in front of the building. Here a broad stair with a wide landing provided a venue for open-air activities sited on the most prominent position at the very apex of the acropolis.

The much narrower lower stair, rising to the top of the lower substructure body projects outward from a masonry block attached to the front of the platform and elaborated with high relief masks. Early Classic formal conventions are initiated here in that outsets carrying the lower masks are set below the first terrace top. The second outset carries up to the platform top where it provides additional surface for the wider upper stair and landing. Stair-side ramps or *alfardas*, illustrated here are assumed on the basis of 22-1st.

The masks, known best on the second terrace, W side (Plates 39 and 40), are modeled only in rough outline in Plates 41-54. Partly human and partly non-human, their significance is debatable. For example, Arthur Miller (1986) considered them as symbols of rulership enduring beyond mortal existence. Haviland (personal communication) proposes that such images may represent therianthropes, humans in the process of transforming into supernaturals.

My own view is that they were not primarily symbols although they surely would have possessed a symbolic dimension. I see them as similar to the larger

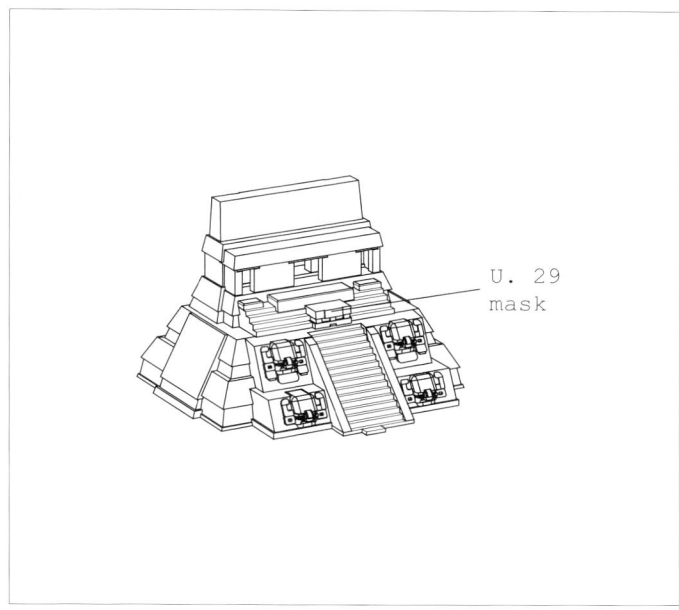

Figure 41. Structure 5D-22-3rd-D.

masks flanking the axial acropolis stair and installed not long before these masks as devices intended to reveal presence of supernatural beings or forces within the fabric.

A problem is that we do not know whether the 22-3rd masks were all identical or whether there was some difference between E and W sides and upper and lower terraces, as with the Cerros masks (Schele and Freidel 1990:104-15). Discovery of variation in mask details would greatly affect interpretation. Plate 40 shows the upper W side mask after excavation in 1965. The eyes appear realistically human but the mouth elements are non-human.

Upper zones of 22-3rd probably would have been elaborated with sculptural detail, particularly on the frontal body but I have not attempted to suggest this in my rendering of it. Similarly, if there really was a roof comb, it too would have displayed sculptural imagery.

The exterior space in front of the 22-3rd building (Plate 41 and Figure 41) underwent a series of modifications, not all of which are illustrated here (TR.14: fig. 93-100). Among these changes the white plaster finish was covered with red paint and a spectacular stair-block mask (U. 29) was installed at the base of the building platform stair, or perhaps more significantly, at the head of the lower stair.

The U. 29 mask appears in Plate 42 with Coe looking at it immediately on its excavation. The top shows heavy burning suggesting use as an altar. Most of the paint is gone. The eye cruller, indicates the deity known

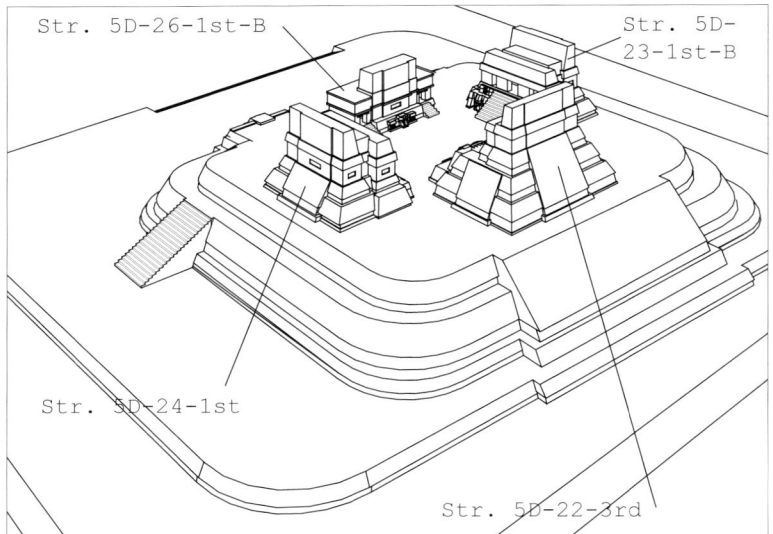

Figure 42. Platform 5D-4-4th-A.

as GIII, the jaguar god of the underworld. Initially this figure was associated with one of the hero twins of the Popol Vuh (Lounsbury 1985). It has been connected also with the sun and with sacrificial ritual (Schele and Miller 1986:50-1).

The top part of this mask is a rectangular block that provides a horizontal surface very heavily burned. The term "altar" might be appropriate for this feature. It raises images of offerings made at the stair head where space had been made available by drastically curtailing width of the front room. To repeat, the deity image on the axis and the humanoid images on the terraces can be considered as not merely decorative, but fundamentally utilitarian.

Interpretations advanced above imply that these features were meant to increase the fundamental functionality of the whole structure in relation to power and influence over human affairs as well as natural phenomena.

The overall character of 22-3rd is that of an essentially vertical structure, higher than it is wide, particularly when seen from either side or from the rear. This satisfies a very simplistic definition of a "temple," a term that has been widely used for a range of structures suspected to have served ritual purposes. A more precise definition, specific to the ancient Maya context, may be that of a structure designed to attract the presence of supernatural entities. The 22-3rd features discussed above as serving this purpose likely provide only a small sample of equivalent features presented by other structures correctly classified as "temples." Although still horribly vague and subjective, "ritual purposes" at least identifies functional "temple" criteria even though inferential and based to a great degree on formal properties.

During the 3rd century AD, with Fl. 5 continuing in use, the summit complex developed as a tightly enclosed quadrangle with open corners (Plate 43 and Figure 42). Probably coeval with 22-3rd, original E and W features, 24-2nd and 23-2nd, were replaced by much larger three-roomed structures with a roof comb definitely present on 23 and therefore probably also on unexcavated 24 which, until data are available, is assumed to have been identical. Features discussed below are those of 23-1st-B.

The 23-1st-B substructure is in two bodies, like so many earlier North Acropolis precedents, but now, the frontal body, though still lower than the rear, extends farther laterally, so that the front façade is wider than the rear, like 26-3rd. On this lower substructure arrangement the building platform has two bodies separated by an inset element that roughly corresponds to the middle room in the set of three rooms. The front room walls stand on the frontal building platform body and the rear room walls, higher up, rise from the rear building platform body. As a result the structure appears to be made up of two separate buildings one tightly placed in front of the other.

For the ancient Maya this arrangement may have evoked imagery of tandemly placed thatch structures. Whatever its associations, the format must have satisfied doctrinal considerations since it re-appears frequently in structures built during subsequent centuries at Tikal. They appear also at Río Azul (Adams 1999:43) and Piedras Negras (Satterthwaite 1941:183-208). The great majority of later examples, however, occur at Tikal and in no other Maya center can we see such repetition of one particular architectural format.

To me this phenomenon seems to indicate that, while displaying features common to ancient Maya monumental architecture generally, the particular format exemplified by 23-1st-B, the earliest known instance, held a very special value for Tikal ritual specialists. As far as I know all the structures formed like 23-1st-B, that is, with the side inset feature, can be classified as ritual structures, or "temples." The North Acropolis summit, then, can now be characterized as comprising three temples, a triad of ritual structures, with the fourth side defined by portal structure 26-1st-B.

As can be seen in Plate 43, the rear façade of 26-1st-B presents a central mask on the N-projecting substructure body that sustains the rear room. This poorly preserved feature appears to consist of a deity head set between two wide spaced deity eyes (TR.14:298, fig. 80c). Although there are numerous examples of rear façade sculptural treatment at Tikal, none appear on substructure bodies. Therefore I wonder if the N façade of 26-1st should not be regarded as a second front so that all four structures forming the acropolis summit complex would face into the inner precinct. This would be consistent with the idea advanced earlier that costumed figures might have entered from the "rear" to appear dramatically in the S doorway openings.

As a secondary speculation the two N doorways flanking the substructure mask might have provided access to accoutrements stored in 26-1st. In any case, entry into the acropolis precinct did not require passage through the building.

The side inset (Appendix II; Loten 2006; Loten and Pendergast 1984:13) is the feature that causes the superstructure to project an image of two "buildings," one in front of the other (Plate 44). This is a format applied to the exterior whether or not it corresponded to interior arrangements. For example, 23-1st-B, the Great Temples I, II, and IV all have three rooms, not two rooms as the exterior form would suggest. Other examples of this architectural model have only one room; for example, Structure 5D-96, the central member of the so-called Seven Temples, a Late Classic group of structures immediately W of the South acropolis (TR.11:Great Plaza quadrangle). Others have two rooms conforming exactly to the exterior form; for example Str. 5D-3 (Great Temple III) and 3D-40, a late Classic structure in the North Group at Tikal (Loten 2002:fig. 1).

My subjective assessment of why such a detailed and formally specific exterior architecture had such enduring value at Tikal comes back to matters of duality and complementary in ancient Maya natural philosophy, as discussed earlier. Perhaps these ideas were particularly strong in the eschatological doctrines followed by Tikal ritual specialists.

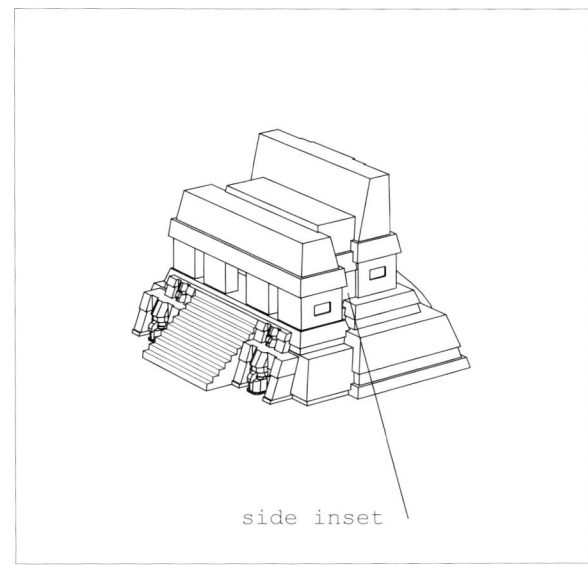

Figure 43. Structure 5D-23-1st-B

Plate 45 illustrates Str. 5D-23 shortly before consolidation work, undertaken by the Guatemalan government and directed by Swiss archaeologist George Guillemin, had been completed in the 1960s. This view emphasizes the vaulting, and in particular the very high narrow vault rising up above the rear room. Structural considerations alone would not lead to such a high vault. The room is so narrow that a much lower vault would be able to span it easily. The effect of the high vault is to hide the upper limit of the space in darkness, like the space of certain cave chambers. This may have been its symbolic role, so that the structure could be regarded as a kind of "mountain" containing a cave and accessed as a portal to the underworld (Bassie-Sweet 1996). In other words, this rear room may have been seen as a place where presence of supernatural beings could be expected.

Details of the vaulting masonry will be treated in TR.34B (in preparation). The high vault may simply reflect intention to raise the roof comb to a conspicuous height and vaulting would save on the material needed for this and would reduce the load on the walls.

8

Platform 5D-4-3rd

Early in the 4th century AD, possibly during tenure of a relatively well documented ruler long known to Mayanists as "Jaguar Paw", more recently as Chak Tok Ich'aak I (Martin and Grube 2000:28), authorities embarked on an ambitious renewal program (Plate 46 and Figure 44) affecting all the lower parts leading up to the summit complex (TR.14:103-28, 832-838, fig. 6j). The acropolis that emerged from this work, essentially a massive face-lift capped by Fl. 4, endured through the 4th century and most of the 5th (AD 325-475, TR.14: chart 1).

New U. 56 masks, similar to the previous set but larger and surrounded by more intricate details, occupy the S front beside new axial stair U. 32. New U. 317 side stairs, inferred from fragmentary evidence, now serve a revised path running across the S front to the new acropolis court at the head of the new axial stair using lateral stair U. 176, and its assumed eastern counterpart, tucked in behind the front masks. Strangely, though, this involved treading on the heads of the two massive masks flanking the axial stair, something that might seem disrespectful to us but apparently did not bother the ancient Maya.

The most conspicuous, innovative move made at this time, aside from re-alignment of the basal stair, daringly involved redesign of the main acropolis stair, perhaps the most impressive feature of the old acropolis, to install a new element within it, the acropolis court. This stair-head feature might be described as a mini-precinct set below the summit level and prominently located at the acropolis front. Its use may be unclear but apparently it served as a locus of intense ritual activity, if that can be reliably judged from abundance of cache deposits (TR.14:fig. 85).

This looks so much like a theatrical setting that I wonder if it does not strengthen my earlier suspicion that this axial stairway locus had already served as a setting for ritual. An earlier landing placed part way up the stair (Figure 36) may have inspired this new, higher setting.

Plate 49 shows Str. 5D-26-1st and the acropolis court after consolidation. The stair system in front of 26-1st, the acropolis court, is clearly designed to facilitate circulation around the building as well as through it and perhaps also from it.

Flanked by two even more impressive and elaborate mask installations, it must have conveyed a very strong sense of monumentality. In addition this setting faced on to the basal terrace expanse, and beyond that, the Great Plaza, so that dramatic ritual performances could have been witnessed by large numbers of people.

From its longevity, the arrangements and architectural character, partly established earlier but now brought to a greater level of refinement with these early 4th century developments, must have seemed particularly effective. Ironically, however, during the time that this seemingly more stable and fully resolved architectural setting functioned, Tikal's political establishment underwent the most dramatic upset that limited records allow us to see.

Earlier accession of Yax Ehb' Xook may have posed an equally profound dislocation but no known texts reveal it. I refer to an event known as "the arrival of strangers" first sniffed out by Proskouriakoff, though fully published only many years later (1993). Subsequently other scholars (Culbert 1991; Coggins 1975; Martin and Grube 2000; Martin 2003; Stuart 2000) have clarified it. Archaeological investigations active after the University

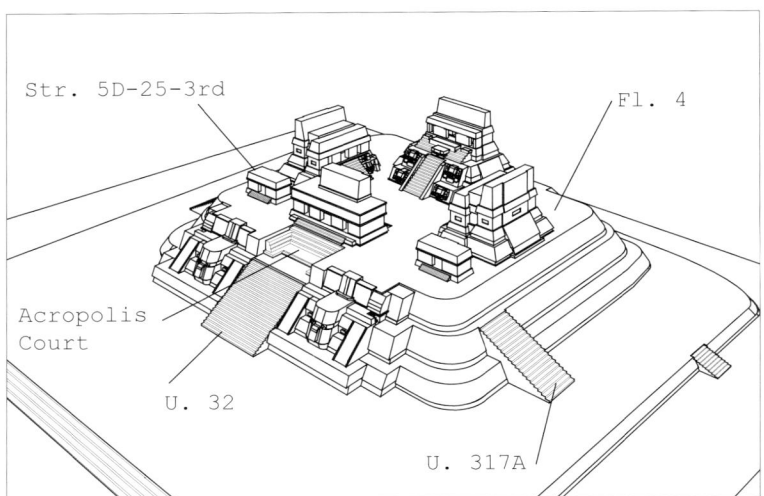

Figure 44. Platform 5D-4-3rd.

Museum Tikal Project had wrapped up (Laporte, 2003) have added vital information.

From physical and epigraphic evidence it appears that in AD 378 the old Tikal ruling dynasty was overthrown and a new rulership, with Teotihuacan connections took power. These "strangers," however, claimed traditional Tikal roots including descent from Yax Ehb' Xook and continued the old "count of kings". The new (15th) ruler, known in archaeological literature as "Curl Nose," more recently as Yax Nuun Ayiin I (Martin 2003:15), apparently grew up at Tikal (Haviland, personal communication).

Whether this also involved a change in either ritual or personnel may be debatable, but architectural developments following the AD 378 event suggest to me that the old acropolis authorities remained in place.

Architectural development now enters the domain of history in the sense that epigraphic texts presenting apparently historical material connect with construction from the early 5th century on. This begins with Structure 34-2nd (Fig. 45) an architectural entity of uncertain character (TR.14:467-68) illustrated in Plate 47, somewhat arbitrarily, as the first terrace of 34-1st. What is certain about the core material of this entity is that it sealed Bu. 10.

A horizontal layer at the level of the first terrace of 34-1st indicates a pause of uncertain nature and duration before the bulk of 34-1st was put in place. A feature something like the 34-2nd shown in Plate 47 certainly existed for some time. Whether days, weeks, months or years, remains unclear.

Burial 10 has been identified with the above-mentioned ruler Yax Nuun Ayiin I, deceased in AD 404, or perhaps 406. The son of the enigmatic "Spearthrower Owl" he took office in AD 374 at some unspecified center and may have married a Tikal woman (Martin and Grube 2000:32). He appears to be associated in some way with the great Mexican center of Teotihuacan (Stuart 2000:481). Through the fog of numerous cryptic inscriptions it seems clear that Yax Nuun Ayiin I did not succeed as Tikal ruler through the traditional line of dynastic descent. In this light, placement of Bu. 10 off the central axis and even off the acropolis is suggestive.

The new dynastic succession may have been no more able to claim burial in the acropolis summit than many of the earlier rulers. I imagine that the son of Yax Nuun Ayiin I, Siyak Chan K'awiil II, wanted his father's tomb in the acropolis, and that acropolis authorities, traditionalists, vetoed this but were unable to prevent interment close enough so that some kind of connection with the venerable institution could be claimed by the new regime. Implicit in this reconstruction is my assumption that ritual specialists held positions of political power at Tikal, a view best known from accounts of Aztec practices (Townsend 1993:192-207), and therefore debatably applicable to Classic Maya contexts.

Plate 47, Figure 44, and Figure 45 include two new summit features, Str. 5D-25-3rd and its eastern, unexcavated equivalent, 27-3rd. Scant details of 25-3rd architectural form (TR.14:334-38, fig. 143) indicate a one-room building with a single axial doorway on the S and two off-axis doorways on the N, as previously seen in Str. 5D-26. Steps below the W doorway on the north side are decorated with crossed sky-symbol bands on their risers, a detail unique at Tikal. Innovative implications are considered below. On the other hand, a rich dedicatory cache (Ca. 74, TR.14:435-7) similar to one found in 22-3rd links this structure to more traditional North Acropolis practice.

Installation of these two very small structures in the open corners of the summit quadrangle appears to have been a departure from traditional patterns of development on the North Acropolis. Earlier structures such as Sub.11, near the corner position were never placed squarely on the diagonal and were not considered to have possessed symmetrically balanced eastern equivalents. Thus the appearance of 25-3rd and presumed 27-3rd might be taken as influence of the new

Tikal rulership. The character of Ca. 74, however, seems to argue against this and these new corner structures actually enhance the quadrangular composition.

Certainly traditional North Acropolis authorities had always been open to novel developments. Therefore it seems reasonable to suppose that this too sprang from the same perpetual effort, documented from the earliest acropolis fabric, to continuously adjust the architectural setting, either to improve functional effectiveness, or perhaps in response to on-going doctrinal revisions emerging from esoteric studies and calculations of ritual specialists. Possibly reflecting a new doctrinal measure, 25-3rd and 27-3rd might have acted as portal structures for entry into the acropolis precinct on the diagonal lines, something that had long been possible but not previously formalized. The informal alternative still remained open in that one could still walk around these corner installations (Plate 48).

The rulership descending from Yax Nuun Ayiin I may have somewhat diverted investment in monumental construction away from the North Acropolis and into the Lost world complex to the SW where several "rich" chamber burials predate BU. 10 (Laporte 2000:281-318). But North acropolis interests did not stagnate entirely. Around AD 450 or 460, the N axial summit feature, 5D-22 (TR.14:363-72, fig. 102), acquired a new superstructure, 22-2nd (Plate 48). To support it new frontal terraces were fitted around the old stair-side masks, the entire 3rd superstructure was dismantled, a new building platform slightly higher than the previous one was built, and on it, a new building, probably vaulted and topped by a roof comb, although no details of these upper parts survived the final stage of N axial renewal. The alteration transforming 3rd into 2nd seems to have been done in order to provide a building with three tandemly placed rooms where previously there had been only two. They did this very ingeniously without enlarging the whole substructure, perhaps on a restricted allowance of resources. Conspicuous side outsets of 3rd are still visible in 2nd, as are the frontal stair-side masks.

Despite limited space available for expansion the new front room was made much deeper than the other rooms of the new building. This may point to some particular functional consideration perhaps connected with the altar at the head of the earlier stair. Respect

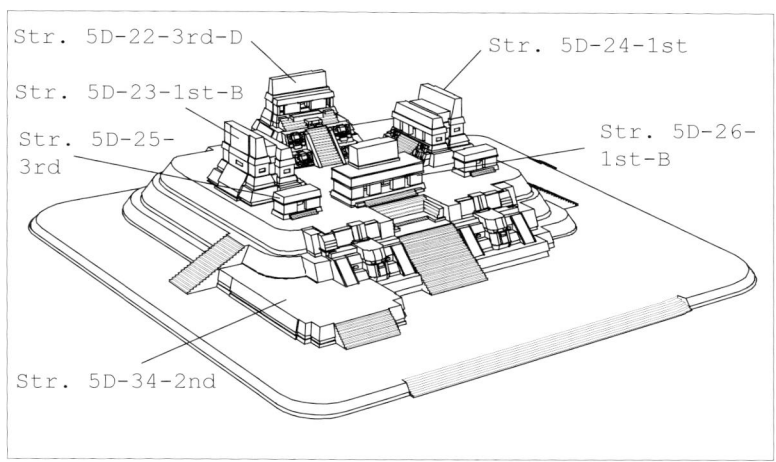

Figure 45. Platform 5D-4-3rd-A.

for the exterior format recently established on 23-1st and 24-1st, with their side insets, may have exerted the determining pressure.

With this renewal 22-2nd now presented a similar exterior image. Two house-like bodies presumably satisfy dualistic doctrines concerning compound or complementary identities of the mythological references. Substantial scale of constructional investment dedicated to this architectural refinement, despite hinted-at suggestions of restrictions, nevertheless indicates either that North Acropolis authorities still commanded substantial power and influence, or that ritual conducted on 22-2nd still seemed essential to the success of Tikal in its state enterprises.

Plate 50 and Figure 47 illustrate a face the acropolis might have presented to the Great Plaza toward the end of AD 457, though by no means certain. In February of the previous year, AD 456, the ruler Siyaj Chan K'awiil II died (Valdés, Fahsen, Munoz Cosme 1997). His tomb is now thought to be that of Bu. 48, cut into the basal platform at the base of the great stair on the acropolis axis with the date 9.1.1.10.10 by the Maya calendar painted in black line on the plaster tomb chamber wall. This corresponds to March AD 457, more than a year later than the death date and is generally assumed to mark placement of the body, sans head and hands, in the tomb.

The interment completed, the cut was repaired and finished with a well-made seal patching over the hole that had been made in the basal platform floor (TR.14:118-19). Then, some time later, this floor patch, together with the bottom steps of stair U. 32, disappeared beneath core masonry of 33-3rd. Therefore it is clear that 33-3rd post-dated Bu.48 by some interval of

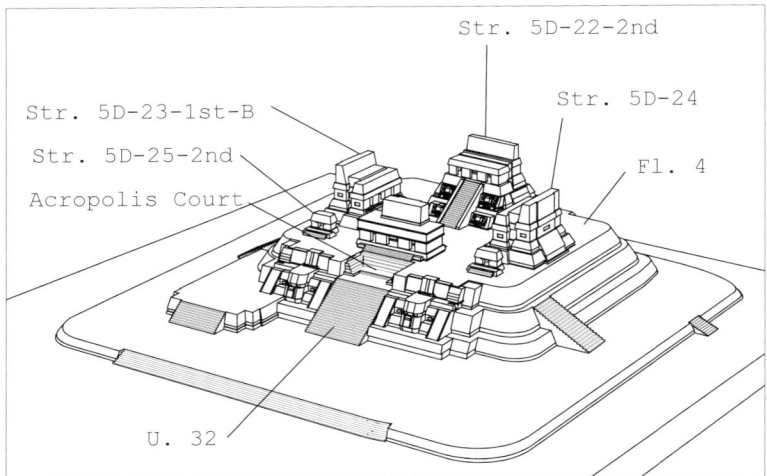

Figure 46. Platform 5D-4-3rd-A.

time that remains undetermined. The acropolis front shown in Plate 50 might have emerged by the end of the year, or perhaps at some time during the following year, AD 458.

Architectural form of 33-3rd (TR.14:507-10, fig. 168a, 179, 180, 183) is somewhat debatable. The S face survived but the E and W faces had been removed. It was at least one terrace high, capped with a good floor surface that had been renewed, and on the basis of this evidence apparently was used for a period of time. But if it ever included a superstructure no trace remained in the areas examined, and Tikal Project conventions could classify it as a "Platform" like 34-2nd.

The terrace profile, extant at the edges of the stair-side masks (below), is of a progressive type. That is, apron and basal moldings lie in the same inclined plane and the sub-apron appears as a horizontal slot, a form that became standard in Late Classic work. But here the apron profile is slightly convex, an attribute allying it with more traditional conventions. In effect, Str. 5D-33-3rd provides a surface on which activities could be staged closer to the Great Plaza than those performed in the Acropolis Court.

Flanking the stair are two relatively well-preserved masks, apparently identical (Plate 51). They depict humanoid figures with either animal snouts or bird beaks and have the mouth curls commonly included in images of supernatural beings. Arthur Miller sees these latter as fish barbels and suggests that the masks refer to the watery underworld realm (Miller 1986:42). Plate 51 shows the west mask WU 4A (TR.14:fig. 183) shortly after excavation. Some plaster remains but all color has gone. The blend of human and non-human features is quite conspicuous.

If 33-3rd existed as depicted in Plate 50 its function must have been connected with entry to the acropolis on the principal NS axis. One would have first ascended between the two masks described above and thence between the larger masks on the acropolis platform. This adjustment to the main stair recalls the earlier precedent of Sub.3 structures that once stood in a similar relation to the acropolis. In the 33-3rd case, however, particularly if there really was only the large "stage" and no superstructure, performances located there may have referred to the masks and tomb. If these were indeed conceptually related, then the masks may have depicted Siyaj Chan K'awiil II as a supernatural power. Martin and Grube point out that the images painted in black line on the tomb chamber walls represent "the flowery ether of divine space" (2000:36). I take the term "divine space" to mean the supernatural realm, where the deceased ruler was thought to have gone in death, presumably retaining favor with the forces of nature, as an advocate for Tikal interests.

The ruler Siyaj Chan K'awiil II is depicted on the front of Stela 31, a monument found within 33-2nd (below) displaying both Teotihuacan and traditional Tikal Maya iconography including the Yax Ebh' Xook name glyph. A possible interpretation is that this ruler, buried headless, claimed both traditional Tikal dynastic descent, through his mother, and access to the supernatural powers that supported Teotihuacan. This might explain location of Bu. 48 on the acropolis axis, a position more favorable than that of his father in non-axial Bu. 10.

A shadowy 32-2nd existed on the same stratigraphic level as 34-2nd and 33-3rd and therefore, if not built contemporaneously must have been in use at the same time (TR.14:554-58; fig. 199). Due to demolition its architectural character is as unclear as that of 34-2nd, but unlike the latter there is no burial associated with it. It seems like a gratuitous assault on the S front of the acropolis, perhaps built to claim a right of access to this prestigious location, or maybe for symmetry with 34 and 33.

The archaeological record is similar enough in these three features, 34-2nd, 33-3rd, and 32-2nd, to suggest that perhaps they were similar architectural entities. For this reason they appear as similar forms in Plate 50. On stratigraphic evidence they could have been contemporaneous.

As mentioned previously this image of the acropolis front is highly conjectural. The form of 32-2nd, in

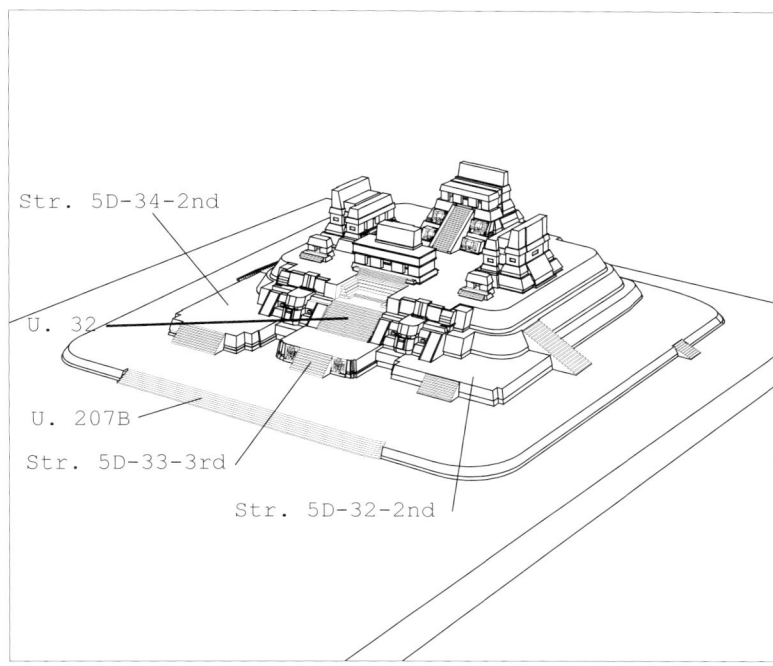

Figure 47. Platform 5D-4-3rd-A.

particular, might have been very different. There was, for example, nothing proving, or even suggesting, that 32-2nd did not have additional terraces and a superstructure. But in the absence of other data, I have illustrated the one basal terrace that did show up in the excavations. From an architectural viewpoint these features deployed across the front of the acropolis did not obscure its bulk and were not high enough to stand between it and the Great Plaza. A desire to retain the long-established relationship between the plaza and the acropolis might stand behind the otherwise puzzling decision to erect features of such minimal height over two burials of apparently powerful rulers. Traditional North Acropolis ritual specialists still may have possessed significant influence at Tikal. If so, this was about to change.

9

Platform 5D-4-2nd

The time span covered by Platform 5D-4-2nd (TR.14:128-39, 838-40, Fig. 6k) extends from AD 475 to 600 (TR.14:Chart 1). Massive construction projects were undertaken and a decisive shift developed in the relationship between the North Acropolis and the Great Plaza. Work completed within this developmental stage set the final appearance of the acropolis, particularly on the E, W and N sides of the platform.

With the coming of 34-1st and 33-2nd venerable North Acropolis fabric began to disappear behind new frontal features (Plate 52 and Figure 48). Either traditional status no longer obtained, or specialized esoteric function was becoming more strongly guarded. The timing of these two disruptive developments is somewhat unclear, but they must refer to the latter part of the 5th century, at least in terms of their presence and function. Sequence is equally unclear although 34-1st might have preceded 33-2nd.

In its architectural form 34-1st combines both early and late features. Innovation is most evident in the lower substructure of three terraces. Previously only the acropolis platform had possessed this format. The three are not the same however; the uppermost terrace has a frontally expanded element absent on the lower two. This may have been done to provide for a wider, more prominent, stair, another feature that, if not particularly innovative was not revivalist either. Apron moldings, however, display the innovative, or at least relatively recently established, character formed by basal moldings and straight-line profiles. Outsets on the lower terraces are proportioned so that the overall effect is that of inset corners. Contrast this with the side outsets on 22-3rd. The outsets appear as distinct entities and rise through both terraces.

On 34-1st it is the terraces that carry through, rather than the outsets and the corners appear emphasized rather than the outsets. This was definitely an innovative treatment and probably indicates a change in the iconography of either the terraces or the outsets. Perhaps the diagonals implied by the inset corners had taken on a greater significance at this time, as already noted in connection with 25-2nd and 27-2nd. This use of outsets to emphasize the corners typifies later work at Tikal. It can be seen in the Great Temples and in Str. 5D-33-1st. Structure 5D-34-1st appears to initiate this pattern.

At the building level older precedents prevail. The single doorway recalls precedents such as Sub. 8-2nd, an anachronism also seen in relatively recent 25-3rd and 27-3rd. Exterior wall surfaces are elaborated with inset panels, features that look like images of windows, and had been seen earlier on 23-1st. Other well established conventions would include the side insets, deeply cut into the building and continuing down through the building platform.

On the innovative side, walls were made thicker than in earlier buildings, perhaps implying existence of a roof comb though no details had survived. The roof illustrated is entirely conjectural.

A very different and unusual architectural form was adopted for 33-2nd, a very broad substructure platform sustaining a much less expansive building and building platform. This cannot really be considered innovative in the sense of initiating a new convention followed subsequently. This was more likely a response to a particular setting at the base of the main acropolis stair. The wide substructure allowed for circulation around the building and on to the stair, somewhat similar to

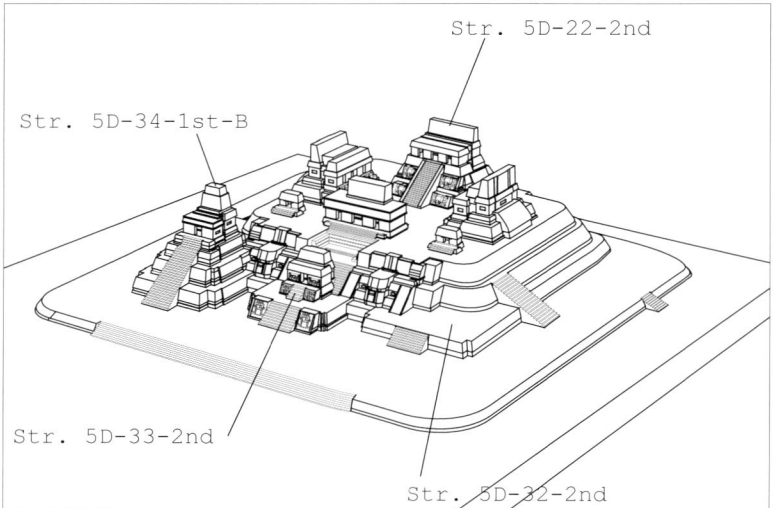

Figure 48. Platform 5D-4-2nd.

the much earlier Sub.3 setup, but with no provision for circulation through the building.

A series of spectacular mask panels is displayed across the front of 33-2 not only on the substructure but also, uniquely at Tikal, on the building walls. Masks also adorn the building platform recalling temporally remote Str. 5D-Sub.1-1st. These masks were uncovered in an excellent state of preservation and have been much discussed. Schele and Freidel (1990:169) point out cave imagery and the cleft in the earth from which ancestors emerge, together with vegetation, corn, blood, and "witz" (mountain) symbols. Bassie-Sweet (1996:63-110) reviews the cave iconography in relation to places the supernaturals would choose to occupy. Miller (1986:41-46) adds venus, the sun at sunrise, and the sun in the underworld. The witz image is said to mark a structure as a "portal to the underworld" (Freidel, Schele and Parker 1993:149-50). The interior presents numerous graffiti in which humans, perhaps in a state of trance, interact with supernaturals (Trik and Kampen 1983:fig. 44).

This suggests a place where humans enter the supernatural realm. I suspect for the ancient Maya it might have worked equally in reverse. That is, as a place where supernaturals enter this world. Perhaps both processes operated at once. The supernaturals would then be present to witness ritual and accept offerings made by humans. Their presence would be the decisive factor reifying human-made settings for invocation rites. Such rites could also be associated with deceased rulers. Structures incorporating tombs, then, can be regarded both as memorials to rulers and as installations equipped to enhance effectiveness of ritual through presence of supernaturals (Becker 1992).

If the acropolis stair had previously provided a theatrical setting for prominent ritual performance, 33-3rd may have supplanted it but 33-2nd must have entirely disrupted it. The relatively cramped Acropolis court is now hidden from the Great Plaza and perhaps earlier its activities had already descended to the 33-3rd "stage."

The 33-2nd building has space immediately in front where performances could be staged closer to the plaza. Iconography of 33-2nd masks may well reveal some aspects of rituals performed at this location. Supernaturals, ancestors, blood, and agricultural energy all are evoked by these images. The complex of ritual trajectories involved very likely includes many that had long been conducted on the North Acropolis. Construction of 33-2nd may have brought some of these activities closer to the Great Plaza. At the same time others, perhaps more esoteric, probably continued in the more restricted summit venues (Plate 54).

Plate 53 shows the superstructure and upper parts of the substructure of Str. 5D-34-1st. To its left, grass covers debris of unexcavated Str. 5D-35. The rear façade of Str. 5D-23-1st appears behind it. In centre background the building component of Str. 5D-22-1st stands on terraces of 22-3rd. In right background is unexcavated Str. 5D-24 and to the right of 34-1st is partially excavated Str. 5D-33-1st.

Discontinuities in stratigraphy make it difficult to be certain about the sequence of events across the front of the acropolis. A clue providing evidence of a different sort, less certain but at least suggestive, emerged in 1996 when Proyecto Nacional Tikal excavations subsequent to the University of Pennsylvania Tikal Project turned up Stela 40 buried in collapse debris in front of (W of) structure 5D-29 (Valdés et al. 1997).

The principal represented on this stela is K'an Chitam, son of Siyaj Chan K'awiil II. His date of death is not recorded but his birth date (8.18.19.12.1–26 Nov. AD 415, Martin and Grube 2000:37) is. Stela 9 dated to AD 475 refers to this same ruler (TR.33A:23-25, fig. 13) who would have been 60 years old by that time. So his age at death might be in the 70s or even 80s. In any case, his would logically be the next major interment after Bu. 48, and perhaps his tomb lies beneath Str. 5D-29.

Structure 5D-29 (Plate 54) is the southernmost of a set of three all built on a platform (U. 288B) squeezed onto the SE corner of the acropolis where it was slightly too big to fit easily (TR.14:583-85, fig. 207, 208, 209). An access stair from the E is assumed in response to a western feature that seems to be a stair image, with treads too shallow for actual use. The three structures were not excavated so the known details mainly relate to the superstructures. These are buildings similar to 34-1st, with similar inset panels in exterior wall surfaces.

Presumably a set of three structures would embody a triadic symbolism, as can be seen in the presence of three tandem rooms in each. Alternatively, there may have been three deaths associated with these structures.

Such awkward placement on the SE corner implies conflicting pressures. Desire for proximity to the North Acropolis is clear. A more prominent site may have been denied. Obliteration of existing summit structures is equally denied. That is, there is no further architecture development at summit level with this platform addition any more than there had been with structures 33, and 34.

No burial is known in association with these structures, but then, no excavation has yet been done.

Apart from 34-1st and 22-1st, major projects in this developmental stage focused on the acropolis platform. Massive side and rear outsets were added at this time (Plate 55 and Figure 50). It remains unclear whether the side outsets were entirely new features or renewed versions of earlier outsets. Preceding plates have illustrated the acropolis without these side outsets, mainly because their presence prior to 2nd has not been determined. Rear outsets, on the other hand were there from the beginning.

If the side outsets appeared here for the first time, they were preceded and presumably inspired by 22-3rd (Plate 38). This admittedly hypothetical sequence not only implies that powerful medicine was embodied in these directionally significant forms but that this significance was attached to the acropolis platform, not only to features such as stairs and summit structures. Iconography carried by side outsets, reviewed above in relation to 22-3rd, relates to the four-directional and eight-directional aspects of supernatural forces as embodied in summit structures. Needless to say, if excavations show side outsets to have been present earlier on the acropolis, a slightly different interpretation might be called for. But the fundamental reading would still apply. That is, as previously stated, ancient Maya architects developed forms designed to enhance

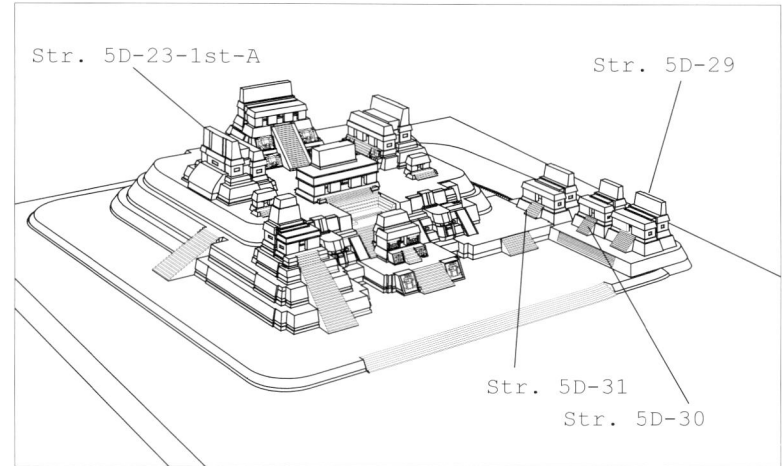

Figure 49. Platform 5D-4-2nd.

the function of the acropolis as a place that would attract the presence of supernatural beings conceptually associated with natural forces, and believed to be crucial to success of enterprises carried out by the people of Tikal.

At the same time that the outsets illustrated in Plate 55 were installed, new rear outsets and substructure platforms were applied to Str. 5D-23 and presumably also 24. The new substructures appear to do nothing more than support new, larger rear outsets, although at the same time they obliterated the old side inset in the building platform component. Perhaps the controlling factor was the association of the rear outsets on these E and W summit features with the side outsets below them on the acropolis platform. As Plates 55 and 61 illustrate, the rear outsets on 23-1st and 24-1st rise up above the acropolis E and W side outsets in a highly unified manner, as though summit structure and acropolis platform had been designed simultaneously.

These unifying elements initially installed at different times must have been an architectural triumph in their day. They present a vision of monumental architectural power that emerged slowly over decades and even centuries. Curiously, again with the caveat regarding earlier acropolis side outsets, this development, strengthening acropolis architectural form seems to have coincided with relegation of the summit to a less prominent position with respect to the Great Plaza. Perhaps it had evolved as a setting of more mystery and exclusiveness than was deemed appropriate for Great Plaza activities.

Professional ritual specialists conducting more or less secret offerings, rites and studies on the acropolis summit may have been the primary human audience

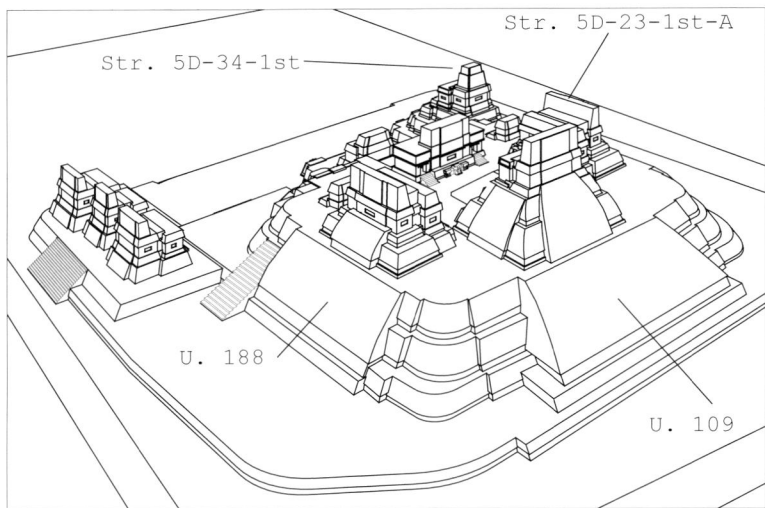

Figure 50. Platform 5D-4-2nd/1st.

for these outsets. They may have been the only ones who knew what the forms really meant. Others, laypersons, able only to glimpse the summit precinct from a distance, would have been impressed by its inaccessibility. Perhaps they might have understood that these outsets were highly potent items. But they might not have known their real import.

As with 34-1st, treatment of the acropolis terraces at this time by addition of outsets resulted in the appearance of inset corners, particularly on the N façade. At least this is my impression. Plates 55 and 61, chosen to make this point, show the NE acropolis platform corner. The rounded corner appears inset between sharp-cornered terrace elements on either side of it. In terms of construction, the flanking elements were added as outsets, but the inset corner architectural reading they produced was the opposite. By these changes emphasis was placed more heavily on the rounded corners and the diagonals connecting them. General appreciation of the esoteric importance associated with inset corners and diagonal, intercardinal, directions might have been even more restricted than that of the side outsets. It is noteworthy, however, that the side stairs, carefully retained during these changes, arrive on the diagonals at the front corners. No doubt processional ceremonies had long recognized these significant points.

The new side outsets reveal something quite different about treatment of architectural form on the acropolis. They rise up some fifteen meters with the only break fairly low down at the apron corbel course. This demonstrates that the builders did not need to subdivide a high platform into terraces. Advantages gained by terracing can easily be seen. Shorter profiles are easier to keep true. Construction tasks can be organized incrementally. A requisite summit area can be maintained by adjusting the amount of batter at each terrace level. So terracing probably assisted in the construction process. But these considerations did not make terracing absolutely necessary even on high platforms. The fundamental consideration was, I imagine, the value that terraces held for the primary function of the acropolis. If they were seen as setting out territories that particular supernatural beings could claim, or might choose to occupy, then it would be absolutely necessary to provide those domains within the fabric. Additionally, it would be logical that they should be displayed prominently so that presumed supernatural presence would be persuasively demonstrated.

The new outsets display traditional forms of apron moldings even though newer forms had already appeared on Str. 5D-34-1st and 5D-33-2nd. This may be another instance of a long-established authority on the acropolis maintaining a clear distance from the "stranger" lineage fronting the Great Plaza.

The rear axial outset illustrated in Plate 55, U. 109, was actually the second such element constructed as part of Platform 5D-4-2nd. A new rear outset had been built along with the U.188 outsets while 22-2nd was still standing. Then, when it was decided to build over 22-2nd to install the structure designated as 22-1st, the recently installed rear outset was ripped out and a new larger one built in its place, to provide room for the necessary expansion and a stable base to support it (Plate 56).

A decision to enlarge Str. 5D-22-2nd may have been prompted by encroachment of new structures along the S front facing the Great Plaza (Plate 54), to make sure that the north axial feature retained its dominant position. This may have coincided with accession of the ruler "Double Bird" in AD 537 (Jones and Satterthwaite 1982:127) a.k.a. Wak Chan K'awiil (Martin 2001), but there is no evidence confirming this. The dating is right for Double Bird's death as is the dating of the tomb later intruded into it.

The new structure was essentially a replay of the previous one, somewhat bulkier and somewhat higher. All features of 2nd were obliterated; its plaster was removed, and the upper parts of its building demolished. But then, all features of 2nd appear to have been repeated in the new fabric, although the masks had eroded so badly that their similarity to 2nd masks cannot be confidently asserted.

The new N axial feature, 22-1st, must have been built in the early part of the 6th century, perhaps some twenty years prior to a military defeat of AD 562 (Culbert 1991:135). A tomb (Bu. 200) was cut into 22-1st, through the floor of the building, but it had been opened and its contents removed, perhaps during this period of dark times for Tikal. However, it seems likely that the structure would have been in use during these years of adversity and this may be attested by the unusual number of caches that were placed within its rooms (TR.14:fig. 114-122). If this structure was associated with Double Bird the cache activity may have been intended to compensate for his defeat.

Moholy-Nagy (2003a:96) interprets this heightened cache activity as evidence of increasing material wealth at Tikal. I wonder if it might not reflect adversity and a perceived need to curry greater favor with supernaturals. Obviously they possessed the means to undertake lavish offerings but these might reflect stored wealth rather than increasing prosperity at a time of military adversity.

Plate 57 shows the west end of the middle room of Str. 5D-22-1st. Unspecialized vault stones can be seen. They are slab-like units, each projecting out beyond the one below as true corbels. They differ very markedly from typical vault stones of the Late Classic at Tikal. These latter do not employ the corbel technique (a subject further developed in TR.34B).

A striking feature of this vault is its low height, absolutely, but also as compared with wall height. It contrasts greatly with the very high rear room vault in earlier Str. 5D-23-1st and indicates that vault height was not calculated by structural considerations alone, but varied to reflect other factors. Presumably the middle room of 22-1st held associations quite different from those attached to the rear room of 23-1st.

The rear room vault is similar in height, quite unlike the rear room vault of Str. 5D-23-1st. This suggests to me that vault design was as loaded with iconographic significance as other parts of these structures. Rear rooms of Str. 5D-23, and 24 where a similarly high vault can be seen above debris, must have carried some association not present in the N axial structure.

There is no plastered wall-top, although a plastered lintel bed is visible above the doorjamb leading into

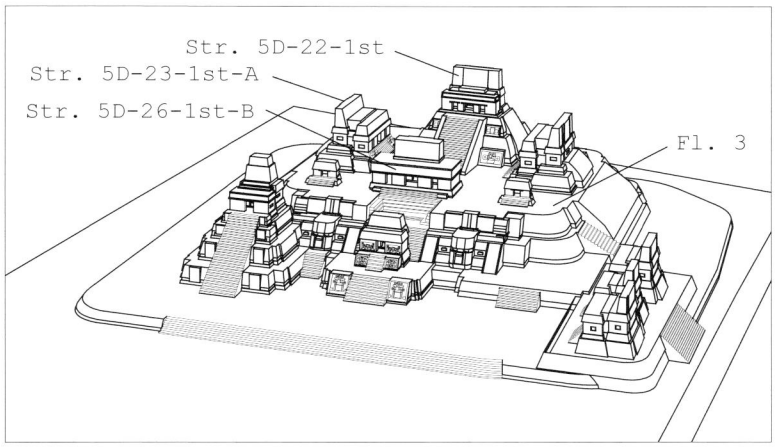

Figure 51. Platform 5D-4-2nd/1st.

the rear room, which also has a relatively low vault. Parts of the central rear bench can be seen within the doorway, and in front of it gapes the hole left by ancient intrusion into Bu. 200. Debris in the west end of the middle room covers the interior platform (bench) seen in Plate 58.

Plate 58 shows the west end of the middle room of Str. 5D-22-1st after debris had been removed to expose the bench. Differential staining on the end wall shows the height of debris at the time of initial excavation. The circular hole in the floor before the bench, P.D. 139 (TR.14:fig. 114), probably represents removal of a cache in Early Postclassic times. The bench had been installed some time after construction of the building and beneath it three intact caches were found

Cache 185 (TR.14:386), shown in Plate 59, is the largest of the three under the west bench. Its contents, illustrated sectionally in TR.14 (fig. 119) include marine materials, obsidian shapes, flint shapes and items of jade. The marine material may invoke the watery "underworld" domain of deceased rulers such as the personage laid to rest in Bu. 200, most likely Double Bird, though identity remains unknown.

Hardly any original floor surface had survived the intensity of cache activity. This might have been due to a perceived need for accelerated ritual in an attempt to reverse Tikal's fortunes. Such activity, if my interpretation is correct, stands as solid evidence for the kind of concrete benefits that were expected to flow from enormous investment of capital and labor. Constant work of ritual specialists, and heavy investment in monumental construction constitute this investment.

Monumentality carried not only symbolism. Recovery from defeat and occupation would not have been seen as merely symbolic. A more materially useful

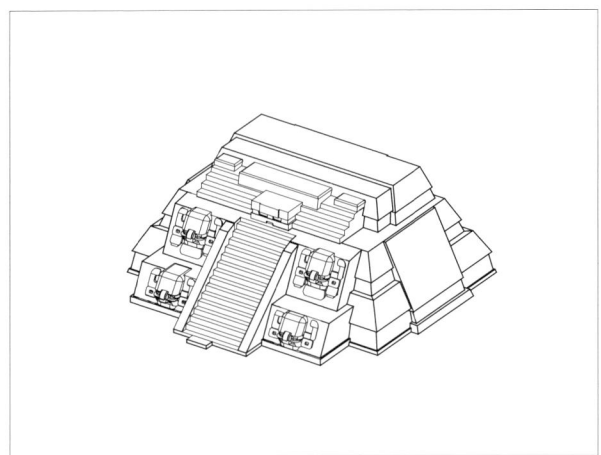

Figure 52. Structure 5D-22-3rd Substructure.

result can hardly be imagined. This is the epitome of functional architecture. Monumentality is clearly one category in a whole suite of activities aimed at a most practical outcome.

The rear axial interior platform or bench can be seen in Plate 60 following excavation. It had evolved through an intricate developmental process detailed in TR.14:fig. 121. The final result has a throne-like character that might have been quite appropriate for placement of cult objects as described by Carmack at Utatlan (1981:186).

Whether or not architectural forms were expected to yield material goods, the builders of 22-1st applied established conventions in an entirely new way. Earlier builders, on 23-1st for example, had completed the building-platform with its frontal and rear bodies separated by side insets and had plastered all top and face surfaces prior to starting on the walls of the building as illustrated in Fig. 50.

As a result exterior elements were simply the exposed parts of the building-platform projecting out beyond the outer faces of the walls. Builders of 22-1st did not follow this practice. They applied plaster surfacing only on the areas that would eventually be exposed as floors within the rooms, leaving rough masonry where the walls would go. They then built the walls together with exterior faces of the building-platform, shaping these so that they would roughly correspond to the three interior room levels. The side insets in the building-platform were modeled as purely exterior elements, no longer merely the exposed faces of the building-platform.

Removal of the 22-1st building would not expose a complete building-platform but rather a discontinuous set of terrace faces and floor surfaces, approximately aligned but separated by the unfinished strip where the walls had been. Implicit in this change is ancient recognition of a specific exterior architectural format as an iconographic entity carrying specific meaning of some sort. Probably, as mentioned earlier, this had to do with duality in some way.

The three rooms of 22-1st all have large interior platforms, or benches installed secondarily (TR.14:fig. 119, 120, 121). These certainly provide evidence for function, but as ever, such evidence requires a great deal of interpretation. Carmack (1981:186) describes how, at Utatlan, potent icons were hidden away and placed in temples only when ritual events were about to be staged. If it is legitimate to draw inferences from the Late Post Classic highlands, the benches in the front room and in the second room of 22-1st building, placed at the ends of the rooms, could have provided the settings for icons and cult objects during ceremonial performance. At the same time they are large enough to serve as sleeping platforms, and this cannot be ruled out as a possible function. The central bench in the rear room, mentioned above, would have provided a most prominent position for cult objects and never at any time provided a surface suitable for sleeping. Its initial form, indicated by U. 84 (TR.14:fig. 121c) would seem too small for anything other than a cult object. After subsequent enlargement it could have functioned as a throne.

10

Platform 5D-4-1st

Symmetry, a persistent fact of North Acropolis architecture, demands that Chapter 10 mirror Chapter 1. Hence, where Chapter 1 (Platform 5D-4-10th) extended temporally from the time of earliest known occupation to the first recognizable acropolis platform, Chapter 10 (Platform 5D-4-1st, TR.14:139-160, 840-6} is similarly conceived as running from the final acropolis platform to the last known occupation (TR.14:157). In terms of architectural development, however, only a small fraction of this period is actually engaged here. In TR.14 Platform 5D-4-1st-C-B corresponds to AD 600-900, with 5D-4-1st-A open-ended (TR.14:Chart 1) to include present-day use of the acropolis by international tourists (Plate 3).

Structures 5D-27-1st, 25-1st, 21-2nd, 20-2nd, and 22-1st all stand on Fl. 3 (Plate 61) and therefore their installation can not be sequentially ordered by means of stratigraphy. Adverse fortunes during the second half of the 6th century and first half of the 7th suggest that these features likely predate Tikal's Intermediate Classic difficulties (see below), and hence may represent projects carried to completion early in the 6th century. Compared with cache activity involving imported material dated to this period, architectural development, at least at this locus, seems relatively modest. Cache materials may have been already on hand and architectural projects require larger mounts of labor. The work force may have been dedicated to military endeavors at this time.

This inference may be strengthened by the observation that 27-1st and 25-1st merely renewed earlier fabrics, as did 22-1st. The N corner pair, 21-2nd and 20-2nd, seem to be new installations lacking known antecedents. They complete the pattern initiated by the southern corner pair. Almost nothing except its existence is known about 5D-20-2nd. It had been almost completely dismantled prior to installation of much larger 20-1st (below), well into the Late Classic Period. The form depicted in Figure 53 with a single body and single doorway, is entirely hypothetical. Doctrinal authorities on the acropolis may have considered that the lack of these N diagonal features had contributed to their political setbacks. Supernatural support certainly seemed to have been withdrawn.

As discussed earlier, structures 5D-25 and 27 occupy the open corners of the long established summit quadrangle. The correct form for these features seems to have been a subject for greater than usual debate and revision. Within a fairly short space of time they were changed radically, finally ending up as three-room tandem buildings, stepping up front to rear into progressively higher rooms of smaller size.

The northern corner pair mark the diagonal intercardinal directions. Structures 5D-23 and 24 perhaps embody sunrise and sunset references. The N and S structures, 22 and 26 offer less obvious correlates but, because of burial locations and intensity of cache activity, the N position seems focused on deceased ancestors and possibly also related to the vertical direction. The south position deals with entry and hence may signify descent into the mythical underworld. The S building in Twin Pyramid groups may have held similar associations.

The ancient Maya may have considered the four initial features as stable positions relating to aspects of supernatural power while the diagonals might have signified passages between them. Pages 76/75 of the Madrid Codex may substantiate this (Paxton 2001:32-

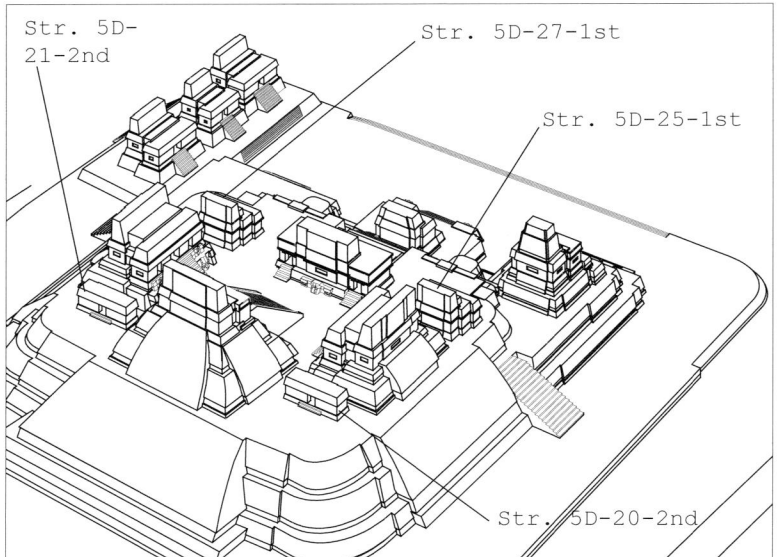

Figure 53. Platform 5D-4-1st-C.

40). In Paxton's analysis of this famous diagram the E and W positions - understood as sunrise and sunset zones rather than cardinal points – are occupied by figures of supernaturals seated within buildings. The N position illustrates a sacrificial act. There are many other features of this diagram but these two correspond remarkably with the North Acropolis summit composition. The diagonals in the Madrid diagram contain footprints, generally understood as ancient Mesoamerican signifiers of movement, and numerals that correspond to calendric units in the 260 day ritual calendar. As mentioned earlier, Schele, Freidel, and Parker (1995:96-99, fig. 2:29, 2:30) relate the diagonals to positions taken by the visible Milky Way galaxy, from one extreme to the other, during the solar year. This, again, is a theme of movement. It is notable that the diagonally sited structures conform to the NS alignment of all acropolis architecture. This probably reflects the power of the NS axial direction.

Ritual specialists using the acropolis no doubt constantly consulted the ritual calendar and galactic positions among other observations. They surely possessed a rich and detailed mythology summarized by diagrams like the Madrid Codex figure cited above. Physical manifestation of this pattern in architectural features on the acropolis calls for interpretation and my guess is that enhancement of acropolis function accounts for its presence. It seems to me that these developments represent continuity with longstanding North Acropolis traditions and ongoing efforts to improve functionality of the complex. It must surely stand as a supreme irony that precisely at the time the acropolis had reached this point of maximally iconic architectural form the supernaturals turned against Tikal and supported their enemies (Culbert 1991:134-40; Schele and Mathews 1998:67-72). Collapse of the Classic order in the early ninth century may have resulted, in part at least, from some similar betrayal by the supernaturals. The resurgence that developed in the eighth century (Plate 62) reflects their renewed support (see below).

Structure 5D-32-1st is shown in Plate 63 during initial clearing and after removal of a large tree growing out of the top of extant remains. That so much of the superstructure survived under these conditions is a testament to the quality of construction, in particular the quality of the mortar.

As the next major architectural development, after roughly a century of inaction, 32-1st appeared on the E side of the S front, sealing a royal interment, Bu. 195. The ruler, identified by inscriptions carved in wooden boards and painted on pottery vessels within the tomb, is known colloquially as "Animal Skull." His name glyphs have been tentatively glossed as "K'inich ?(Te-?)(Martin and Grube 2000:40). He is identified on a vessel description as ruler number 22 in the succession from Yax Ebh' Xook but was not the son of ruler number 21, Double Bird (Jones and Satterthwaite 1982:129; Jones 1991:117; Haviland 1992:73). He had jade inlaid teeth (the inlays removed), features also found in Bu. 23 and 24 in the 5D-33 locus, and features of these burials are similar (Coggins 1975). These three rulers may have been connected somehow, since no other royal burials at Tikal have such inlays.

Plate 64 shows Str. 5D-32-1st following restoration work in the late 1960s. This view particularly emphasizes the new type of apron molding, which, in certain sun angles, that is, when the sun is directly at the zenith, appears as a horizontal slot (Plate 64). The date 9.8.0.0.0 (AD 593) on wooden boards in the tomb may precede the time of the burial but perhaps not by very long (Haviland 1992:74).

Structure 5D-32-1st would have risen to completion in the years immediately following Bu. 195, years of political adversity marked archaeologically by intense cache activity interpreted by Moholy-Nagy (2003a:96) as evidence for prosperity among non-elites but by me as a sign of desperation. Jones (personal communication) suggests that the ruler associated with this structure may have been Animal Skull, number 22 in the succession from Yax Ehb' Xook.

The arrival of 32-1st during this time of reversal, defeat, even possibly foreign occupation, must have shed a brief, flickering light amid the enveloping gloom. Lack of supernatural support must have severely challenged the claims for which massive investments in North Acropolis architecture and ritual activity had been justified over many centuries. Nevertheless, despite severe reverses during the 6th and 7th centuries, 32-1st was built, perhaps as a desperate, but ineffectual effort to induce a return to better times; further defeats followed on its construction (Martin 2003:28).

Erection of 32-1st continued the earlier trend of development whereby the acropolis platform remained essentially static, progressively screened by new construction on its south façade toward the Great Plaza. Architecturally, 32-1st emulated 34-1st but without its archaic superstructure attributes. Substructure terracing of 32-1st resembles that of 34-1st, with similar apron profiles, inset corners, and prominent fully outset stair. Unlike 34-1st, stair-side outsets feature sculptural elaboration, known only for the basal terrace, and illustrated accordingly in Plate 62, but probably present at all terrace levels. Such masks are archaic features. However, the proportions of the substructure are quite unlike those of Str. 5D-34-1st. The whole is more compact and pyramid-like in form. This aspect appears distinctly forward looking, anticipating the character of subsequent structures such as 33-1st (Plate 66).

Plate 65 shows the long narrow proportions of the rooms in the 5D-32-1st building component (looking east). The building component then emerges as very broad, though entered through a single axial doorway opening. A roof-comb seems called for by the amount of debris and by wall thickness greater than room width in distal parts. Otherwise, the traditional three-room plan externally formed as two house-like bodies, prevails.

Extreme breadth may have been determined by stair width. My guess is there was no pressure for deeper rooms but that great frontal width was necessary to accommodate the wide stair. That is to say, designers may have primarily desired a wide, impressive stair while at the same time other design criteria called for a single doorway rather than the triple openings that had

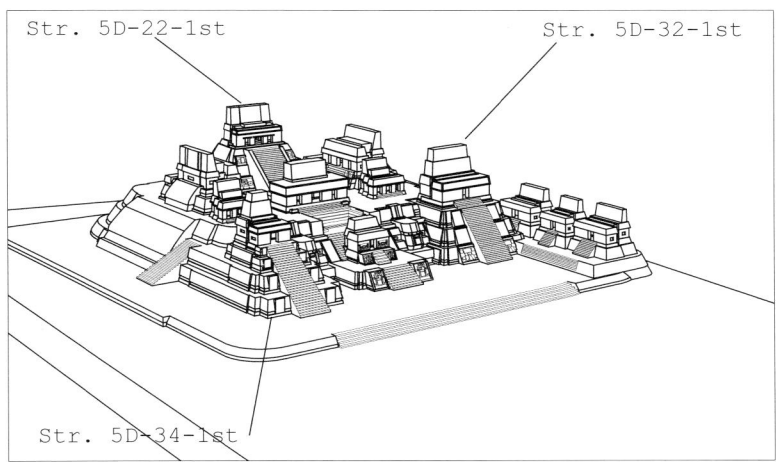

Figure 54. Platform 5D-4-1st-C.

been in vogue prior to 5D-34 and 33-2nd.

The wide stair seems to have been a short-lived preference. Great Temple V, possibly built at around the same time, also has a similarly wide stair (http://www.mesoweb.com/reports/ temple5.html). Later structures such as 33-1st and Great Temple I have relatively narrow stairs.

Ritual observances served by Str. 5D-32-1st may have related to deceased ruler Shield Skull and perhaps this single individual focus found expression in the single axial doorway. Earlier structures such as 5D-22-1st, for example, with triple doorway systems, may have served a less narrowly focused ritual program that may have been somewhat altered when Bu. 200 was intruded beneath the floor of the 22-1st building.

If the reported dating of Great Temple V is correct then this represents an even greater investment at a time of political difficulty. Moholy-Nagy's assessment of this period as a time of prosperity must be correct to the extent that resources were available for very large scale construction. But I would still argue that this type of investment might not represent prosperity so much as determination to overcome the problems and reverses that had been recently experienced. A very large ritual structure might be seen as something that could help to correct an adverse balance of supernatural influences considered responsible for military defeats.

Throughout North Acropolis development those responsible for decisions about architectural form seem to have wavered on the matter of color. Red paint appeared at some times and not at others. Generally though, the trend was toward less use of red at later times. This is strongly exemplified in 32-1st. Its white plaster finish, carefully smoothed and burnished, must have generated intolerable glare on sunny days, and at

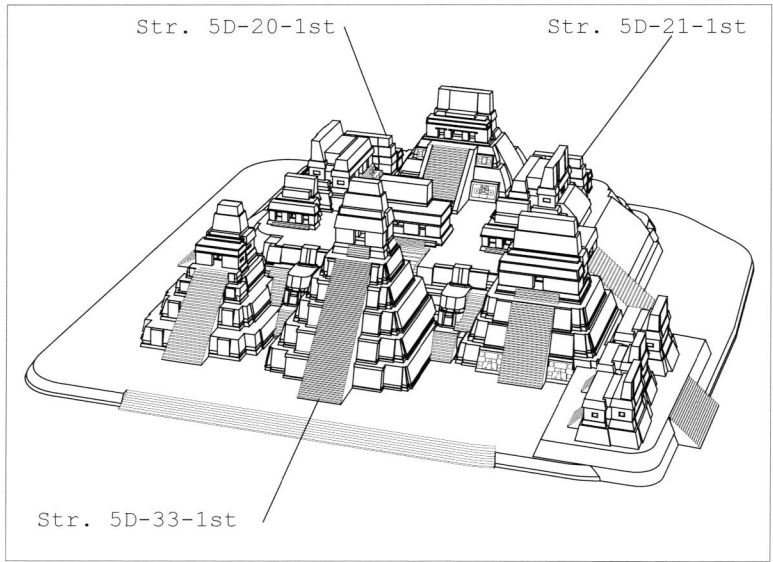

Figure 55. Platform 5D-4-1st.

the same time saved the effort and expense associated with producing red pigment.

A high level of glare must have always characterized the Great Plaza when its plaster flooring was new, clean and reflective. The uncomfortable experience of this space in daytime with the sun overhead may have been very impressive for the ancient Maya. They may have felt the presence of the sun very proximally. This highly desirable condition, though extremely unpleasant, even painful, may have exactly suited the attitude considered appropriate in the presence of supernatural forces. A white finish on 32-1st, as on earlier 22-1st, may have been intended to further extend this experiential aspect of design. As a corollary of this solar effect white finished structures, particularly large ones, may have been almost impossible to look at directly in daytime under strong sunlight. This too might have been seen as a desirable condition, even at times when the structures were considered to be asleep, or the supernaturals were not in residence (Carmack 1981:186).

The mere fact that supernaturals might at times choose to be present in the fabric of these structures would remove them so completely from "this world" that innocently looking at them might have been seen as a kind of violation. It might have been even dangerous. The experience of high glare in the plaza during daytime may have helped induce an altered state condition desirable for participation in ritual activities.

In the grassy Great Plaza today (Plate 3) tourist groups do not experience the high glare of the Classic Period because reconstructions have not employed plaster finishes. Such reflective surfaces generated glare but also protected the stone, encouraged runoff of rainwater, and deterred growth of mould.

Return of good times to Tikal is marked architecturally on the North Acropolis by 33-1st (TR.14:527-54, fig. 168-77) a development that raises contradictory interpretive possibilities (Plate 66 and Figure 55). Placement on the central axis, obliterating both 33-2nd and the main acropolis stair could be seen either as slighting the acropolis or as bringing it forward into a new and more intense relationship with the Great Plaza.

Coe (TR.14:844-45) considered Str. 5D-33-1st as the culmination of a scheme intended to more or less duplicate the by now historic summit composition directly on the Great Plaza. Architectural format of the 33-1st building with its lack of side insets might argue against this (see discussion below). Temples I and II would have been predicted in the scheme proposed by Coe and their construction much later than 33-1st implies continuity of architectural intentions.

Coe's view may be supported by the striking difference in architectural form between 33-1st and 2nd. Verticality of the final structure makes such a contrast with its predecessor that some intention other than renewal of the earlier fabric seems implicated. The situation recalls formal discontinuity between Str. 5D-26-3rd and 4th. In both cases siting may have been the determining factor. The 5D-26 structures stand at the head of the axial acropolis stair while the 33 series occupy its foot. These locations are so distinctive that structures sequentially occupying them would seem surely to have been related conceptually.

Construction of 33-1st (Plate 67) followed immediately on completion of a large, rich tomb, Bu. 23 (TR.14:536-40, fig. 176), cut into the floor of the acropolis basal platform (Terrace South). Jones (2003:220) proposes that the ruler known as Shield Skull might be the individual stretched out in this tomb. Haviland (personal communication) doubts this identification, citing dental evidence linking Shield Skull with Animal Skull rather than Jasaw Chan K'awiil I (jade inlays). He considers that Bu. 23 and 24 may relate to the 23rd and 24th rulers whose tombs have not been identified. He points out that Shield Skull was killed away from Tikal and his remains may never have been brought back.

Burial 24, made subsequently to Bu. 23 (TR.14:540-43), is primary to construction of 5D-33-1st and therefore might be expected to contain an individual closely related to Jasaw Chan K'awiil the ruler in office when it was built.

Shield Skull, a.k.a. Nuun Ujol Chaak (Martin and Grube 2000:42), was the father of Jasaw Chan K'awiil I, the ruler buried under Great Temple I, famed as the Tikal ruler who defeated Calakmul in AD 695 (Schele and Freidel 1990:205-15). If Jones's contention is correct 33-1st would have been built in the years just after Jasaw Chan K'awiil took office as ruler of Tikal in AD 682. By the time of the victory over Calakmul, 33-1st might have been in place, but equally might have been built immediately afterward. If it had already been built both Calakmul and Tikal factions would have believed in a causal relationship between the new, formally powerful temple and the military success.

Tikal ritual specialists probably believed that they had finally come up with an architectural model, and perhaps also a form of ritual, pleasing to the unseen but strongly felt forces that, in their worldview, either withheld or granted success. The victory over Calakmul might have been interpreted as a sign of supernatural support for Jasaw Chan K'awiil I justifying investment in a major structure to facilitate continuation of this favorable influence.

Since efforts represented by Str. 5D-32-1st, Great Temple V, and the intense cache activity in 22-1st had not yielded results, something more ambitious must have seemed called for. Structure 5D-33-1st (Plate 66) may have been the response.

Novel features include a pyramidal substructure of five terraces, a two-bodied building platform with the frontal body narrower than the distal body–a reversal of recent practice, and a building of two rooms stepping up front to rear, but without the traditional side inset. Recently established conventions include the fully outset, very prominent stair, single doorway, continuous terrace levels, and inset lower substructure corners. The most venerable, longest established convention still considered essential is the rear axial outset running vertically through all parts of the structure.

Probably the most radical architectural departure from established convention would have been the extreme verticality of the lower substructure. With 33-1st the term "pyramid" seems entirely appropriate even though not completely accurate as a precise geometrical form. To achieve this degree of verticality very long-established modes of construction had to be upgraded. From the earliest known acropolis (Sub 1-2nd, Plate 7) core material had been assembled in task units defined by rough masonry facings. For the lower substructure of 33-1st this practice was radically reviewed and followed with unprecedented rigor (TR.14:fig. 170, 171). Core material was assembled in the form of nested walls running through substructure hearting in different patterns at each terrace level. This procedure (Plate 68) ensured that each unit of core material established its own stability.

In Plate 68 some core units have been taken down, others still stand. Excavators were able to remove core units without causing collapse of other units. All core material is bedded masonry, roughly broken to size. Each unit has a rough facing of stones slightly better shaped than those of inner unit heartings. No task unit depended on its neighbor or retained its neighbor. At the exterior surface of terraces, material employed for the final terrace forms did not have any retentive function. In fact, nearly all the outer layer had collapsed, leaving inner core masonry exposed through most of the pyramid height (Plate 67). The small amount of outer facing that remained, in the lowest terrace, consisted of large relatively thin blocks approaching the proportions of veneer masonry (Jones 2003:217).

Installation of 33-1st completely obliterated the still exposed portions of the old, and probably highly regarded axial stair. Ritual specialists might have justified this as a replacement for the stair. That is, significance previously attached to the stair might have been transferred to 33-1st and added to the import conveyed by the three tombs (Bu. 48, 23 and 24) or "chamber burials" (Moholy-Nagy 2003:5) beneath it. Architectural innovation in 33-1st might have emerged from an effort to more effectively embody the forces that might choose to occupy the axial stair position. Designers, who probably were ritual specialists, faced the challenge of finding a way to make those forces more likely to choose to be present and to be favorably disposed toward Tikal interests. The client for architectural design then was neither the ruler the priests, nor the public, but unseen supernatural beings that might choose to support the Tikal Polity if they felt inclined to do so. The argument presented earlier in connection with the number of doorways in the front façade of the building implies that the deceased individual in one of the three chamber burials, as a supernatural, might have been this putative client.

Whether or not the above fanciful analysis comes anywhere near the reasons for doing it, construction of 33-1st effectively removed the North Acropolis from the Great Plaza. A very broad stair confronts the plaza at the basal platform level (Terrace S), but above it two inconspicuous stairways (U. 198A,B) thread their way around the ancient great masks that had for so long dominated the acropolis façade. The acropolis court still exists behind 33-1st, still accessible from plaza level, but it no longer commands the plaza.

Separation of the acropolis from the plaza may have allowed for development of new ritually specialized institutions. More esoteric studies and activities might have been relegated to the acropolis summit while more publicly oriented ceremonies took place in the plaza. The line of new structures in front of the old acropolis cut the basal platform so that it now appeared as a terrace connected to the Great Plaza. This was the impression initially noted when the area was cleared of vegetation for Tikal Project operations, and this explains why the acropolis basal platform was designated as the North Terrace (Terrace South in earlier developments).

Structure 5D-35 is sited on this terrace to the west of 5D-34. It has not been excavated and extant features appear late. Therefore I have not included it in illustrations.

A new locus for ritual activity in the plaza did not terminate activity and development on the acropolis summit. Well into the Late Classic Period Str. 5D-20-1st, and its eastern counterpart 21-1st arrived on the N corners as renewals of much earlier and smaller structures (TR.14:451-59, fig. 137-41). Construction took place on Fl. 1, the final acropolis upper surface, probably some time around AD 700 (TR 14:458).

The only other structure on this floor is Str. 5D-28, the small portal building at the head of the E side stair (TR.14:fig. 150, 151), an addition that either ignores or intentionally destroys long-maintained EW symmetry. Structure 5D-28 is either unique or very unusual among Tikal buildings in that it has no building platform. Its walls rise directly from the stair with the front wall standing on the second tread down from the top while the rear wall stands atop the acropolis summit (Plat. 5D-4 Fl. 1). Summit access via this stair (U. 189) is through the building with no possibility of bypassing it. In this sense Str. 5D-28 is the purest example of a portal structure in the North Acropolis sequence.

Access to the summit is still possible via older and smaller W side stair and U. 198A and B stairs on the S front between structures 32, 33, and 34 by means of an indirect and perhaps one could say informal flight partly obscuring the S façade masks. The east side stair with 5D-28 at its head has now become the most formalized path of access to the summit, a path not rising from the Great Plaza. The implication may be that those now using the summit did not control the Great Plaza. Perhaps the traditional ritual specialists who had always conducted affairs on the acropolis still continued to do so while other, less arcane events, designed for wider participation, were staged in the Great Plaza.

Some attributes of Late Classic architecture at Tikal are well exemplified in features of Str. 5D-20-1st. Walls are relatively thick, building platform relatively low and projecting minimally from wall faces, all face masonry is finished with a thin coat of hard white plaster. Vaults are still a little low in relation to wall height, and the rear axial outset at upper zone level contains a variant of the inset panel–a thoroughly archaic feature, though slightly modified by presence of a projecting ledge at the top. The frontal upper zone contains sculptural treatment, and probably also the roof comb. Presence of three frontal doorways constitutes another deferment to tradition.

Although Str. 5D-20-1st presents a blend of early and late attributes in terms of architectural form, constructional techniques are generally typical of Late Classic work. Walls are built together with the outer facings of the building platform and capped off at wall-top level with plaster that runs through from exterior to interior. Interior wall facings are similar to exterior wall facings. Vaults are built in half-vault units with finished vault-back surfaces and closed at the top with pre-plastered capstones. Then upper zone material was set in place. This unitized approach to superstructure construction had not been used in Early Classic features on the acropolis. It typifies all Late Classic work at Tikal.

Conclusions

Judging by architectural attributes, mainly morphological features such as structure format and layout or planning, seven distinct episodes of development can be discerned.

The first, spanning the centuries from about 800 BC to roughly 350 BC (TS 15 and part of TS 14), left no undisturbed evidence in the restricted exposures that were sampled. Hence, we have no *in situ* architecture from this period. Secondarily redeposited materials suggest both residential and ritual activity.

The second period, dating from about 350 to about 200 BC (most of TS 14), appears in Plates 5/Figure 5 and 6/Figure 6. Although a circular structure may be present (Plate 6, Str. 5D-Sub.14-2nd), this cannot be established with much confidence. The only other architectural fragment from this time (Str. 5D-Sub. 14-1st, Plate 6), largely hypothetical in the reconstruction illustrated, seems like unspecialized architecture that might have served either residential or ritual functions.

Structure 5D-Sub.1-2nd defines the third episode (Plates 7/Figure 7–12/Figure 12) roughly 200–80 BC (TS 13 and the first third of TS 12). Lack of data hampers judgment as to whether this structure could be considered residential or ritual. The whole complex looks very formal but this would certainly not be inappropriate for elite occupancy. Triple stairs (seen best in Plates 9/Figure 8 and 10/9) may argue for ritual use. The circular platform (U. 94, Plate 10) together with rear outset (Plate 8/Figure 7) may weigh in on the side of ritual. The two terraces comprising the platform U. 96 (Plate 10), with apron moldings may also count as ritual indicators. Twinned altar-like Str. 5D-Sub.24 (Plate 10), and the extensiveness of lower substructure platforms (Plate 11/Figure 10) seem ritual-related to me. Rounded platform corners and twinned frontal stairs may argue for a further level of formality (Plate 11). Rounded corners would not be seen as ritual forms were it not for persistence of such corners in later developments where ritual functioning seems indicated. Such corners appear to be absent in the Tikal residential contexts that have been investigated (Haviland 1985).

The format of Str.5D-Sub.1-2nd, the little that we know of it, seems very like an ordinary residential dwelling persistent through more than a century of change. If indeed ritual function was a primary consideration designers chose not to emulate very much more developed architectural forms already in place at sites not far distant (El Mirador, Nakum, Lamanai, and others). Prior occupation of the acropolis site, its evidence destroyed by these developments, may have been a factor in this conservative treatment. Evolution of kingship and elite status, which might stimulate more monumental construction, may have been less developed at Tikal than at other sites of the region during this period, or may not have involved the North Acropolis.

Structures 5D-Sub.9 and Sub.1-1st (Plates 13/Figure 13-25/26) initiate the fourth episode and here architectural forms appear specialized either for ritual or for some other demand calling for impressive, articulated, forms equipped with prominently placed sculptural imagery. Substructure height, when compared with clearly residential construction (TR.19:fig. 41), stands as persuasive evidence for this. The subject is taken up in greater detail in TR.34B. This developmental stage runs from about 80 BC to about AD 75 (two thirds of TS 12 through TS 11).

Interpretation of these works as ritual architecture may be supported by the tandem plan organization of the two-room buildings. Residential structures show this pattern but perhaps not as frequently and rarely as only two rooms in tandem arrangement. Mask panels flanking the axial stairway provide additional features not known from residential structures (Wauchope 1940).

The Str. 5D-Sub.3 development (Plate 18/Figure 18–29/Figure 30) at the head of the axial stair provides another example of planning not typical of residential installations but perhaps appropriate for ritually specialized ones with their demands for separation from the mundane realm. These structures first appear in episode 5 and continue into episode 6.

Introduction of red paint on a large scale during episode 4 probably indicates ritual function. Possible provision for theatrical appearances in the wide axial doorway of the Sub.3 structures suggests a dramatic role aimed at addressing a larger audience. This could serve both ritual and rulership and may document manipulation of beliefs for political purposes.

Stature of the acropolis as a dominant element in Tikal society may be indicated by the increase in height that marks episode 5 (Plate 26/Figure 27–31/32). Total height only increased modestly subsequently. This development, the 5th seen spanning AD 75–200 (TS 10, 9, and just into 8), gave the acropolis a commanding position topographically and perhaps this corresponded to the civic and ideological roles that its users enjoyed as members of the dynastic line expounded in later inscriptions. Plates 26–31 seem to show a tentative approach to development of this much higher summit that may reflect a search for the architectural arrangement that would embody the ideas, and intentions inherent in the function served, and would support the aspirations that this institution represented for the whole Tikal community. At the same time the impression of unresolved form depicted in these plates partly reflects excavational limitations.

The 6th developmental departure is illustrated in Plate 32/Figure 34–46/44, covering the period from roughly AD 200–340 (first third of TS 8 to first third of TS 7). Plates 32–35/Figure 37 show the beginnings of a formal resolution in a balanced quadrangular layout. In Plate 36/Figure 38, with the arrival of Str. 5D-22-4th as a dominant element its final configuration can be glimpsed. The potentiality of this arrangement was soon developed, as can be seen in Plate 39/Figure 37 with the portal Str. 5D-26-1st introducing a triadic set of similarly formed red-painted structures. Structure 5D-22-3rd easily dominates this group both by magnitude and by distinctive formal properties. This grouping conveys the sense of a strongly established institution in sure command and with no internal conflicts.

Plate 47/Figure 45 signals the end of this regnum and the onset of my final, seventh episode, illustrated in Plates 47- 66/Figure 55 from AD 340-720 (first third of TS 7 through TS 5 and 6 and into TS 4). As is now well known, this period includes a major political upheaval, the famous "arrival of strangers" event. The previously balanced serene composition is now brutally disrupted by large scale, though initially relatively low, construction across the S front of the acropolis. As discussed earlier, I see this development as indicating a real split in institutions claiming the right to use the acropolis to their advantage. My speculative reading is that the old acropolis establishment controlled the summit but was unable to prevent a new rulership from building across the S front.

I ascribe special significance to Plate 55/Figure 49 and 61. These show fine-tuning of acropolis architectural form by the addition of side outsets to form a bi-axial composition that probably held powerful mythic content. If the interpretation sketched above is correct this was done at a time when the traditional local authority had been somewhat eclipsed by a new ruling line with some kind of exotic Teotihuacan connection. It may be that here we can seen a clear separation of powers; a priestly authority performing esoteric rites on the summit and a ruling authority, quite different institutionally, claiming the benefits derived from these rituals as part of their legitimization. It may be significant that the new side outsets on the acropolis platform (Plate 55) have traditional apron moldings rather than the contemporary form as seen on Str. 5D-34-1st (Plate 54/Figure 48). This suggests that apron profiles were not merely stylistic devices changing as fashions evolved but that they denoted different ideologies, or perhaps different agendas. The traditional form may have been associated with sacerdotal affairs and the innovative form with current rulership.

Distinction between rulers and priests may be finally expressed in Plate 66/Figure 54 with Str. 5D-33-1st directly adjacent to the Great Plaza and strongly associated with rulership as shown by the tombs in its fabric and the text of Stela 31 (Jones and Satterthwaite 1982:64-74). Behind it the acropolis could continue to operate but at a visual remove from the plaza and perhaps as a venue for esoteric shamanistic activities that did not require to be witnessed by large groups of people and therefore perhaps of little immediate political significance.

In summation, then, judging from architectural data on a qualitative basis, seven lines of development can be seen as design trajectories investigated over many centuries at the North Acropolis locus. The first lies obscurely in the Middle Preclassic. The next four take place within the Late Preclassic. Prior to any clear evidence of a ruling elite establishment architectural expression during this early episode remained modest with tentative sense of a formally dominant complex. At this time immediately adjacent developments may have been similarly modest and the North Acropolis may have risen dominantly despite its actual modest magnitude.

Acropolis function may have been primarily sacerdotal in these years. The final Late Preclassic development, my episode 5, is marked by amplification of height and includes establishment of the ruling Tikal dynastic line, perhaps usurping an earlier rulership. After hesitant beginnings this stage of development took on a coherent pattern and eventually established the final lineaments of the acropolis. Early in this phase the ruling lineage holding power throughout most of the Early Classic Period took office and the acropolis probably served both ritual and rulership functions. It is at this time that development emerges as a historical record. Finally, in episode 7, a new ruling lineage appeared and detracted from architectural form by a series of frontal additions that did nothing to increase the sense of power and coherence established earlier. Ironically though, the final refinements of form, aiming to embody ideological content (the cosmic diagram) took place during this period and the acropolis, behind the screen of frontal structures, may have reverted to its original sacerdotal identity.

The seven developmental stages outlined above, which I think of as design experiments carried on over varying lengths of time, do not correspond consistently with the ceramic sequence as set out in TR.14:Chart I (see North Acropolis Chronology). The 1st, Middle Preclassic development, lacking intact architecture in the North Acropolis sample, corresponds to the Eb and Tzec ceramic complexes and ends only slightly later. Architectural episode two, within the Late Preclassic, falls entirely within the time of Chuen ceramics, as does the 3rd episode, also in the Late Preclassic. Three of the four subsequent stages span periods in which ceramic complexes change. The 4th architectural episode, still within the Late Preclassic, begins at a time of Chuen ceramics but continues into Cauac times. The 5th, starting in Cauac times ends during production of Cimi ceramics. The 6th falls within Manik and the 7th, up to construction of Str. 5D-34-1st, spans Manik and Ik (a Double Bird development) and lasts into Imix times, although these ceramics only appear with Bu. 116 and Great Temple I. North Acropolis ceramics remain somewhat conservative, perhaps due to use of heirloom material in burials.

This final development opens with the arrival of a new type of apron molding (Str. 5D-34-2nd, Plate 47) that persists throughout later monumental architecture at Tikal. In this regard we see an architectural detail that remains constant while ceramic forms and techniques change markedly (Culbert 2003:59-62).

In TR.14 stages in North Acropolis development are summarized as Time Spans (TR.14:chart 1). Fifteen Time Spans are defined. Time Span 15 is the earliest and Time Span 1 is the latest. The architectural record that I have discussed in preceding chapters starts with Time Span 14 and ends early in Time Span 4B. I refer to the divisions within this record as "episodes" because, looking primarily at morphology, I think of them as design vectors. The earliest is episode 1 and the latest is episode 7. They are different design formulations, experimented with and followed for varying lengths of time. As outlined above my seven design episodes relate only loosely to the TR.14 Time Spans. Episode 4 extends through TS 12 and 11; episode 5 spans TS 10, 9 and part of 8; episode 7 begins early in TS 7 and runs through TS 5 into TS 4. In terms of architectural morphology I see somewhat less change than is evident in the more comprehensive TR.14 analysis. Careful reading of TR.14:813-74 yields repeated warnings about uncertainty as to sequences of events. The series illustrated in the plates that accompany this volume, therefore, can be taken at best as only one possible succession among others equally valid.

Apparent asynchronicity between architectural development on the North Acropolis and the Tikal ceramic sequence may not carry great significance. Morphological episodes in North Acropolis architecture may not coincide with constructional changes in architectural attributes and a pattern apparent in the North Acropolis may not characterize Tikal generally. A chronology of Tikal architecture based on change in attributes is taken up in TR.34B. Nevertheless, lack of agreement between morphological episodes on the North Acropolis and the Tikal ceramic sequence is suggestive. It seems to imply that changes in ceramics do not reflect the sorts of change responsible for different design strategies followed at different times in this particular locus. The fact that we know what social, or political changes were involved only in a few cases, as for example the "arrival of strangers" event, does not help interpretation. Firm conclusions, obviously, are not called for. Part B of TR.34 examines architectural attributes at a finer level detail, controlled by Time Spans. This work is still underway. Hopefully it will produce more definite results either for or against the relation between architecture and ceramics, hinted at here.

Finally, as a closing observation, the three "alien" structures, 5D-34-1st, 5D-33-1st and 5D-32-1st, while somewhat obscuring the old North Acropolis, nevertheless make a most impressive N edge to the Great Plaza. They provide a setting for ceremonies that could be witnessed by large numbers of people. With the rise of kingship as a possibly contentious element of Late Classic Maya society there may have been a need to impress people just as much as supernaturals. Societal stresses indicated by skeletal studies (Haviland personal communication) may have prompted rulers to exert greater efforts to retain their position of authority. The stelae standing along the N boundary of the plaza testify to kingship as a focus of events in this area. Architectural development of the North Acropolis may have ceased because pressures of a political and secular nature overcame the old priority of esoteric priest-astronomers and mathematicians who probably continued their arcane studies just behind this screen of formally innovative new structures. After all, the overriding intention of North Acropolis development was that of getting in good with supernatural forces for the benefit of the whole community.

Bibliography

Adams, Richard E. W. 1999. *Rio Azul: An Ancient Maya City*. Norman, OK: University of Oklahoma Press.

Ashmore, Wendy 1992. Deciphering Maya Architectural Plans. In *New Theories on the Ancient Maya*, edited by Elin C. Danien, and Robert J. Sharer, pp. 173-84. Philadelphia, PA: University of Pennsylvania Museum of Archaeology and Anthropology.

Bassie-Sweet, Karen 1996. *At The Edge of the World: Caves and the Late Classic Maya World View*. Norman, OK: University of Oklahoma Press.

Becker, Marshall J. 1992. Burials as Caches: Caches as Burials. In *New Theories on the Ancient Maya*, edited by Elin C. Danien, and Robert J. Sharer, pp. 185-96. Philadelphia, PA: University of Pennsylvania Museum of Archaeology and Anthropology.

___2003. Plaza Plans at Tikal. In *Tikal: Dynasties, Foreigners, & Affairs of State*, edited by Jeremy A. Sabloff, pp. 253-80. Santa Fe, NM: School of American Research.

Breton, Adela 1989. The Wall Paintings at Chichen Itza. In *The Art of Ruins*, edited by Sue Giles and Jennifer Stewart. Bristol: City of Bristol Museum and Art Gallery.

Carmack, Robert M. 1981. *The Quiché Mayas of Utatlán*. Norman, OK: University of Oklahoma Press.

Carr, Robert F., and James E. Hazard 1961. *Tikal Report No. 11: Map of the Ruins of Tikal, El Peten, Guatemala*. Philadelphia, PA: University of Pennsylvania Museum of Archaeology and Anthropology.

Carrasco, David 1990. *Religions of Mesoamerica*. San Francisco, CA: Harper and Row.

Chase, Diane Z., and Arlen F. Chase 1992. *Mesoamerican Elites: An Archaeological Assessment*. Norman, OK: University of Oklahoma Press.

Coe, Michael 1989. The Olmec Heartland: Evolution of Ideology. In *Regional Perspectives on the Olmec*, edited by Robert J. Sharer, and David C. Grove, pp. 68-82. Cambridge: Cambridge University Press.

Coe, William R. 1967. *Tikal: A Handbook of the Ancient Maya Ruins*. Philadelphia, PA: University of Pennsylvania Museum of Archaeology and Anthropology.

___1965. Tikal, Guatemala, and Emergent Maya Civilization. *Science* 147 3664: 1401-19.

___1990. *Tikal Report 14: excavations in the Great Plaza, North Terrace and North Acropolis of Tikal*. Philadelphia, PA: University of Pennsylvania Museum of Archaeology and Anthropology.

Coe, William R., and William A. Haviland 1982. *Tikal Report 12: Introduction to the Archaeology of Tikal, Guatemala*. Philadelphia, PA: University of Pennsylvania Museum of Archaeology and Anthropology.

Coe, William R., and J. J. McGinn 1963. Tikal: The North Acropolis and an Early Tomb. *Expedition* 5(2):24-32.

Coggins, C. 1975. Painting and Drawing Styles at Tikal. Ph.D. dissertation, Harvard University.

___1980. The Shape of Time. *American Antiquity* 45(4):727-39.

Culbert, T. Patrick 1991. Polities in the northeast Peten, Guatemala. In *Classic Maya Political History*, edited by T. Patrick Culbert, pp. 128-46. Cambridge: Cambridge University Press.

___1993. *Tikal Report No. 25: The Ceramics of Tikal*. Philadelphia, PA: University of Pennsylvania Museum of Archaeology and Anthropology.

___2003. The Ceramics of Tikal. In *Tikal: Dynasties, Foreigners and Affairs of State*, edited by Jeremy A. Sabloff, pp. 47-82. Santa Fe, NM: School of American Research.

Falkenhausen, Lothar von 1985. Architecture. In *A Consideration of the Early Classic Period in the Maya Lowlands*, edited by Gordon R. Willey and Peter Mathews. Albany, NY: Institute for Mesoamerican Studies, State University of New York at Albany.

Frankfort, H. and H. A., John A. Wilson, Thorkild Jacobsen, and William A. Irwin 1946. *The Intellectual Adventure of Ancient Man*. Chicago: The University of Chicago Press.

Freidel, David, and Linda Schele 1988. Symbol and Power: A History of the Lowland Maya Cosmogram. In *Maya Iconography*, edited by Elizabeth P. Benson and Gillet G. Griffin, pp. 44-93. Princeton, NJ: Princeton University Press.

Freidel, David, Linda Schele, and Joy Parker 1993. *Maya Cosmos: Three Thousand Years on the Shaman's Path*. New York: William Morrow.

Gerhart, Juliette Carwright 1988. *Preclassic Maya Architecture at Cuello, Belize*. Oxford: BAR.

Gerhart, Juliette Cartwright, and Norman Hammond 1991. The Community of Cuello: the ceremonial Core. In *Cuello an Early Maya Community in Belize*, edited by Norman Hammond, pp. 98-117. Cambridge: Cambridge University Press.

Gossen Gary H. 1986. Mesoamerican Ideas as a Foundation for Regional Synthesis. In *Symbol and Meaning Beyond the Closed Community: Essays in Mesoamerican Ideas*, edited by Gary H. Gossen, pp. 1-8. Albany, NY: Institute for Mesoamerican Studies.

Hansen, R. D. 1984. Excavations on Structure 34 and the Tigre Area, El Mirador, Petén, Guatemala: A New Look at the Preclassic Lowland Maya. Master's thesis, Brigham Young University.

___1998. Continuity and Disjunction; The Pre-Classic Antecedents of Classic Maya Architecture. In *Function and Meaning in Classic Maya Architecture*, edited by Stephen D. Houston, pp. 49-122. Washington, DC: Dumbarton Oaks.

Harrison, Peter 1999. *The Lords of Tikal*. London: Thames & Hudson.

Haviland, William A. 1985. *Tikal Report 19. Excavations in Small Residential Groups of Tikal: Groups 4F-1 and 4F-2*. Philadelphia, PA: University of Pennsylvania Museum of Archaeology and Anthropology.

___1992. From Double Bird to Ah Cacao: Dynastic Troubles and the Cycle of the Katuns at Tikal, Guatemala. In *New Theories on the Ancient Maya*, edited by Elin C. Danien, and Robert J. Sharer, pp. 71-80. Philadelphia, PA: University of Pennsylvania Museum of Archeology and Anthropology.

___2003. Settlement, Society and Demography at Tikal. In *Tikal: Dynasties, Foreigners and Affairs of State*, edited by Jeremy A. Sabloff, pp. 111-42. Santa Fe, NM: School of American Research.

Haviland, William A., and Hattula Moholy-Nagy 1992. Distinguishing the High and Mighty from the Hoi Polloi at Tikal, Guatemala. In *Mesoamerican Elites: An Archaeological Assessment*, edited by Diane Z. Chase and Arlen F. Chase, pp. 50-60. Norman, OK: University of Oklahoma Press.

Haviland, William A., and Anita de Laguna Haviland 1995. Glimpses of the Supernatural; Altered States of Consciousness and the Graffiti of Tikal, Guatemala. *Latin American Antiquity* 6(4):295-309.

Hendon, Julia A. 1999. The Pre-Classic Maya Compound as the Focus of Social Identity. In *Social Patterns in Pre-Classic Mesoamerica*, edited by David C. Grove and Rosemary A. Joyce, pp. 97-125. Washington, DC: Dumbarton Oaks

Houston, Stephen 1998. Depictions of the Built Environment. In *Function and Meaning in Classic Maya Architecture*, edited by Stephen D. Houston, pp. 333-72. Washington, DC: Dumbarton Oaks.

Jones C. 1977. Inauguration Dates of Three Late Classic Rulers of Tikal, Guatemala. *American Antiquity* 42:28-60.

___1991. Cycles of Growth in Tikal. In *Classic Maya Political History: Hieroglyphic and Archaeological Evidence*, edited by T. P. Culbert, pp. 102-27. Cambridge: Cambridge University Press.

___2003. The Tikal Renaissance and the East Plaza Ball Court. In *Tikal; Dynasties, Foreigners, & Affairs of State*, edited by Jeremy A. Sabloff, pp. 207-25. Santa Fe, NM: School of American Research.

Jones, C., and Linton Satterthwaite 1982. *Tikal Report 33A. The Monuments and Inscriptions of Tikal: The Carved Monuments*. Philadelphia, PA: University of Pennsylvania Museum of Archaeology and Anthropology.

Kelemen, Pál 1943 (1969). *Medieval American Art*. New York: Dover.

Kowalski, Jeff Karl, Alfredo Barrera Rubia, Heber Ojeda Más, and José Huchim Herrera 1996. Archaeological Investigations of a Round Temple at Uxmal: Summary Discussion and Implications for northern Maya Culture History. In *Palenque Round Table-1993 Vol.X*, edited by Merle Green Robertson, Martha Macri, and Jan McHargue, pp. 281-96. San Francisco, CA: Pre-Columbian Art Research Institute.

Kubler, George 1962. *The Art and Architecture of Ancient America*. Harmondsworth: Penguin.

Laporte, Juan Pedro 2003. Thirty Years Later: Some Results of Recent Excavations in Tikal. In *Tikal: Dynasties, Foreigners, and Affairs of State*, edited by Jeremy A. Sabloff, pp. 281-318. Santa Fe, NM: School of American Research.

Laporte, Juan Pedro, and Vilma Fialko 1995. Un Reencuentro con Mundo Perdido, Tikal, Guatemala. *Ancient Mesoamerica* 6(1):41-94.

León-Portilla, Miguel 1963. *Aztec Thought and Culture*. Norman, OK: University of Oklahoma Press.

___1988. *Time and Reality in the Thought of the Maya*. Norman, OK: University of Oklahoma Press.

Loten, H. Stanley 1985. Designation of Architectural Entities. *Cuadernos de Arquitectura Mesoamericana* 5.

___2002. *Tikal Report 23A: Miscellaneous Investigations in Central Tikal*. Philadelphia, PA: University of Pennsylvania Museum of Archaeology and Anthropology.

___2003. The North Acropolis: Monumentality, Function and Architectural Development. In *Tikal: Dynasties, Foreigners, & Affairs of State*, edited by Jeremy A. Sabloff, pp. 227-52. Santa Fe, NM: School of American Research.

___2006. A Distinctive Architectural Format: The Lamanai Temple. In *Reconstructing the Past*, edited by David M. Pendergast and Anthony P. Andrews, pp. 89-106. BAR International Series, Oxford: John and Erica Hedges Ltd.

Loten, H. Stanley, and David M. Pendergast 1984. *A Lexicon for Maya Architecture*. Toronto, ON: Royal Ontario Museum.

Lounsbury, Floyd G. 1985. The Identities of the Mythological Figures in the Cross Group Inscriptions of Palenque. In *Fourth Palenque Round Table, 1980*, edited by Merle Greene Robertson and Elizabeth P. Benson, pp.45-58. San Francisco, CA: Pre-Columbian Art Research Institute.

Love, Bruce 1992. Divination and Prophecy in Yucatan. In *New Theories on the Ancient Maya*, edited by Elin C. Danien, and Robert J. Sharer, pp. 205-16. Philadelphia, PA: University of Pennsylvania Museum of Archaeology and Anthropology.

Maler, Teobert 1911. *Explorations in the Department of Peten, Guatemala*. Cambridge, MA: Peabody Museum of Archaeology and Ethnology, Harvard University.

Marquina, Ignacio 1964. *Arquitectura Prehispanica*. Mexico. Instituto Nacional De Antropologia E Historica, Secretaria De Educacion Publica.

Martin, Simon 1996. Tikal's "Star War" against Naranjo. In *Palenque Round Table–1993 Vol. X*, edited by Merle Greene Robertson, Martha Macri, and Jan McHargue, pp. 223-36. San Francisco, CA: Pre-Columbian Art Research Institute.

___2001. Unmasking "Double Bird," Ruler of Tikal. *The Pari Journal* 2(1): 7-12.

Martin, Simon, and Nikolai Grube 2000. *Chronicle of the Maya Kings and Queens*. London: Thames & Hudson.

Matheny, R.T. 1980. *El Mirador, Peten, Guatemala: An Interim Report*. Papers of the New World Archaeological Foundation 46. Provo, UT: Brigham Young University.

___1987. El Mirador: An Early Maya Metropolis Uncovered. *National Geographic* 172 (3):317-39.

McAnany, Patricia A. 1995. *Living With the Ancestors: Kinship and Kingship in Ancient Maya Society*. Austin, TX: University of Texas Press.

___1998. Ancestors and the Classic Maya Built Environment. In *Function and Meaning in Classic Maya Architecture*, edited by Stephen D. Houston, pp. 271-98. Washington, DC: Dumbarton Oaks.

Miller, Arthur G. 1986. *Maya Rulers of Time*. Philadelphia, PA: University of Pennsylvania Museum of Archaeology and Anthropology.

Mock, Shirley Boleter 1998. Prelude. In *The Sowing and the Dawning*. edited by Shirely Boleter Mock, pp. 3-18. Albuquerque, NM: University of New Mexico Press.

Moholy-Nagy, Hattula 2003a. Beyond the Catalogue: The Chronology and Contexts of Tikal Artifacts. In *Tikal: Dynasties, Foreigners, and Affairs of State*, edited by Jeremy A. Sabloff, pp. 83-110. Santa Fe, NM: School of American Research.

___2003b. *Tikal Report 27B. The Artifacts of Tikal: Utilitarian Artifacts and Unworked Material*. Philadelphia, PA: University of Pennsylvania Museum of Archaeology and Anthropology.

Moholy-Nagy, Hattula, and William R. Coe Forthcoming *Tikal Report 27A. The Artifacts of Tikal: Ornamental and Other Special Material.* Ms. Forthcoming. Philadelphia, PA: University of Pennsylvania Museum of Archaeology and Anthropology.

Morley, Sylvanus Griswold, and George W. Brainerd 1946. *The Ancient Maya*. Palo Alto, CA: Stanford University Press.

Paxton, Meredith 2001. *The Cosmos of the Yucatec Maya: Cycles and Steps from the Madrid Codex*. Albuquerque, NM: University of New Mexico Press.

Pendergast, D. M. 1981. Lamanai, Belize: Summary of Excavation Results 1974-1980. *Journal of Field Archaeology* 8:29-53.

___1992. Nobless Oblige: The Elites of Altun Ha and Lamanai, Belize. In *Mesoamerican Elites*, edited by Diane Z. Chase and Arlen F. Chase, pp. 61-79. Norman, OK: University of Oklahoma Press.

Pollock, H. E. D. 1936. *Round Structures of Aboriginal Middle America*. Publication 471. Washington, DC: Carnegie Institution of Washington.

___1965. Architecture of the Maya Lowlands. In *Handbook of Middle American Indians Vol. 2*, edited by Robert Wauchope, Margaret A. L. Harrison, and Inis Pickett, pp. 378-440. Austin, TX: University of Texas Press.

Powis, Terry 1996. Excavation of Middle Formative Period Round Structures at the Tolok Group, Cahal Pech, Belize. Master's thesis, Trent University.

Proskouriakoff, Tatiana 1963. *An Album of Maya Architecture*. Norman, OK: University of Oklahoma Press.

___1993. *Maya History*, edited by Rosemary A. Joyce. Austin, TX: University of Texas Press.

Rice, Prudence M. 2006. *Maya Political Science: Time, Astronomy, and the Cosmos*. Austin, TX: University of Texas Press.

Ringle, W. M., and E. Wyllys Andrews V 1988. Formative Residence at Komchen, Yucatan, Mexico. In *Household and Community in the Mesoamerican Past*, edited by R. R. Wilk and W. Ashmore, pp. 171-99. Albuquerque, NM: University of New Mexico Press.

Roberston, Donald 1963. *Pre-Columbian Architecture*. New York: George Braziller.

Sabloff, J. A. 1973. Continuity and Disruption During Terminal Late Classic Times at Seibal: Ceramic and Other Evidence. In *The Classic Maya Collapse*, edited by T. P. Culbert, pp. 107-32. Albuquerque, NM: University of New Mexico Press.

___2003. Preface. In *Tikal: Dynasties, Foreigners, and Affairs of State*, edited by Jeremy A. Sabloff, pp. 83-110. Santa Fe, NM: School of American Research.

Saturno, William, A., Karl A. Taube, and David Stewart 2005. *The Murals of San Bartolo, El Petén, Guatemala Part 1: The North Wall*. Barnardsville, NY: Center for Ancient American Studies.

Satterthwaite, Linton, Jr. 1937. Identification of Maya Temple Buildings at Piedras Negras. *Twenty-Fifth Anniversary Studies*, pp. 161-77. Philadelphia, PA: Philadelphia Anthropological Society.

___1941. Some Central Peten Maya Architectural Traits at Piedras Negras. In *Los Mayas Antiguos*, edited by César Lizardi Ramos, pp. 183-208. Mexico City: El Colegio de Mexico.

___1943. *Piedras Negras Archaeology: Architecture*. Philadelphia, PA: University of Pennsylvania Museum of Archaeology and Anthropology.

Sharer, Robert J. 1994. *The Ancient Maya*, 5th ed. Palo Alto, CA: Stanford University Press.

Schele, Linda 1976. Accession Iconography of Chan-Bahlum in the Group of the Cross at Palenque. In *The Art, Iconography & Dynastic History of Palenque Part III*, edited by Merle Greene Robertson, pp. 9-34. Pebble Beach, CA: Pre-Columbian Art Research, the Robert Louis Stevenson School.

___1992. Lineages at Copan and other Maya Sites. *Ancient Mesoamerica* 3(1):133-44.

Schele, Linda, and David Freidel 1990. *A Forest of King*. New York: William Morrow.

Schele, Linda, and Mary Ellen Miller 1986. *The Blood of Kings*. New York: George Braziller.

Shook, Edwin M., and William R. Coe 1961. *Tikal Report 5. Tikal: Numeration, Terminology, and Objectives*. In *Tikal Reports 5-10*, pp. 1-13. Philadelphia, PA: University of Pennsylvania Museum of Archaeology and Anthropology.

Spinden, Herbert J. 1913 (1975). *A Study of Maya Art: Its Subject Matter & Historical Development*. New York: Dover.

Stuart, David 1998. Fire Enters His House. In *Function and Meaning in Classic Maya Architecture*, edited by Stephen Houston, pp. 373-425. Washington, DC: Dumbarton Oaks.

___2000. The Arrival of Strangers: Teotihuacan and Tollan in Classic Maya History. In *Mesoamerica's Classic Heritage: From Teotihuacan to the Aztecs*, edited by David Carrasco, Lindsay Jones, and Scott Sessions, pp. 465-513. Niwot, CO: University Press of Colorado.

Taube, Karl 1998. The Jade Hearth: Centrality, Rulership, and the Classic Maya Temple. In *Function and Meaning in Classic Maya Architecture*, edited by Stephen D. Houston, pp. 427-78. Washington, DC: Dumbarton Oaks.

Tedlock, Dennis 1985. *Popol Vuh*. New York: Simon & Schuster.

Thompson, J. E. S. 1955. *The Rise and Fall of Maya Civilization*. Norman, OK: University of Oklahoma Press.

___1960. *Maya Hieroglyphic Writing: An Introduction*. Norman, OK: University of Oklahoma Press.

___1970. *Maya History and Religion*. Norman, OK: University of Oklahoma Press.

___1988 (1968). Foreword. In *Time and Reality in the Thought of The Maya*. Edited by Miguel León-Portilla Norman, OK: University of Oklahoma Press.

Tikal Reports
   TR.5: Shook and Coe 1961.
   TR.11: Carr and Hazard 1961.
   TR.14: Coe 1990.
   TR.19: Haviland 1985.
   TR.23A: Loten 2002.
   TR.33A: Jones and Satterthwaite 1982.
   TR.25: Culbert 1993.
   TR.27A: Moholy-Nagy and Coe forthcoming.
   TR.27B: Moholy-Nagy 2003b.
   TR.31 Trik and Kampen 1983.

Totten, George Oakley 1926. *Maya Architecture*. Washington, DC: The Maya Press.

Tozzer, Alfred M. 1911. *Preliminary Study of the Ruins of Tikal, Guatemala*. Cambridge, MA: Peabody Museum of Archaeology and Ethnology, Harvard University.

Trigger, Bruce 2003. *Understanding Early Civilizations*. Cambridge: Cambridge University Press.

Trik, Helen, and Michael E. Kampen 1983. *Tikal Report 31: The Graffiti of Tikal*. Philadelphia, PA: University of Pennsylvania Museum of Archaeology and Anthropology.

Valdés, Juan Antonio 1987. Uaxactún: recientes investigaciones. *Mexicon* 8(6):125-28.

___1989. El Grupo H de Uaxactún: Evidencias de un Centro de Poder Durante el Preclasico. In *Memorias Del Segundo Coloquio Internacional De Mayistas*, edited by Mercedes de la Garza et al., pp. 603-24. México: Universidad Nacional Autonoma de México.

Valdés, J. A., F. Fahsen, and G. Munos Cosme 1997. *Estela 40 de Tikal: Hallazgo y Lectura*. Guatemala: Instituto de Antropología e Historiaa.

Van Zantwijk, Rudolph 1981. The Great Temple of Tenochtitlan. In *Mesoamerican Sites and World Views*, edited by Elizabeth P. Benson, pp. 71-86. Washington, DC: Dumbarton Oaks.

Villacorta, J. A. 1962. *Popol Vuh*. Guatemala: Ministerio de Educación Publica.

Wauchope, Robert 1940. Domestic Architecture of the Maya. In *The Maya and Their Neighbours*, edited by C. L. Hay, R. L. Linton, S. K. Lothrop, H. L. Shapiro, and G. C. Vaillant, pp. 232-41. New York: Appleton-Century.

Willey, Gordon R., W. R. Bullard, J. B. Glass, and J. C. Gifford 1965. *Prehistoric Maya Settlements in the*

Appendix 1

Content of Architectural Episodes

Architectural Episode Contents (cited in text)
Episode 7: AD 340-720
Plat. 5D-4-2nd and 1st-C/D
Str. 5D-34-1st; Str. 5D-33-3rd, 2nd, and 1st; Str. 5D-25-2nd and 1st; Str, 5D-23-1st-A; Str. 5D-22-2nd and 1st; Str. 5D-29; Str. 5D-30; Str. 5D-31; Str. 5D-32-1st; Str. 5D-20-2nd and 1st; Str. 28; Str. 5D-5 (Great Temple V)
Bu. 10; Bu. 48; Bu. 200; Bu. 23; Bu. 24; Bu. 195
U. 288B; U. 109; U. 188; U. 84; U. 198A and B; U. 189
P.D. 139
Fl. 3; Fl. 2; Fl. 1
Episode 6: AD 200-340
Platform 5D-4-4th and 3rd
Str. 5D-8-1st; Str. 5D-22-5th, 4th and 3rd; Str. 5D-23-2nd and 1st B; Str. 5D-24-2nd and 1st; Str. 5D-26-2nd and 1st
Bu. 85
U. 35; U. 115; U. 149; U. 2; U. 33; U. 150; U. 29
Fl. 6; Fl. 5; Fl. 4
Episode 5: AD 75-200
Platform 5D-4-5th and 6th
Str. 5D-Sub.3-B and A; Str. 5D-Sub.6; Str. 5D-22-6th; Str. 5D-26-5th and 4th; Str. 5D-Sub.21; Str. 5D-Sub.8-2nd; Str. 5D-Sub.7
Bu. 125
U. 91B; U. 40
Fl.9; Fl. 8; Fl. 7
Episode 4: 80 BC-AD75
Platform 5D-4-8th
Str. 5D-Sub.3-F-B; Str, 5D-Sub.12-2nd; Str. 5D-Sub.4; Str. 5D-Sub.5; Str. 5D-Sub.9; Str. 5D-Sub.1-1st
Bu. 164
U. 59; U. 111; U. 49; U. 232/83; U. 64; U. 46B; U. 63; U. 42' U. 41
Fl.13
Episode 3: 200-80 BC
Platform 5D-4-9th
Str. 5D-Sub.1-2nd; Str. 5D-Sub.24
U. 110; U. 82; U. 96; U. 305
Episode 2: 350-200 BC
Platform 5D-4-10th-A
Str. 5D-Sub.14-2nd and 1st
U. 80; U, 71; U. 74; U. 78
Fl. 17; Fl. 16
Episode 1: 800-350 BC
Platform 5D-4-10th-B
Bu. 120
P.D. 83
U. 223; U. 224A

Appendix 2

Glossary of Architectural Terms

For a more comprehensive glossary see Loten and Pendergast 1984.

Acropolis

This term, referring to the North Acropolis, Tikal, appears as "Northern Acropolis" in the Tikal sketch map made by Tozzer and Merwin (Tozzer 1911). It is meant to identify a group of structures raised on a relatively high common sustaining platform. The term Plazuela (Falkenhausen 1985:115; Willey et. al. 1965), which I have not used, is essentially equivalent. The terms "Complex" and "Group" are often used for similar arrangements not raised as high. An example of this usage is Group A-V at Uaxactun. In TR.14 "acropolis" is used as a term for the uppermost of the platforms that sustain the summit complex of structures. I have used "acropolis" loosely in the text to refer to the entire set of North Acropolis architectural features. There may be some objection to "acropolis" as an Old World term applicable to classic architecture and therefore to be avoided in New World studies, but for Tikal the term is long established.

Alfarda

This is the Spanish term used for shallow ramp-like elements placed at the side of stairs. The terms "stair-side ramp" and "balustrade" are sometimes used for this feature. An alfarda is essentially a low, solid balustrade with no balusters (uprights). An example can be seen on Str. 5D-22-3rd (Figure 40/Plate 38).

Apron

A term applied to a distinctive type of molding particularly conspicuous on terrace facings in the Maya area. An "apron" consists of an upper part and a recessed lower part sometimes noted as a "sub-apron." Although the outset upper part provides the name, "apron," as I have used it here, refers to the entire profile, top to bottom.

There are two chronologically sequent apron types in the architecture of the North Acropolis. The earlier form is the simple apron/sub-apron well illustrated in the terracing of Str. 5D-Sub.1-1st (Figure 15/Plate 15). Its initial appearance is on the Second Supplementary Platform of Platform 5D-4-9th. The later form appears for the first time in the substructure of Str. 5D-34-2nd (Figure 45/Plate 47). It is created by insertion of a horizontal slot below the mid-height of the terrace.

Aprons do not appear to have any structural value and therefore I suspect they have iconographic significance. One particularly striking property is the shadow pattern they generate when the sun is at zenith. For this reason I speculate that iconographic associations, if any, might be solar.

Architectural Development

I believe this term can be credited to Wm. R. Coe, Tikal Project Director (TR.5). It refers to a series of superimposed structures or platforms that for various reasons seem to show some kind of conceptual continuity through sequential rebuilding episodes. In these cases the surface structure has "1st" appended to its map number, as for example Str. 5D-22-1st, or Platform 5D-4-1st. Then, as excavation proceeds and if earlier versions of the structure appear, they are designated "2nd," "3rd," etc., counting from latest to earliest. Unmodified map numbers designate features that are either unexcavated or do not overly earlier versions.

Ambiguous situations emerge in cases where earlier features at the same locus have radically different architectural forms. Examples include the Str. 5D-26 series and the 5D-33 series in the North Acropolis. As seen in Figure 30/Plate 29, Str. 5D-26-4th bears no resemblance to Str. 5D-26-3rd (Figure 31/Plate 30) directly above it. A similar relationship can be seen in the case of Str. 5D-33-2nd (Figure 48/Plate 52) directly beneath Str. 5D-33-1st (Figure 55/Plate 66). Here, assumed continuity seems primarily dictated by the prominent site on and atop the S axial acropolis stair.

An opposite condition prevails in the Str. 5D-22 series rising above Str. 5D-Sub.1-1st. Here the change in scale of the acropolis as a whole accounts for the shift in designation despite the fact that both series occupy comparable N axial positions and probably were dominant features of their respective complexes.

Architectural development in the specialized sense outlined above is the central theme of TR. 34A. It seems to me the many different versions of the acropolis all represent re-embodiments of a fabric that carried very strong conceptual continuity throughout the nine centuries documented by the architectural remains that were uncovered in the excavations.

Axis

As used here, and in TR. 14, an "axis" is an imaginary line traced through the front and rear centers structures. Coe identified four North Acropolis axes (TR.14: fig. 5).

Very often structures facing each other across a plaza or patio space appear to occupy the same axial lines but when carefully measured are found to be not exactly collinear. In some cases I suspect that the offsets are intentional so that each feature possesses its own axis yet both generate an apparent alignment.

Some sub-assembly features such as outsets appear to exist solely for the purpose of marking axes. Structure 5D-22-1st (Figure 50/Plate 55) provides a prime example of this. The rear outset and the frontal stair mark the NS axis. The two very prominent side outsets mark an EW axis. The stair fulfills a function of access, but the outsets have no other purpose that I can see.

Axes raise an ambiguous interpretive issue. They can be understood as marking a direction that the structure faces toward, perhaps to some astronomical target. Conversely, the ancient Maya might have arranged things so that some astronomical feature appears to face toward the structure as some specific point in the year. This might have been intended to demonstrate a claimed connection with the astronomical feature.

Body

I use this term as a convenient referent to various parts of structures at various levels of complexity. I find the term appropriate because some parts of structures have an appearance of wholeness although they are integral parts of a larger whole. For example, consider the rear part of the substructure of Str. 5D-Sub.1-1st (Figure 16/Plate 17). It is easy to imagine these terraces as forming an architectonically complete entity. The same can be said of the front and rear parts of the Str. 5D-22-1st building.

I suspect the ancient Maya thought in terms of visual whole entities. Their glyphic writing is constructed in this way. The scribes who developed the writing probably had close connections with the designers of structures, particularly those for ritual purposes.

Balustrade

In modern usage this is an open railing at the side of a stair consisting of a handrail supported on balusters. The closest thing to this in ancient Maya architecture is a low ramp-like feature sometimes placed at the sides of stairs. The Spanish term "alfarda" (above) is sometimes preferred in that is does not suggest so alien a feature. "Balustrade" is useful in that it immediately directs attention to a stair-side.

Basal Platform

This term can be applied to the bottom member of a structure if that member has the properties of a platform as defined below. A potentially confusing condition arises when the larger architectural entity is also designated as a Platform rather than a Structure. We then have a Basal Platform as a component of a Platform. This is the case with U. 92, the acropolis platform body in Platform 5D-4-9th-B (Figure 7/Plate 7). Many other parts of ancient Mesoamerican structures are conveniently designated as platforms because they are satisfy the general understanding of that term (see "Platform" below).

Building

This is normally part of a structure, and normally contains the rooms. The North Acropolis does not present any arrangement calling for more than one "Building" in any one Structure. A multi-building pattern appears, for example, at Lamanai in Structure N10-43 (Pendergast 1981:fig. 12). Hypothetically, a

"Structure," properly defined, can consist of a Building and nothing else. That is, there might be no substructure. An example of this is Str. 5D-28 (Figure 55/Plate 66). It stands partly on a stair designated as part of the acropolis platform and partly on acropolis Fl.1. It has walls and was vaulted but has no substructure of its own. This is quite exceptional. The great majority of buildings are component parts of structures that include other features.

Several North Acropolis structures have rooms that were not enclosed. Pole and thatch superstructures present this condition. The earliest appear in Platform 5D-4-8th-D (Figure 11/Plate 11).

Some room-like spaces are present in roof combs and very likely some North Acropolis structures had them but noe have survived. Structure 5D-22-1st probably had such spaces in its roof-comb. They are designated as chambers rather than rooms since they were not accessible.

Building Platform

Except for Str. 5D-28, all North Acropolis buildings stand on substructure bodies that conform to them in plan either fully or partly. The Str. 5D-Sub.1-1st substructure (Figure 16, 18) is a Building Platform. Examples of partial building platforms are afforded by Str. 5D-23-1st (Figure 43/Plate 44) and Str. 5D-22-1st (Figure 47/Plate 50). In these cases some parts of the substructure conform to the building plan but other parts do not. In TR.34B I contemplate designating these as pseudo building platforms.

Core

I apply this term to the inner hearting material in platforms, walls, vaults and interior platforms. There are two extremes of core types in the North Acropolis architecture-loose core and bedded core. The former can be seen in structures immediately above bedrock and in Str. 5D-Sub.3 (TR.14:fig. 10). These are relatively low constructions. Loose core does not cause any great stablility problem in works of this type. In higher constructions, however, loose core would require very substantial retaining walls at the outer edges. High structures exhibit various types of coursed core made of masonry units bedded in mortar. The outstanding example of this is Str. 5D-33-1st (TR.14:fig. 9b(right)). Here, in a strikingly vertical substructure, core assembly is so inherently stable that no retaining walls are needed at the outer faces. Indeed, the outer facing material had largely fallen long before the Tikal project operations began leaving core masonry exposed and still firmly in place after centuries of exposure (Plate 67.10).

Doorway

The openings provided for access to rooms are "doorways." Evidence for doors in the form of wooden slabs placed between the jambs does show up at Tikal (TR 23A:23, fig. 16b) but not on the North Acropolis. These doorjambs (in other parts of the site) have beam holes indicating that solid doors of slab form were used. On the North Acropolis, in contrast, it seems either curtains or slabs placed on inside wall surfaces were the preferred method of doorway closure though even these appear exceptional.

Str. 5D-22-1st (TR.14:fig. 108c) and Str. 5D-26-1st (TR. 14:fig. 81) have cord holders on inner wall faces of rooms. These indicate that fabrics or slabs had been used to close these doorway openings, held by cords fastened to the cord holders. Closing and opening could only be done from the inside. This could mean that people were sleeping in these rooms, perhaps fasting, or engaging in some kind of purification ritual.

Facing

I refer to the masonry installed to establish a surface for plaster finishing as "facing" masonry. North Acropolis provides a wide variety of facing characteristics. Wall facings are made of relatively small stones. Terrace facing stones are much larger and more regular in shape. All North Acropolis structures considered in TR.34A require relatively thick plaster for finishing.

To compare facings between different structures it is necessary of control for facing type. These include exterior wall, interior wall, building platform, upper zone, roof comb, stair side, and substructure terracing. In any structure, dimensions, shapes, and degree of dressing vary between these categories.

Substructures frequently include Core Facings. These are withes of masonry that mark task units both deep within core bodies and at the outer edges of core assemblies. These are usually relatively rough and were never intended to be exposed as finished surfaces. They appear early in North Acropolis construction (Platform 5D-4-9th-B) and show that a sophisticated construction industry already existed at Tikal. Core facings of Str. 5D-33-1st clearly demarcate task units (see "Task Unit," below). They are further discussed above (see "Core" article).

It is my impression that no facing masonry of finish surfaces was ever left exposed. I think all were covered with plaster.

Floor

Activity surfaces, the tops of platforms and floors in rooms, are designated as Floors, and numbered in order of their discovery during excavations, if finished with plaster surfacing. This is the minimal requirement for a North Acropolis "Floor." Most, particularly those capping platform cores and exposed to weathering, are built up with a body of aggregate, ballast, and a topping of plaster. Others are mere skin coats. There are a few activity surfaces that did not have plaster finishing.

Lintel

Lintels, the beams that span doorway openings, certainly were present in North Acropolis buildings but none had survived. A number of lintel beds are evident and they prove the existence of lintels. It is unfortunate that the North Acropolis builders used only wood lintels and no stone lintels. Indeed, as far as I know there are no stone lintels at Tikal.

Mortar

The matrix employed to bond masonry units together is called "mortar" regardless of its composition and adhesiveness. Some are mere earth, mud or clay. Others are almost pure lime similar in composition to the best plasters and relatively strong. These latter mortars tend to retain their adhesiveness to this day while those with a larger proportion of earth tend to be rather friable. The better mortars are used for facings. Inner core material generally displays weaker mortar.

Outset

North Acropolis structures display rear axial outsets, side outsets, and stair-side outsets. These are facets of architectural form projecting beyond adjacent elements. I suspect they carry iconographic content. They do not satisfy any other obvious function. In this they are similar to apron moldings.

Paint

Aside from sculptural features approximately half of the North Acropolis structures are finished with red paint. Specular hematite is the pigment most commonly used for this body paint. Traces and flakes of other colors are found on sculptural features. Colors, apart from red, include cream, blue, black, and green.

Platform

A "Platform" in Tikal Project usage is an architectural entity on a par with "Structure," "Terrace," "Plaza," and "Court" (TR.5:7; TR.14: 4). Hence the North Acropolis structures are raised up on Platform 5D-4, and the Great Plaza is the upper surface of Platform 5D-1. They are designated as "Platforms" because they engage with or appear to sustain other entities separately designated as numbered "Structures." In effect, this avoids having structures that engage or sustain other "Structures."

The term "platform," without a map square number, applies to parts of structures, as for example, Building Platform, Supplementary Platform, Basal Platform, and Interior Platform. For these component entities I apply the formal criterion that each must fully contain all sub-assemblies that engage with it. This is the reason why I define the 5D-22-1st substructure as a single platform entity, since its Rear Axial Outset extends from base to top (Figure 53/Plate 61). Stairs are other features that often bind various parts together into single platforms. Platform 5D-4-9th-B (Figure 7/Plate 7) U. 96 illustrates the need for this criterion. It appears to me to be a distinct platform entity of a kind that could not properly be labeled as a "terrace." To accomodate this feature in a consistent designation system (Loten 1985) I have expanded the category of Supplementary Platform by simply numbering such entities according to their position above the sustaining surface of the structure. Thus U.96 can be designated as Second Supplementary Platform of Platform 5D-4-9th-B. The feature designated in TR.14 as U. 92, the Acropolis Platform (Figure 7/Plate 7) I designate, for general Tikal architecture purposes, as a Third Supplementary Platform. Terrace South (U.305) could be either a Basal Platform or a First Supplementary Platform. In the text I have used these general terms and the TR.14 designations.

Plaster

Plasters are reconstituted lithic materials made by grinding or dissolving limestone and then allowing it to harden again. I understand that chemical analysis fails to conclusively prove that limestone had been burned to produce pure lime. My impression is that native soft limestone, or marl in the Tikal area is so high in lime content that merely by breaking it up and grinding it small very good hard plaster could be made.

In cuts that I have made through some plasters at Tikal I have observed curving pressure lines. I think this indicates that the plaster had been pounded to harden it and make it denser. In these cases exterior plaster surfaces were pounded, rubbed and burnished after the material had hardened sufficiently. This would have rendered freshly completed structures somewhat reflective and glossy. Such reflectivity may have possessed a certain value due to the glare of full sunlight and perhaps also moonlight. This issue is considered at various points through chapters 1-10.

Shrine Room

Some structures include a single room placed low down on the axial stair. This feature is generally designated as a "Shrine Room." The North Acropolis does not provide any precise examples of this but several small structures placed at the foot of axial stairs may have served the same function. Examples include Str. 5D-Sub.7 (Figure 31), Str. 5D-Sub.10-2nd and 1st (Figure 21/22), Str. 5D-Sub.2-2nd and 1st (Figure 23/24). Structure 5D-33-3rd and 2nd may fall into this category as well.

Stair

An uninterrupted series of treads and risers constitutes one stair. Two or more stairs make a stairway if they are aligned as one path of ascent. Stairs placed off-axis on the front façade, whether running parallel to the axis or not, are designated as lateral stairs. Stairs placed on side façades are designated as side stairs. Stairs placed on rear façades are designated as rear stairs whether on or off axis.

Structure

Individual architectural entities that appear to be whole and complete works are designated as structures and numbered in sequence of encounter within map squares. All North Acropolis structures are in square 5D. Comparable features beneath later constructions, not members of an architectural development (see above), are designated as "sub." structures.

Modifications to structures are designated as "A," "B," etc. counting from the final change ("A") to earlier ones. A disadvantage of this system is that primary structures do not have consistent designations. Thus Str. 5D-23-1st-B, and Str. 5D-33-1st are both primary structures but their designations do not suggest this.

Stucco

This is a material similar to plaster but coarser. Fine aggregate may be included. Typically, stucco is employed for modeling while plaster is used on plain surfaces. Aprons on the acropolis platform of Platform 5D-4-9th-B are modeled in stucco.

Substructure

The set of elements or bodies sustaining a building is designated as a substructure. There are various forms of substructure as yet not formalized. A fine example of a substructure formed as two bodies is Str. 5D-Sub.1-1st (Figure 15/Plate 15). Establishing a comprehensive Tikal substructure typology is one task of TR.34B.

Superstructure

A building is a superstructure even though there may be no substructure (cf. Str. 5D-28, Figure 55/Plate 66a).

Supplementary Platform

The term "supplementary platform was coined specifically for Str. 5C-4 (Great Temple IV) to designate the member coming in between the Pyramid and the Building Platform. To accommodate some North Acropolis features I have expanded this category to include First, Second and third supplementary platforms counting from the bottom up (see "Platform," above).

Sustaining Surface

The surface on which a feature is built is known as the sustaining surface.

Task Unit

Core material frequently shows subdivisions, or subassemblies within the hearting of features such as platforms. Core faces (see "Facing" and Core," above) mark these subdivisions. I refer to them as task units. They indicate that the work of construction was organized in discrete increments. In a few cases I have noted that adjacent units show differences in core characteristics such as mortar color. I wonder if this means that different task units were installed by different groups of workers preparing their own materials. It is my impression that the very highly organized core assembly of Str. 5D-33-1st (TR.14: FIG. 9b (right)) shows that several work crews were operating at the same time on this major project.

Temple. Recognition of multiple crews affects estimates of the time required for construction.

Temple

This term is often used very loosely in Mesoamerican studies and carries an assumption of ritual function that rarely can be substantiated objectively. Presence of caches and signs of burning may be evidence of ritual function. In terms of Tikal architectural form, my guess is that rear axial outsets, side outsets, and side insets probably mark ritual structures. High pyramidal substructures seem like the surest ritual attribute. Location is another prime factor though lacking certainty.

In general terms I suggest the attempt to establish linkages with supernatural powers is the fundamental role played by temples. There are so many ways that such attempts might be made that it may never be possible to confidently identify all temples. Structures with none of the attributes that suggest ritual function may well have served temple roles. My personal bias is that all structures on the North Acropolis at all times served ritual purposes but only some of them could properly be labeled as temples. Some seem to me like support structures, perhaps housing ritual accoutrements but maybe not serving directly at attract supernaturals. These include Str. 5D-20, Str. 5D-Sub.21, Str. 5D-28, Str. 5D-Sub.3, and perhaps Str. 5D-26.

Terrace

In North Acropolis literature there are two distinct usages for the term "terrace." A problematic feature encountered in Platform 5D-4-9th-B is designated in TR.14 as Terrace South (U. 305 in Figure 7). This seemed appropriate at the time because only one face (U. 110 in Figure 7) of U. 305 showed up in the excavations. Additionally it appeared likely that the feature would die against rising grades like an agricultural terrace. I did not find this to be the case when I constructed the model for Figure 7, so in my reconstruction U. 305 appears fully four sided like a Basal Platform or First Supplementary Platform.

The other, more common, usage of "terrace" in architectural contexts is that employed in substructure assembly. Most substructures whether tall like Str. 5D-33-1st, or relatively low like Acropolis Platform U. 92 (Figure 7) are subdivided vertically into terraces, in most Maya cases, with apron moldings. Terraces no doubt served as task units useful in organizing the work. By dividing a platform into terrace levels it was possible to adjust the angle of each to ensure that the top surface area would not be smaller than desired. At the same time this strategy resulted in apron moldings of manageable height and made it easier to obtain desired profiles. In addition, as I have suggested in the text, terraces may have incorporated iconographic references central to the basic meaning of the architecture.

Unit

Features lacking an established designation, or of uncertain nature, are labeled as "Units" and numbered within a category such as "Structure," or "Platform." The unit references in the text are tabulated in TR.14: Appendix E. Unit numbers are attached to major feature designations such as Platform 5D-4 or a structure number. I have omitted these cumbersome qualifiers on grounds that the context is evident in the line figures.

Upper Zone

The vaulted structures of the North Acropolis always have a band of masonry above the wall level that projects out beyond the wall face. Some of these upper zone surfaces were treated sculpturally but very little of this has survived. From scant evidence it appears that frontal upper zones were carved while rearward ones were left plain. This pattern is very evident in later work that has preserved more of these surfaces. A conspicuous exception is Str. 5D-96, the central member of the Seven Temples group in the SW quarter of central Tikal (Coe 1967:89).

They are sometimes referred to as "friezes" but I have not used this term and indeed many of them are plain.

Vault

Masonry assemblies spanning spaces such as rooms, chambers (in roof combs), tombs, and doorways, are designated as "vaults." North Acropolis vaulting is suspected as early as Str. 5D-Sub.1-1st (TR.14:fig. 23) but the earliest substantial surviving vaults are on Str. 5D-23-1st-B (TR.14:fig. 130a) and 5D-24 (TR.14:fig. 136b).

North Acropolis vaults are built up using relatively unspecialized masonry units. The term "corbelled vaulting" is appropriate for these vaults. In contrast, Late Classic vaulting uses specialized masonry units that are not corbelled (TR.23A:fig.2, 6, 17b, 52a).

Except for Str. 5D-20-1st (ca. AD 720) North Acropolis vaults lack vault-back surfaces. This means simultaneous installation of upper zone masonry and vault masonry. I suspect this practice reflects use of modeled stucco for upper zone relief work rather than carved stone.

Wall

I restrict the term "wall" for application to elements that enclose rooms and divide spaces. That is, I do not apply "wall" to the facings of solid members such as terraces or platforms. In TR.34A, an element that might otherwise be called a platform "wall," is noted as a platform face (see "Face" article above). Except for Str. 5D-Sub.1-1st, all North Acropolis walls have both facing and core masonry (Sub.1-1st has solid block walls, unique at Tikal as far as I know).

Wall-top

In typical Late Classic construction at Tikal building walls were assembled, faced, dressed, and plastered before any work on vaulting or upper zones was begun. As a result a plaster coat extends across the top surface of the walls and lintel beds.

Index

Access, 7, 12, 20, 24, 26, 30, 68
Acropolis, 9, 81
Acropolis court, 51, 58, 67
Acropolis suddenly made higher, 29, 31
Adverse fortunes, 63
Agricultural imagery, 58
Alfarda, 81
Anachronistic developments, 57, 60, 66
Ancestors, xiii, 7, 23, 25, 42, 54, 58, 63
Animal Skull, 64
Animism, xvi, xviii, 9
Apron moldings, 6, 8, 13, 46, 54, 57, 60, 64, 70, 81
Architectural development, 5, 16, 81, 31, 32, 66
Arrival of strangers, 51, 52, 70, 71
Aspect ratio, 29
Asymmetry, 13, 14, 2, 14, 19, 35, 41, 68, 70
Auto.des.sys, x
Axis, 7, 13-14, 19, 41, 47, 82
Axial niche, 18-19, 31
Axial stair absent, 7
Aztec parallel, 52

Bajo Santa Fe, 1
Balustrade, 82
Banner poles, 26
Basal platform, 6, 9, 21-22, 39, 53, 82
Beam and mortar roofing, 10, 18, 31, 43-44
Bedrock modification, 1
Bedrock sculpture, 1
Becker hypothesis, xv, 25, 58
Beliefs displayed, 11
Blood scrolls, 24
Body, 82

Building, 82
Building as offering, 26
Building platform, 83; see also Pseudo building platform
Burials: Bu. 10, 52, 54; Bu. 23, 64, 66; Bu. 24, 64; Bu. 48, 53; Bu. 85, 25, 26, 31; Bu. 120, 1; Bu. 121, 1; Bu. 125, 33, 39; Bu. 164, 13; Bu. 166, 22-23; Bu. 167, 24; Bu. 195, 64; Bu. 200, 61
Burning, 2, 16, 18, 25, 26, 33, 47, 86

Cache activity as sign of desperation, 61, 64
Caches: Ca. 74, 52-53; Ca. 185, 61
Calakmul, Defeat of, 66-67
Calendric influences on design, xviii, 12- 14, 27, 39, 40, 42, 64
Canon of ancient Maya design, 36
Carmack theories, xvii
Cave symbolism, 49, 58
Ceramic associations, 71
Circular structure, 1-2, 10, 30-31, 69
Chak Tok Ich'aak I, 51
Classic Period Collapse, 64
Complete replacement, 5, 10
Concealment of summit features, 31
Corbel, 8, 61
Core, 83
Core units, 8, 29, 66
Cosmic template, 12, 44, 70
Cuello, 10
Cult item repositories, 62

Demolition considered dangerous, 30
Designation of entities, xiv

Developmental episodes, 69-71
Diagonal directionality, 20, 45, 52, 57, 60, 63-64
Doctrinal influences, 53
Doorway, 83
Double Bird, 64
Dresden Codex Venus Table, 27
Dualistic concepts, 16, 19, 62
Duplicate structures, 19
Dyadic form, 16

East-West direction, 8, 10, 12, 14, 27, 32, 44, 46
East-west stairs, 12, 40
El Mirador, 17
Exterior form as façade, 62

Facing, 83
Feature designation, xiv
First appearance of monumental scale, 6
Floor, 84
Four-sidedness symbolism, 44, 59
FormZ modeling program, x
Frontality, 7

Grafffiti, xvii, 58
Great Plaza unpaved, 11
Great Plaza paved, 21
Great Temple V, 65
Green paint, 44

Hearth stones of creation, 7
Historical dimension, 52
House platform, 1

Innovative developments, 12, 33, 54, 57, 64, 68
Inset corners, 57, 60
Inset panels, 57, 59
Inset stairs, 19, 31, 39
Intercardinal directions, 60, 63-64
Interior platform, 61-62

Jade inlaid teeth, 64
Jaguar Imagery, 16-17
Jaguar god of underworld, 49
Jasaw Chan K'awiil I, 66

Kan Chitam, 58
Komchen, 10

Late Classic attributes, 68
Lateral stairs, 7-8, 15, 43
Lintel, 84
Lost World complex, 53

Maya design convention, 36
Milky Way symbolism, 44, 64
Madrid Codex diagram, 63-64
Modeled stucco, 17
Modest scale of early development, 1-2
Monumentality, xv, 7, 9, 16, 21, 36-37, 39, 51, 59, 62
Mortar, 63, 84
Multiple work crews, 8
Mundo Perdido complex, 2-3, 8, 52
Mural painting, xvii, 23- 25, 53, 54

Nocturnal function, 16
North axial dominance, 15, 31, 42, 45-46, 60-61, 63
North Acropolis excavation, xiii
North-South directional significance, xiii, 7, 12, 36
North Acropolis site, 1
Nuun Ujol Chaak, 66

Obliteration of masks, 33, 37
Open-cornered quadrangle, 44
Open Pavilion form, 23
Outset, 19, 84

Paint, 84
Paired structures, 14-15, 19
Partial replacement, 10-11
Pause line, 29
Piedras Negras, 48
Portal structure, 20, 26, 31, 35, 48, 53, 68
Portal to underworld, 58
Plaster, 84
Plaster paving symbolism, 22
Platform, 54, 84
Plazuela, 81
Practical benefit of monumentality, 9, 11
Pre-plastered capstones, 68
Primary occupation, 1
Processional ceremony, 8, 40, 43, 60
Pseudo building platform, 83
Public art, 7
Pyramid form, 29, 65, 66

Quadrangular format, 12, 43, 44, 48, 63
Quetzalcoatl, 30

Radial symmetry, 46
Rear axial outsets, 7, 10, 15, 18-19, 24-25, 31, 45, 59
Rear Doorways, 31, 35, 44, 52
Rear facade mask, 49
Rear stairs, 26
Red Paint, 2, 21, 23, 30-31, 33, 45, 47, 65, 69-70
Residential occupancy, 1, 10

Residential format, 16, 69
Rice proposal seat of the May, 3, 42
Ritual design directives, 2, 5, 10, 13, 23, 24, 69, 70, 86
Rock sculpture, 1
Roof comb, 15, 52, 57
Room proportions determined by stair width, 65
Rounded corners, 12, 33, 60, 69
Rulership associations, 1, 5, 7, 9, 18, 22, 25, 29, 32, 39, 41–42, 46, 53, 55, 70

San Bartolo murals, 24
Scribe lines, 14
Screening of summit, 31–32, 35
Sculpture, functional interpretation of, 17
Sculpture on building walls, 58
Shamanic site, 10
Shield Skull, 66
Short-term arrangements, 42
Shrine room, 25, 85
Side access, 7, 12, 40
Side outsets, 12, 46, 59
Side inset, 48–49, 57, 62, 70
Siyak Chan K'awiil II, 52–54, 58
Sky band on risers, 52
Solar glare, xii, 21–22, 65
South Acropolis, 8
Spearthrower Owl, 52
Stair, 85
Stair block mask, 47, 48
Stair-side masks, 17–19, 23, 32, 41, 47, 51–52, 54, 58
Stair-side outsets, 12, 15, 22, 65
Stela 31, 54
Stela 40, 58
Stratigraphic control, x, 14, 42, 54, 58
Structure, 85
Structures: 5D-Sub.14-2nd, 1; 5D-Sub.14-1st, 2; 5D-Sub.1-2nd, 6; 5D-Sub.24, 8; 5D-Sub.12-2nd, 12; 5D-Sub.4, 12; 5D-Sub.9, 14; 5D-Sub.5, 14; 5D-Sub.1-1st, 15; 5D-Sub.3-F, 18; 5D-Sub.11, 23; 5D-Sub.10-2nd, 23; 5D-Sub.12-1st, 23; 5D-Sub.3-E, 23; 5D-Sub.10-1st, 24; 5D-Sub.2-2nd, 25; 5D-Sub.2-1st, 26; 5D-Sub.3-C, 26; 5D-Sub.3-B, 30; 5D-Sub.6, 30; 5D-26-5th, 31; 5D-Sub.21E and W, 31; 5D-22-6th-B, 31; 5D-26-4th, 32; 5D-Sub.8-2nd, 32; 5D-Sub.7, 33; 5D-22-6th-A, 33; 5D-26-3rd, 35; 5D-Sub.8-1st, 40; 5D-22-5th, 42; 5D-26-2nd, 44; 5D-23-2nd, 44; 5D-224-2nd, 44; 5D-22-4th, 45; 5D-22-3rd, 45; 5D-23-1st, 48; 5D-26-1st, 51; 5D-25-3rd, 52; 5D-34-2nd, 52; 5D-22-2nd, 53; 5D-33-3rd, 54; 5D-32-2nd, 55; 5D-34-1st, 57; 5D-33-2nd, 57; 5D-29, 58; 5D-22-1st, 60; 5D-25-1st, 63; 5D-20-2nd, 23; 5D-32-1st, 64; 5D-33-1st, 66; 5D-35, 68; 5D-28, 68; 5D-20-1st, 68

Stucco, 85
Summit out of scale, 39, 42
Summit screened, 35, 60, 67, 68
Substructure, 85; as home for supernaturals, 46
Supernatural presence, xv, xvii, 15, 17, 21, 30, 22, 58–60, 66, 67
Supernatural impersonation, 34
Superstructure, 85
Supplementary platforms, 6–9, 22, 85
Support facilities, 32
Symbolic house form, 2, 10
Symbolic stair, 59
Symmetry, 9, 13–14, 63

Task units, 66, 85
Temple, 86
Temple attributes, 7, 16, 49
Temple of the Inscriptions date C, 11
Temple of the Jaguars, Chichen Itza, xvii
Temple sanctity, xvii
Temples as houses of gods, xvii
Templo Mayor, 8
Teotihuacan imagery, 52, 54, 70
Termination observances, 30
Terraces as abodes of supernaturals, 8, 13, 16, 41, 60
Terrace access stairs, 40
Terracing as structural expedient, 60
Thatch roofing, 2, 10, 12, 26, 43
Theatrical setting, 19, 26, 34–35, 40, 43–44, 51, 58
Theology and temple design, xvii, 10, 12, 52
Therianthropes, 47
Throne, 62
Time Spans, 72
Tikal epicenter, xvii
Tikal setting, xii
Tikal population, xii
Tikal Project publication plan, x
Triadic organization, 7, 12, 39, 48, 57
Triple doorway, 33, 35, 68
triple stairs, 9, 16, 69
Twinned stairs, 6, 12, 22, 35, 40, 41
Two-body building format, 15, 18, 23, 24, 47, 48, 49, 53
T'zolk'in, 3, 12, 27

Unit, 86
Upper zone, 86
Upper zone sculpture, 47
U-shaped platform, 9
Utatlan, xvi
Uaxactun Group E, 5
Uaxactun Group H, 24
Uaxactun murals, 24

Vaulting, 23, 24, 44, 47, 49, 61, 68, 86
Veneer masonry, 67

Wak Chan K'awiil, 60
Wall, 87
Wall-top, 87

Witz symbol, 58
West associations, 10

Yax Ehb' Xook, 22, 24, 25, 29, 46, 51, 52, 54, 64
Yax Nuun Ayiin I, 52, 53